American Indians

BLACKWELL READERS IN AMERICAN SOCIAL AND CULTURAL HISTORY

Series Editor: Jacqueline Jones, Brandeis University

The *Blackwell Readers in American Social and Cultural History* series introduces students to well-defined topics in American history from a socio-cultural perspective. Using primary and secondary sources, the volumes present the most important works available on a particular topic in a succinct and accessible format designed to fit easily into courses offered in American history or American studies.

American Indians

Edited by

Nancy Shoemaker

First published 2001

2 4 6 8 10 9 7 5 3 1

Blackwell Publishers Inc.
350 Main Street
Malden, Massachusetts 02148
USA

Blackwell Publishers Ltd
108 Cowley Road
Oxford OX4 1JF
UK

Library of Congress Cataloging-in-Publication Data

American Indians / edited by Nancy Shoemaker.
    p. cm.—(Blackwell readers in American social and cultural history; 2)
Includes bibliographical references and index.
ISBN 0–631–21994–3 (alk. paper)—ISBN 0–631–21995–1 (pbk : alk. paper)
    1. Indians of North America—Historiography. 2. Indians of North
America—Government relations. 3. Indians, Treatment of—North
America—History—Sources. 4. United States—History—Sources. 5. United
States—Politics and government. I. Shoemaker, Nancy, 1958– II. Series.

E76.8 .A49 2000
973.04'97—dc21
                                                                                00–036196

British Library Cataloguing in Publication Data
A CIP catalogue record for this book is available from the British Library.

Typeset in Plantin 10 on 12pt
by Kolam Information Services Pvt. Ltd, Pondicherry, India
Printed in Great Britain by
TJ International Ltd, Padstow, Cornwall

This book is printed on acid-free paper.

Contents

Series Editor's Preface

The purpose of the Blackwell Readers in American Social and Cultural History is to introduce students to cutting-edge historical scholarship that draws upon a variety of disciplines, and to encourage students to "do" history themselves by examining some of the primary texts upon which that scholarship is based.

Each of us lives life with a wholeness that is at odds with the way scholars often dissect the human experience. Anthropologists, psychologists, literary critics, and political scientists (to name just a few) study only discrete parts of our existence. The result is a rather arbitrary collection of disciplinary boundaries enshrined not only in specialized publications but also in university academic departments and in professional organizations.

As a scholarly enterprise, the study of history necessarily crosses these boundaries of knowledge in order to provide a comprehensive view of the past. Over the last few years, social and cultural historians have reached across the disciplines to understand the history of the British North American colonies and the United States in all its fullness. Unfortunately, much of that scholarship, published in specialized monographs and journals, remains inaccessible to undergraduates. Consequently, instructors often face choices that are not very appealing – to ignore the recent scholarship altogether, assign bulky readers that are too detailed for an undergraduate audience, or cobble together packages of recent articles that lack an overall contextual framework. The individual volumes of this series, however, each focus on a significant topic in American history, and bring new, exciting scholarship to students in a compact, accessible format.

The series is designed to complement textbooks and other general readings assigned in undergraduate courses. Each editor has culled particularly innovative and provocative scholarly essays from widely scattered books and journals, and provided an introduction summarizing the major themes of the essays and documents that follow. The essays reproduced here were chosen because of the authors' innovative (and often interdisciplinary) methodology and their ability to reconceptualize historical issues in fresh and insightful ways. Thus students can appreciate the rich complexity of an historical topic and the way that scholars have explored the topic from different perspectives, and in the process transcend the highly artificial disciplinary boundaries that have served to compartmentalize knowledge about the past in the United States.

Also included in each volume are primary texts, at least some of which have been drawn from the essays themselves. By linking primary and secondary material, the editors are able to introduce students to the historian's craft, allowing them to explore this material in depth, and draw additional insights – or interpretations contrary to those of the scholars under discussion – from it.

Jacqueline Jones
Brandeis University

Introduction

Before reading further, take minute to jot down the names of famous American Indians of the past, those individuals who have made it into the history books. Who were they? When and where did they live? Which Indian nation did they belong to? And for what act or event are they remembered today? Now what about contemporary Indians from the present or recent past? This mental exercise, though seemingly simple and straightforward, illuminates some deep-rooted prejudices about the place of Indian history in American popular culture. There is a pattern to who is famous. Each person's own list of famous Indians may be unique – a compilation of personal knowledge, education, and regional or national origins – but if we were to survey hundreds of people from varying backgrounds, the most historically prominent Indians would probably be Pocahontas, Squanto, Sacajawea, Tecumseh, Sitting Bull, Crazy Horse, and Geronimo. This list of famous Indians produces a particular narrative of American Indian history. Individual Indians from the past are famous for one of two great acts: they helped Euroamericans settle North America or they fought Euroamerican expansion.

According to this narrative, in the period from 1607 to 1805, Indians welcomed Europeans. Pocahontas saved the life of the English adventurer John Smith when she rescued him from captivity among Virginia Indians. She later married another English colonist, John Rolfe, bore him a son, and then while on a trip to England became ill and died. Hundreds of miles to the north and a few years later, the Indian man Squanto taught the Pilgrims who settled at Plymouth how to grow corn and survive harsh New England winters. In the early nineteenth century, the Shoshone woman Sacajawea showed the explorers Lewis and Clark the way to the Pacific. The wife of the French fur trader whom Lewis and Clark hired as guide, Sacajawea cooked, interpreted, shared her knowledge about the environment and people of the west, and with her newborn child symbolized the peaceful intent of Lewis and Clark's venture. Pocahontas, Squanto, and Sacajawea live on as icons in popular treatments of the American past. Persistently, but erroneously, portrayed as John Smith's ill-fated lover, Pocahontas was recently the subject of a Disney movie. Every Thanksgiving holiday, images of Indians and Pilgrims in amicable fellowship bombard American media. And a newly minted dollar coin commemorates Sacajawea.

According to our list of famous Indians, there was a dramatic switch in Indian sentiment towards Euroamericans in the period from 1805 to 1890 as Indians fought US expansion across the continent. In the years leading up to the War of 1812, the Shawnee warrior Tecumseh attempted to ally all eastern Indians in a war of resistance against the newly formed United States. In 1876, Sitting Bull and Crazy Horse defeated the US Seventh Cavalry at the Battle of Little Bighorn, a shortlived victory in a war the Lakotas were losing. And also in the late nineteenth century, Geronimo's band of Apaches fled their reservation to return to their former homelands, only to be relentlessly hunted down by American soldiers and, when finally captured, imprisoned. In stark contrast to the Pocahontas- and Squanto-inspired mythology of hospitable Indians who encouraged a mingling of New Worlds and Old, this narrative highlighting the feats of tough, but ultimately subjugated, Indian warriors implies that the United States won the American West through conquest.

To turn to our list of contemporary American Indians, we would probably conclude that from 1890 up to the present Indian citizens of the United States have made a distinct ethnic contribution to American art and politics. Indians with national name-recognition – the US Senator Ben Nighthorse Campbell, the Navajo flutist Carlos Nakai, the political activist Russell Means, the writers Louise Erdrich and Sherman Alexie, the actor Wes Studi – present an entirely different image of Indians and of America. As political and cultural leaders, they serve to represent Indians as a minority group within a multicultural America.

By now, it should be apparent that this particular historical narrative, albeit familiar and readily grasped, has problems. First, this is Indian history from a Euroamerican perspective. Whether popular accounts cast Indians as receptive or resistant, the stories end the same way, with Indians dwindling in power while a United States dominated by Americans of European heritage rises in power. Euroamericans are the primary historical actors while Indians constitute the backdrop, the landscape, to Euroamerican settlement in North America. Most tellingly, the history starts in 1607 with the English founding of Jamestown, Virginia. By implication, Indians have no history outside of a Euroamerican presence.

Second, this schematic for telling Indian history simplifies a vastly diverse people – in culture, language, society, religion, political organization, and historical experiences – into a single group of people acting as a cohesive unit. Neither Pocahontas nor Squanto can be considered representative of seventeenth-century Virginia and New England, where English–Indian relations did break down into war. If Pocahontas and Squanto are to be remembered in history, then so should Opechancanough and Metacom, both of whom led Native people, in Virginia and New England respectively, in wars of resistance against English expansion. Similarly, not all nineteenth-century Plains Indians fought the United States. If we elevate only Sitting Bull and Crazy Horse to heroic stature, then we would have to ignore the perspectives of White Man Runs Him and Curley, two Crow Indian scouts who helped Custer locate the site of the Lakota and Cheyenne camp on the Little Bighorn River. Add to this history Sitting Bull's life after the 1876 battle – for example, the years the spent re-enacting "Custer's Last Stand" as a performer with Buffalo Bill's Wild West Show – and we will arrive at a more complex, richer understanding of Indian history than can be had by recounting the achievements of the few Indians memorialized in American popular culture.

In short, we should probably throw out the over-simplified narrative of American Indian history conjured up by our list of famous Indians. However, it contains a few kernels of important truths. It is indeed difficult to separate American Indian history from the dominating presence of Euroamericans. Since Indians north of Mexico had no written form for their languages, non-Indian commentary about Indians makes up the bulk of the historical documents. By the eighteenth and nineteenth centuries, literate Indians were creating their own written records, usually in English but also in Native languages, by using the Cherokee syllabary, which Sequoyah invented in the early nineteenth century, or by borrowing the English alphabet. However, as the number of documents authored by Indians increased, non-Indians still outpaced Indians in the production of relevant written records. The Bureau, or Office, of Indian Affairs (BIA), the US agency appointed to oversee America's colonized peoples, collected voluminous, detailed information on Indians living on reservations in the nineteenth and twentieth centuries. Thus, there is plenty of information available for learning about Indian history; the problem is that so little of it comes directly from Indian speakers or writers.

Unfortunately, the problem of Euroamerican dominance runs much deeper than the issue of sources. Even our most basic vocabulary is a product of European colonization. Christopher Columbus, sailing under the auspices of the Spanish government, was looking for Asia when he landed in the Caribbean in 1492, and so all the Native people of the Americas acquired the label "Indios," translated into English as "Indians." The few Native and non-Native people who object to the word "Indian" will never succeed at eliminating the term, since there is no preferable alternative that would satisfy everybody. "American," whether part of "American Indian" or "Native American," is of similar origins. A European mapmaker named America after Amerigo Vespucci, a contemporary of Columbus's and one of the first European explorers to recognize that he had sailed not to Asia but to a "New World." Today, Native people in the United States generally accept, or even claim, "American Indian" and "Native American" as self-identifying labels. In Canada, the more common terms are "Native People" or "First Nations."

The same issues arise with "tribe," a word that has derogatory connotations in some contexts. In early modern English, "tribe" and "nation" had similar meanings; each referred to a group of people sharing common descent and, usually, a common culture and language. But increasingly, especially in the nineteenth century, Euroamericans began thinking of "tribes" as barbaric, primitive peoples while reserving the word "nation" for peoples and polities of European heritage. Consequently, "tribe" could be considered an insult, since it conjures up an image of a culturally affiliated but politically unorganized group of people, people who did not qualify as "nations" in the eyes of colonizing powers. However, as with the phrase "American Indians," words change meaning over time and can mean different things to different people. Although some Indian polities prefer "Nation" as an assertion of the sovereignty they never surrendered, many Indian communities have depended on the developing legal definition of "tribe" to protect their original sovereignty. In US Indian law, "tribe" defines a level of government subordinate to the national government but independent from states. Federally recognized Indian tribes have a distinct political status within the United States.

The last kernel of truth in the simplified narrative of American Indian history is that receptivity and resistance do indeed capture some of the responses Indians had to Europeans. Several of the chapters in this collection talk about resistance. Other recurring themes are survival, accommodation, and adaptation. These conceptual frameworks for understanding how Indian societies have changed over time are for the most part new to the study of Indian history, having emerged primarily in the 1970s under the rubric "The New Indian History."

Until the 1970s, most academic scholars researching and writing about Indian history came from the discipline of anthropology. Lewis Henry Morgan, who inquired into Iroquois culture and history in the mid-nineteenth century, was a kind of founding father to anthropology. His fieldwork among the Iroquois helped establish a method for studying the diversity of human cultures. In the late nineteenth and early twentieth centuries, Franz Boas was equally influential, especially as a teacher. He inspired innumerable graduate students to undertake fieldwork in Indian communities. In Boas's time, "salvage anthropology" was all the rage. With a great sense of urgency, anthropologists rushed to record, or to "salvage," every scrap of information about Indian cultures before they completely disappeared.

Morgan's and Boas's ideas reflected the biases and presumptions of their own times. Writing at mid-century, Morgan used his collected data about Indians to construct an evolutionary scale explaining human development over time. North American Indians, according to Morgan, were at the "barbarism" stage, one step above "savagism" and one step below "civilization." Although Morgan had great respect for Iroquois cultural traditions, he still regarded the Iroquois as lower on the evolutionary scale than his own "civilized" society, the white, Protestant, middle-class culture of Morgan's upstate New York environs. Boas's ideas mesh better with our own, for Boas asserted that all cultures needed to be respected and studied on their own account, an approach that is called cultural relativism. However, Boas's many working relationships and friendships with Native people did not shake his belief that Indian cultures were dying.

Indeed, both Morgan and Boas relied on paradigms for studying Indian history that have been largely abandoned today. Although Boas did much to dispel hierarchical rankings of cultures, he along with Morgan spoke uninhibitedly about "primitive" and "civilized" cultures, a juxtaposition that most of us now regard as fallacious and prejudicial. In addition, Boas and Morgan used models of culture that could not tolerate change. They described Indian cultures as single entities with clear boundaries, pure and unsullied by contacts with other peoples. They cast innovations or adaptations, especially any customs or ideas borrowed from Europeans, as cultural degeneration or loss. Morgan believed that the Iroquois could progress to a "civilized" state, but then they would no longer be distinguishably Iroquois. This perception of Indians as having static, unchanging cultures differed diametrically from Euroamericans' own sense of a progressive history built upon the cumulation of human invention: the emergence of agriculture, the domestication of livestock, industrialization.

The problem with viewing Indian cultures as static became apparent beginning in the 1950s, when anthropologists studying Native North America began to borrow methods from historians. A postwar federal initiative to resolve Indian land claims led anthropologists, many of whom were hired as researchers and expert witnesses, to use written documents, instead of fieldwork, as their primary source of information. This experience was so new to anthropology that it demanded a label of its own: Ethnohistory. Ethnohistorians combined anthropologists' interest in cultural differences with historical documents providing the evidence. One obstacle to integrating the two disciplinary perspectives proved to be the contrast between anthropological models of static cultures and historical models emphasizing the dynamics of change.

The organizing principle behind most historical studies is time. While Ethnohistory was gaining interest among anthropologists, the few historians who worked on topics in Indian history tended to write narrative accounts of US Indian policy, Indian–European wars, and tribal histories. Rarely did historians wonder in what ways culture shaped the sequence of events or the motivations of participants. Even more problematic, however, was how few and how rarely Indians appeared in narrative accounts of Indian history. This was less often the case in histories focusing on a particular tribe but especially noticeable in any attempt to write a general Indian history. The great diversity of Indian cultures and historical experiences makes it difficult to pull out a single narrative thread that does not at the same time put Europeans or the United States at the forefront of the narrative as the primary actors or initiators of change.

US Indian policy, for example, has a chronological sequence with discrete time periods. During the Removal Period (1820–70), the US government sought to remove all eastern Indians to a designated Indian Territory west of the Mississippi River. During the Assimilation Era (1870–1934), US policymakers tried to eliminate Indian cultures, communally owned landbases, and political sovereignty so as to incorporate Indians as individuals into the American body politic. To "Americanize" Indians, the BIA implemented such policies as the Dawes Act (1887), which called for the allotment of reservation land to individual Indians; off-reservation boarding schools for Indian children; imposition of federal legal jurisdiction for certain "major crimes" Indians committed against other Indians; and the criminalization of polygamy, the Sun Dance, and other customs deemed "uncivilized." The Indian New Deal of the 1930s, spearheaded by the Commissioner of Indian Affairs John Collier, reversed assimilationist policies and aimed to restore

Indian lands, sovereignty, and cultural traditions. In the 1950s, government policies reversed again, as the BIA implemented "termination" of some reservations and oversaw the "relocation" program, which encouraged Indians to leave reservations for cities. Since the 1970s, the US government has swung back yet again with "self-determination," a series of policies and court decisions which recognize tribes as distinct communities with rights to political and economic autonomy.

For historians, such chronological narratives demonstrating change over time provide a comfortable structure for organizing complex material into a coherent story. And indeed, having to deal with fluctuating, sometimes brutally destructive, US Indian policies is one of the few experiences most Indians in the United States have had in common. However, every shift in policy only makes the United States government seem to be the key figure moving history along.

The New Indian History of the 1970s represented a sharp break from past scholarship. Influenced by cultural anthropology and the "New Social History," which was sweeping through the historical profession at the same time, scholars began to generate new models for understanding and explaining Indian history. These "New" approaches put ordinary people – especially disadvantaged social groups such as women, slaves, peasants, the working class, and American Indians – at the center of historical narratives. Like social historians, "New" Indian historians focused on Indian perspectives, voices, actions, and decisions. Instead of studying how Europeans treated Native Americans, the emphasis turned to documenting "agency," which meant showing how Indians were active participants in the making of their own history.

This attention to Indian agency explains why survival, resistance, accommodation, and adaptation are now the prevailing themes informing the work of historians, anthropologists, ethnohistorians, and other scholars of Indian history. Since this collection provides many illustrations of how these paradigms or models of historical change play out in practice, I will explain their impact by confining myself to one example only: how we might interpret the assimilationist policies of the late nineteenth century.

First, if we were to apply nineteenth-century models of historical change to the assimilationist era, we would conclude that Indians were in fact assimilating into the general population of the United States, some at a quicker pace than others. That was, of course, the driving idea behind salvage anthropology, and North American anthropologists were for that reason especially active during the assimilationist period. Coming from the same cultural milieu as the policymakers and social reformers who drew up the blueprint for Indian assimilation, most anthropologists believed that Indians as distinct peoples were disappearing and that their disappearance in the face of modernization was sad but inevitable.

Recent scholarship questions the whole idea of assimilation. Policymakers may have tried to assimilate Indians, but Indians survived, resisted, accommodated, or adapted. To argue for survival, endurance, and persistence, scholars could point to demographic statistics: the Indian population reached its lowest point in 1900 but grew rapidly in the twentieth century until now there are about two million Indians in the United States according to the US Census. Or, historians could show how, despite government efforts to dissolve Indian communities through allotment, Indians continued to live in the same place, interact with the same people, and identify as Indian.

Many Indians openly resisted assimilation policies. The Hopi Indians refused to let their children attend government boarding schools. To coerce their consent, the United States imprisoned nineteen Hopi men at Alcatraz for about a year. Members of the secret Keetoowah Society among the Cherokees refused to sign up for land allotments. Many of them also went to jail for not cooperating. Resistance is easy to find in the historical record of the assimilation period.

Some acts of resistance were more subtle, however, and could instead be thought of as accommodation. That is how we might interpret Kiowa efforts to prevent the sale of the remaining, unallotted portion of the Kiowa-Comanche Reservation. In the US Supreme Court case *Lone Wolf v. Hitchcock* (1903), Lone Wolf's attorneys argued, unsuccessfully, that allotment of the reservation violated a clause of the 1867 Treaty of Medicine Lodge, which required that three-fourths of adult men agree to any future land sales. Protesting allotment policies before the US Supreme Court was a form of resistance that required some accommodation, though perhaps only as a last resort, to the decision-making powers of the American legal system. Accommodation implies an acceptance of some aspects of the dominant culture but not the complete transformation and disappearance that is inherent in the term "assimilation."

Accommodation also might mean upholding cultural traditions in secret or adopting a public persona distinct from how one behaved when among family and friends. Under pressure to surrender religious and social practices, many Indians looked for ways to carry on a traditional way of life outside the purview of BIA agents and white schoolteachers, missionaries, and neighbors who were critical of Indian traditions. The BIA may have outlawed the Sun Dance on Indian reservations on the northern plains, but Sun Dances continued to be held by certain families on their allotted homesteads into the twentieth century.

Accommodation and adaptation are both useful terms for explaining how social and cultural customs adjust to larger political events and economic developments that may be beyond one's control. However, accommodation suggests that the decision to change is undertaken deliberately, whereas adaptation may not be a conscious choice. The Native American Church could be considered an example of adaptation. A pan-Indian (multi-tribal) religion, which originated on the southern plains during the assimilation era, the Native American Church combines traditional Indian religious beliefs with some elements of Christianity. The Native American Church introduced many Indians to new cultural practices – the use of peyote as a religious sacrament, for instance. As a concept, adaptation implies that, in every society, culture is a work in progress. Cultural traditions are constantly being invented and reinvented. The Native American Church is one of many Indian religions to emerge in the past two hundred years. A comparatively new religion, it is no less Indian.

In sum, present-day historians writing about the assimilation era focus less on what the policies intended and more on what Indians themselves were doing. This emphasis on trying to understand Indian perspectives and motivations has led scholars to ask new questions about all aspects of Indian history: What were the patterns of interaction between peoples in America before Columbus? Why did Indians become so deeply involved in trade with Europeans? Why did Indian nations fight with other Indian nations? When and why did they choose to ally with other Indian nations or with Europeans? What were women's roles and statuses within Indian societies, and how did these change, or not change, over time? What explains Indians' varying responses to Christianity? When, where, and why did economic dependence emerge, and how did Indian communities alter their economies to avoid it? How have Indian political systems and institutions changed over time?

The following seven chapters, each consisting of one research article and a set of related documents, deal with many of these topics. One question to ask of each article is which model, or models, of historical change it employs.

Further Reading

Calloway, Colin G. *First Peoples: A Documentary Survey of American Indian History*. Boston: Bedford/St Martin's Press, 1999.

Fixico, Donald L., ed. *Rethinking American Indian History*. Albuquerque: University of New Mexico Press, 1997.

Hoxie, Frederick E. and Peter Iverson, eds. *Indians in American History: An Introduction.* 2nd edn. Wheeling, IL: Harlan Davidson, 1998.

Nabokov, Peter, ed. *Native American Testimony: A Chronicle of Indian–White Relations from Prophecy to the Present, 1492–2000.* Revised edn. New York: Penguin, 1999.

Sturtevant, William C., general ed. *Handbook of North American Indians.* 15 vols. Washington, D.C.: Smithsonian Institution, 1978–forthcoming.

Thornton, Russell, ed. *Studying Native America: Problems and Prospects.* Madison: University of Wisconsin Press, 1998.

1

Ancient America

Introduction

It used to be that American history textbooks and course lectures, if they mentioned America before Columbus at all, focused on the elaborate urban cultures of Central Mexico and Peru, the Aztec and Inca Empires. Increasingly, however, American history narratives now start by surveying the many different Native societies north of Mexico: the Anasazi in the Southwest, who were the ancestors of the Pueblo peoples; the Moundbuilding societies, who resided for the most part east of the Mississippi River; and the Five Nations (Iroquois) Confederacy, which formed around 1450 in the Northeast. Diversity, often a dominant theme in US history courses, existed in America well before 1492.

Neal Salisbury's article "The Indians' Old World: Native Americans and the Coming of Europeans" could be considered part of this revisionist trend to incorporate more pre-Columbian history in how American history is told. Appearing in the premier journal for early American studies, *The William and Mary Quarterly*, this article speaks to an audience consisting mainly of scholars specializing in seventeenth- and eighteenth-century Anglo-American studies. Salisbury argues that American Indian history has been undeservedly neglected and marginalized. By highlighting the continuities in pre- and post-Columbian North America, he reconfigures the standard approach, which has tended to trace colonial American beginnings solely back to Europe.

"The Indians' Old World" is a play on words, the idea for which Salisbury borrowed from James H. Merrell's book *The Indians' New World: Catawbas and Their Neighbors from European Contact Through the Era of Removal* (Chapel Hill,

NC, 1989). Europeans viewed the Americas as their discovery. This was for them a "New World." In turn, Europe, Asia, and Africa became known as the "Old World." Merrell argued that European settlement of the Americas created a New World for Indians, too. European diseases, trade goods, and desire for Indian land disrupted Indian communities and set in motion rapid changes in Native economies, political structures, cultural practices, and identities. Merrell's larger thesis is, however, very much about adaptation. In contrast to, in Merrell's own words, "the tragically plummeting trajectory so commonly charted," the many Indian groups inhabiting the Carolina piedmont region met every challenge and crisis with creative responses that enabled them "to rearrange their lives in accordance with new imperatives."

One issue to consider while reading Salisbury's article is to what extent his interpretation resembles Merrell's. They may seem different on the surface. Merrell starts his narrative with European contact and limits himself to a small region, especially small when compared to Salisbury's vast reach across time and space. But where does Salisbury stand on how Indians and Europeans responded to change? Also notice how much Salisbury depends on archaeological evidence for information about pre-Columbian America. What can archaeology tell us about the past, and what are its limitations? Finally, pay particular attention to Salisbury's discussion of Cahokia and the moundbuilding societies of the Mississippi River Valley and Southeast. The two documents that follow his article shed further light on the significance of mounds to one southeastern people, the Choctaws.

The Indians' Old World: Native Americans and the Coming of Europeans

Neal Salisbury

Scholars in history, anthropology, archaeology, and other disciplines have turned increasingly over the past two decades to the study of native peoples during the colonial period of North American history. The new work in Indian history has altered the way we think about the beginning of American history and about the era of European colonization. Historians now recognize that Europeans arrived, not in a virgin land, but in one that was teeming with several million people. Beyond filling in some

Salisbury, Neal. "The Indians' Old World: Native Americans and the Coming of Europeans." *The William and Mary Quarterly*, 3rd series, 53 (July 1996): 435–58.

of the vast blanks left by previous generations' overlooking of Indians, much of this scholarship makes clear that Indians are integral to the history of colonial North America. In short, surveys of recent textbooks and of scholarly titles suggest that Native Americans are well on their way to being "mainstreamed" by colonial historians.

Substantive as this reorientation is, it remains limited. Beyond the problems inherent in representing Indian/non-Indian interactions during the colonial era lies the challenge of contextualizing the era itself. Despite opening chapters and lectures that survey the continent's native peoples and cultures, most historians continue to represent American history as having been set in motion by the arrival of European explorers and colonizers. They have yet to recognize the existence of a North American – as opposed to English or European – background for colonial history, much less to consider the implications of such a background for understanding the three centuries following Columbus's landfall. Yet a growing body of scholarship by archaeologists, linguists, and students of Native American expressive traditions recognizes 1492 not as a beginning but as a single moment in a long history utterly detached from that of Europe. These findings call into question historians' synchronic maps and verbal descriptions of precontact Indians – their cultures, their communities, their ethnic and political designations and affiliations, and their relations with one another. Do these really describe enduring entities or do they represent epiphenomena of arbitrary moments in time? If the latter should prove to be the case, how will readings of Indian history in the colonial period be affected?

Far from being definitive, this article is intended as a stimulus to debate on these questions. It begins by drawing on recent work in archaeology, where most of the relevant scholarship has originated to suggest one way of thinking about pre-Columbian North America in historical terms. The essay then looks at developments in several areas of the continent during the centuries preceding the arrival of Europeans and in the early phases of the colonial period. The purpose is to show how certain patterns and processes originating before the beginnings of contact continued to shape the continent's history thereafter and how an understanding of the colonial period requires an understanding of its American background as well as of its European context.

In a formidable critique of European and Euro-American thinking about native North Americans, Robert F. Berkhofer, Jr., demonstrates that the idea of "Indians" as a single, discrete people was an invention of Columbus and his European contemporaries that has been perpetuated into our own time without foundation in historical, cultural, or ethnographic reality. On the contrary, Berkhofer asserts,

> The first residents of the Americas were by modern estimates divided into
> at least two thousand cultures and more societies, practiced a multiplicity
> of customs and lifestyles, held an enormous variety of values and beliefs,
> spoke numerous languages mutually unintelligible to the many speakers,
> and did not conceive of themselves as a single people – if they knew about
> each other at all.[1]

While there is literal truth in portions of Berkhofer's statement, his
implication that Indians inhabited thousands of tiny, isolated communities in ignorance of one another flies in the face of a substantial body of
archaeological and linguistic scholarship on North America and of a
wealth of relevant anthropological literature on nonstate polities, non-
market economies, and noninstitutionalized religions. To be sure, indigenous North Americans exhibited a remarkable range of languages,
economies, political systems, beliefs, and material cultures. But this
range was less the result of their isolation from one another than of the
widely varying natural and social environments with which Indians had
interacted over millennia. What recent scholars of precolonial North
America have found even more striking, given this diversity, is the extent
to which native peoples' histories intersected one another.

At the heart of these intersections was exchange. By exchange is meant
not only the trading of material goods but also exchanges across community lines of marriage partners, resources, labor, ideas, techniques,
and religious practices. Longer-distance exchanges frequently crossed
cultural and linguistic boundaries as well and ranged from casual
encounters to widespread alliances and networks that were economic,
political, and religious. For both individuals and communities,
exchanges sealed social and political relationships. Rather than accumu-
late material wealth endlessly, those who acquired it gave it away,
thereby earning prestige and placing obligations on others to reciprocate
appropriately. And as we shall see, many goods were not given away to
others in this world but were buried with individuals to accompany them
to another.

Archaeologists have found evidence of ongoing exchange relations
among even the earliest known Paleo-Indian inhabitants of North
America. Ten thousand years before Columbus, in the wake of the last
Ice Age, bands of two or three dozen persons regularly traveled hundreds
of miles to hunt and trade with one another at favored campsites such
as Lindenmeier in northern Colorado, dating to ca. 8800 B.C. At the
Lindenmeier site, differences in the flaking and shaping of stone points
distinguished regular occupants in two parts of the camp, and the
obsidian each used came from about 350 miles north and south of
Lindenmeier, respectively. Evidence from a wide range of settlement

sites makes clear that, as the postglacial warming trend continued, so-called Archaic peoples in much of the continent developed wider ranges of food sources, more sedentary settlement patterns, and larger populations. They also expanded their exchanges with one another and conducted them over greater distances. Highly valued materials such as Great Lakes copper, Rocky Mountain obsidian, and marine shells from the Gulf and Atlantic coasts have been found in substantial quantities at sites hundreds and even thousands of miles from their points of origin. In many cases, goods fashioned from these materials were buried with human beings, indicating both their religious significance and, by their uneven distribution, their role as markers of social or political rank.

While the Archaic pattern of autonomous bands persisted in most of North America until the arrival of Europeans, the complexity of exchange relationships in some parts of the continent produced the earliest evidence of concentrated political power. This was especially so for peoples who, after the first century A.D., developed food economies that permitted them to inhabit permanent, year-round villages. In California, for example, competition among communities for coveted acorn groves generated sharply defined political territories and elevated the role of chiefs who oversaw trade, diplomacy, and warfare for clusters of villages. Similar competition for prime fishing and trading locations strengthened the authority of certain village chiefs on the Northwest Coast. Exchange rather than competition for resources appears to have driven centralization in the Ohio and Illinois valleys. There the Hopewell peoples imported copper, mica, shell, and other raw materials over vast distances to their village centers, where specialists fashioned them into intricately crafted ornaments, tools, and other objects. They deposited massive quantities of these goods with the dead in large mounds and exported more to communities scattered throughout the Mississippi Valley. Hopewell burials differentiate between commoners and elites by the quantity and quality of grave goods accompanying each. In the Southwest, meanwhile, a culture known as Hohokam emerged in the Gila River and Salt River valleys among some of the first societies based primarily on agriculture. Hohokam peoples lived in permanent villages and maintained elaborate irrigation systems that enabled them to harvest two crops per year.

By the twelfth century, agricultural production had spread over much of the Eastern Woodlands as well as to more of the Southwest. In both regions, even more complex societies were emerging to dominate widespread exchange networks. In the Mississippi Valley and the Southeast, the sudden primacy of maize horticulture is marked archaeologically in a variety of ways – food remains, pollen profiles, studies of human bone (showing that maize accounted for 50 percent of people's diets), and in material culture by a proliferation of chert hoes, shell-tempered pottery for storing and cooking, and pits for storing surplus crops. These developments were accompanied by the rise of what archaeologists term "Mississippian" societies, consisting of fortified political and ceremonial centers and outlying villages. The centers were built around open plazas featuring platform burial mounds, temples, and elaborate residences for elite families. Evidence from burials makes clear the wide social gulf that separated commoners from elites. Whereas the former were buried in simple graves with a few personal possessions, the latter were interred in the temples or plazas along with many more, and more elaborate, goods such as copper ornaments, massive sheets of shell and ceremonial weapons. Skeletal evidence indicates that elites ate more meat, were taller, performed less strenuous physical activity, and were less prone to illness and accident than commoners. Although most archaeologists' conclusions are informed at least in part by models developed by political anthropologists, they also draw heavily from Spanish and French observations of some of the last Mississippian societies. These observations confirm that political leaders, or chiefs, from elite families mobilized labor, collected tribute, redistributed agricultural surpluses, coordinated trade, diplomacy, and military activity, and were worshipped as deities.

The largest, most complex Mississippian center was Cahokia, located not far from the confluence of the Mississippi and Missouri rivers, near modern East St. Louis, Illinois, in the rich floodplain known as American Bottoms. By the twelfth century, Cahokia probably numbered 20,000 people and contained over 120 mounds within a five-square-mile area. One key to Cahokia's rise was its combination of rich soil and nearby wooded uplands, enabling inhabitants to produce surplus crops while providing an abundance and diversity of wild food sources along with ample supplies of wood for fuel and construction. A second key was its location, affording access to the great river systems of the North American interior.

Cahokia had the most elaborate social structure yet seen in North America. Laborers used stone and wooden spades to dig soil from "borrow pits" (at least nineteen have been identified by archaeologists), which they carried in wooden buckets to mounds and palisades often more than half a mile away. The volume and concentration of craft activity in shell, copper, clay, and other materials, both local and imported, suggests that specialized artisans provided the material foundation for Cahokia's exchange ties with other peoples. Although most Cahokians were buried in mass graves outside the palisades, their rulers were given special treatment. At a prominent location in Mound 72, the largest of Cahokia's platform mounds, a man had been buried atop a platform of shell beads. Accompanying him were several group burials: fifty young women, aged 18 to 23, four men, and three men and three women, all encased in uncommonly large amounts of exotic materials. As with the Natchez Indians observed by the French in Louisiana, Cahokians appear to have sacrificed individuals to accompany their leaders in the afterlife. Cahokia was surrounded by nine smaller mound centers and several dozen villages from which it obtained much of its food and through which it conducted its water-borne commerce with other Mississippian centers in the Midwest and Southeast.

At the outset of the twelfth century, the center of production and exchange in the Southwest was in the basin of the San Juan River at Chaco Canyon in New Mexico, where Anasazi culture achieved its most elaborate expression. A twelve-mile stretch of the canyon and its rim held twelve large planned towns on the north side and 200 to 350 apparently unplanned villages on the south. The total population was probably about 15,000. The towns consisted of 200 or more contiguous, multistoried rooms, along with numerous kivas (underground ceremonial areas), constructed of veneered masonry walls and log beams imported from upland areas nearly fifty miles distant. The rooms surrounded a central plaza with a great kiva. Villages typically had ten to twenty rooms that were decidedly smaller than those in the towns. Nearly all of Chaco Canyon's turquoise, shell, and other ornaments and virtually everything imported from Mesoamerica are found in the towns rather than the villages. Whether the goods were considered communal property or were the possessions of elites is uncertain, but either way the towns clearly had primacy. Villagers buried their dead near their residences, whereas town burial grounds were apparently located at greater distances, although only a very few of what must have been thousands of town burials have been located by archaeologists. Finally, and of particular importance in the arid environment of the region, the towns were located at the mouths of side canyons where they controlled the collection and distribution of water run-off.

The canyon was the core of an extensive network of at least seventy towns or "outliers," as they are termed in the archaeological literature, and 5,300 villages located as far as sixty miles from the canyon. Facilitating the movement of people and goods through this network was a system of roads radiating outward from the canyon in perfectly straight lines, turning into stairways or footholds rather than circumventing cliffs and other obstacles.

What archaeologists call the "Chaco phenomenon" was a multifaceted network. Within the canyon, the towns controlled the distribution of precious water. The abundance of rooms reinforces the supposition that they stored agricultural surpluses for redistribution, not only within the canyon but to the outliers. The architectural uniformity of towns throughout the system, the straight roads that linked them, and the proliferation of great kivas point to a complex of shared beliefs and rituals. Lithic remains indicate that the canyon imported most of the raw materials used for manufacturing utilitarian goods and ornamental objects from elsewhere in the Southwest. Particularly critical in this respect was turquoise, beads of which were traded to Mexico in return for copper bells and macaws and to the Gulf of California for marine shells. The Chaco phenomenon thus entailed the mobilization of labor for public works projects and food production, the control and distribution of water, the distribution of prestige goods of both local and exotic origin, and the control of exchange and redistribution both within and outside the network. In distinct contrast to Cahokia and other Mississippian societies, no evidence exists for the primacy of any single canyon town or for the primacy of certain individuals as paramount leaders.

Given the archaeological record, North American "prehistory" can hardly be characterized as a multiplicity of discrete microhistories. Fundamental to the social and economic patterns of even the earliest Paleo-Indian bands were exchanges that linked peoples across geographic, cultural, and linguistic boundaries. The effects of these links are apparent in the spread of raw materials and finished goods, of beliefs and ceremonies, and of techniques for food production and for manufacturing. By the twelfth century, some exchange networks had become highly formalized and centralized. Exchange constitutes an important key to conceptualizing American history before Columbus.

Although it departs from our familiar image of North American Indians, the historical pattern sketched so far is recognizable in the way it portrays societies "progressing" from small, egalitarian, autonomous communities to larger, more hierarchical, and centralized political aggregations with more complex economies. That image is likewise subverted when we examine the three centuries immediately preceding the arrival of Europeans. In both American Bottoms and the San Juan River basin, where twelfth-century populations were most concentrated, agriculture most productive, exchange most varied and voluminous, and political systems most complex and extensive, there were scarcely any inhabitants by the end of the fifteenth century. What happened and why?

Cahokia and other Mississippian societies in the Upper Midwest peaked during the late twelfth and early thirteenth centuries. Data from soil traces indicate that even then laborers were fortifying Cahokia's major earthworks against attack. At the same time, archaeologists surmise, Cahokia was headed toward an ecological crisis: expanded settlement, accompanied by especially hot dry summers, exhausted the soil, depleted the supply of timber for building and fuel, and reduced the habitat of the game that supplemented their diet. By the end of the fourteenth century, Cahokia's inhabitants had dispersed over the surrounding countryside into small farming villages.

Cahokia's abandonment reverberated among other Mississippian societies in the Midwest. Fortified centers on the Mississippi River from the Arkansas River northward and on the Ohio River appear to have been strengthened by influxes of people from nearby villages but then abandoned, and signs from burials indicate a period of chronic, deadly warfare in the Upper Midwest. One archaeologist refers to the middle Mississippi Valley and environs during the fifteenth century as "the vacant quarter." A combination of ecological pressures and upheavals within the alliance that linked them appears to have doomed Cahokia and other midwestern Mississippian centers, leading the inhabitants to transform themselves into the village dwellers of the surrounding prairies and plains observed by French explorers three centuries later.

The upheavals may even have extended beyond the range of direct Mississippian influence to affect Iroquois and Hurons and other Iroquoian speakers of the lower Great Lakes region. These people had been moving from dispersed, riverside settlements to fortified, bluff-top villages over the course of several centuries; the process appears to have intensified in the fourteenth century, when it also led to the formation of the Iroquois and Huron confederacies. The Hurons developed fruitful relations with hunter-gatherers to the north, with whom they exchanged agricultural produce for meat and skins, and Iroquois ties with outsiders appear to have diminished except for small-scale interactions with coastal peoples to the south and east. Across the Northeast, political life was characterized by violence and other manifestations of intense competition. Whether the upheavals in exchange ties occasioned by the collapse of Cahokia were directly linked to the formation of the Iroquois and Huron confederacies, as [archaeologists] Dena Dincauze and Robert Hasenstab have suggested for the Iroquois, or were simply part of a larger process generated by the advent of farming and consequent demographic and political changes, the repercussions were still evident when Europeans began to frequent the region during the sixteenth century.

Violence and instability were also apparent across the Southeast. Unlike in the Midwest, where enormous power had been concentrated in a single center, southeastern Mississippian societies were characterized by more frequently shifting alliances and rivalries that prevented any one center from becoming as powerful as Cahokia was from the tenth to thirteenth centuries. A pattern of instability prevailed that archaeologist David Anderson terms "cycling," in which certain centers emerged for a century or two to dominate regional alliances consisting of several chiefdoms and their tributary communities and then declined. Whole communities periodically shifted their locations in response to ecological or political pressures. Thus, for example, the great mound center at Etowah, in northwestern Georgia, lost its preeminence after 1400 and by the time of Hernando de Soto's arrival in 1540 had become a tributary of the nearby upstart chiefdom of Coosa.

From the mid-twelfth century through the fourteenth, the demographic map of the Southwest was also transformed as Chaco Canyon and other Anasazi and Hohokam centers were abandoned. Although southwesterners had made a practice of shifting their settlements when facing shortages of water and arable land and other consequences of climatic or demographic change, they had never done so on such a massive scale. Most archaeologists agree that the abandonments followed changes in the regional cycle of rainfall and drought, so that agricultural surpluses probably proved inadequate. They point to signs that the centralized systems lost their ability to mobilize labor, redistribute goods, and coordinate religious ceremonies and that such loss was followed by outmigration to surrounding and upland areas where people farmed less intensively while increasing their hunting and gathering. Trade between the Southwest and Mesoamerica was disrupted at the same time, though whether as a cause or an effect of the abandonments is unclear.

Most Anasazi peoples dispersed in small groups, joining others to form new communities in locations with sufficient rainfall. These communities are what we know today as the southwestern pueblos, extending from Hopi villages in Arizona to those on the Rio Grande. These dispersals and convergences of peoples reinforced an emerging complex of beliefs, art, and ceremonies relating to kachinas – spirits believed to have influence in both bringing rain and fostering cooperation among villagers. Given their effort to forge new communities under conditions of severe drought, it is not surprising that southwestern farmers placed great emphasis on kachinas. The eastward shift of much of the southwestern population also led to new patterns of trade in which recently arrived Athapaskan speakers (later known as Apaches and Navajos) brought bison meat and hides and other products from the southern Great Plains to semiannual trade fairs at Taos, Pecos, and Picuris pueblos in exchange for maize, cotton blankets, obsidian, turquoise, and ceramics as well as shells from the Gulf of California. By the time of Francisco Vásquez de Coronado's *entrada* in 1540, new ties of exchange and interdependency bound eastern Pueblos, Athapaskans, and Caddoan speakers on the Plains.

When Europeans reached North America, then, the continent's demographic and political map was in a state of profound flux. A major factor was the collapse of the great centers at Cahokia and Chaco Canyon and elsewhere in the Midwest and Southwest. Although there were significant differences between these highly centralized societies, each ran up against the capacity of the land or other resources to sustain it. This is not to argue for a simple ecological determinism for, although environmental fluctuations played a role, the severe strains in each region resulted above all from a series of human choices that had brought about unprecedented concentrations of people and power. Having repudiated those choices and dispersed, midwestern Mississippians and Anasazis formed new communities in which they retained kinship, ceremonial, and other traditions antedating these complex societies. At the same time, these new communities and neighboring ones sought to flourish in their new political and environmental settings by establishing, and in some cases endeavoring to control, new exchange networks.

Such combinations of continuity and change, persistence and adaptability, arose from concrete historical experiences rather than a timeless tradition. The remainder of this article indicates some of the ways that both the deeply rooted imperatives of reciprocity and exchange and the recent legacies of competition and upheaval informed North American history as Europeans began to make their presence felt.

Discussion of the transition from pre- to postcontact times must begin with the sixteenth century, when Indians and Europeans met and interacted in a variety of settings. When not slighting the era altogether, historians have viewed it as one of discovery or exploration, citing the achievements of notable Europeans in either anticipating or failing to anticipate the successful colonial enterprises of the seventeenth century. Recently, however, a number of scholars have been integrating information from European accounts with the findings of archaeologists to produce a much fuller picture of this critical period in North American history.

The Southeast was the scene of the most formidable attempts at colonization during the sixteenth century, primarily by Spain. Yet in spite of several expeditions to the interior and the undertaking of an ambitious colonizing and missionary effort, extending from St. Augustine over much of the Florida peninsula and north to Chesapeake Bay, the Spanish retained no permanent settlements beyond St. Augustine itself at the end of the century. Nevertheless, their explorers and missionaries opened the way for the spread of smallpox and other epidemic diseases over much of the area south of the Chesapeake and east of the Mississippi.

The most concerted and fruitful efforts of the interdisciplinary scholarship entail the linking of southeastern societies that are known archaeologically with societies described in European documents. For example, Charles Hudson, David Hally, and others have demonstrated the connections between a group of archaeological sites in northern Georgia and the Tennessee Valley and what sixteenth-century Spanish observers referred to as Coosa and its subordinate provinces. A Mississippian archaeological site in northwestern Georgia known as Little Egypt consists of the remains of the town of Coosa; the town was the capital of the province ("chiefdom" to the archaeologists) of the same name, containing several nearby towns, and this province/chiefdom in turn dominated a network of at least five other chiefdoms in a "paramount chiefdom." These conclusions would not have been as definitive if based on either documentary or archaeological evidence alone.[2]

Coosa, as previously noted, attained regional supremacy during the fifteenth century, a phase in the apparently typical process whereby paramount chiefdoms rose and fell in the Mississippian Southeast. But Coosa's decline was far more precipitate than others because Spanish diseases ravaged the province, forcing the survivors to abandon the town and move southward. By the end of the sixteenth century, several new provincial centers emerged in what are now Alabama and western Georgia, but without the mounds and paramount chiefs of their predecessors. As with earlier declines of paramount chiefdoms, a center had declined and, out of the resulting power vacuum, a new formation emerged. What differed in this case were the external source of the decline, its devastating effects, and the inability or unwillingness of the survivors to concentrate power and deference in the hands of paramount chiefs. At the same time, the absence of Spanish or other European colonizers from the late sixteenth century to late seventeenth meant that the natives had a sustained period of time in which to recover and regroup. When English traders encountered the descendants of refugees from Coosa and its neighbors late in the seventeenth century, they labeled them "Creek."

Patricia Galloway has established similar connections between Mississippian societies farther west and the Choctaws of the eighteenth century. She argues that the well-known site of Moundville in Alabama and a second site on the Pearl River in Mississippi were the centers of chiefdoms from which most Choctaws were descended. She argues that, unlike Coosa, these centers were probably declining in power before the onset of disease in the 1540s hastened the process. Like the Creeks, the Choctaws were a multilingual, multiethnic society in which individual

villages were largely autonomous although precedents for greater coales-
cence were available if conditions, such as the European presence,
seemed to require it.[3]

As in the Southeast, Spanish colonizers in the sixteenth-century
Southwest launched several ambitious military and missionary efforts,
hoping to extend New Spain's domain northward and to discover additional sources of wealth. The best-documented encounters of Spanish
with Pueblos – most notably those of Coronado's expedition (1540–
1542) – ended in violence and failure for the Spanish who, despite
vows to proceed peacefully, violated Pueblo norms of reciprocity by
insisting on excessive tribute or outright submission. In addition, the
Spanish had acquired notoriety among the Pueblos as purveyors of
epidemic diseases, religious missions, and slaving expeditions inflicted
on Indians to the south, in what is now northern Mexico.

The Spanish also affected patterns of exchange throughout the Southwest. Indians resisting the spread of Spanish rule to northern Mexico
stole horses and other livestock, some of which they traded to neighbors.
By the end of the sixteenth century, a few Indians on the periphery of the
Southwest were riding horses, anticipating the combination of theft and
exchange that would spread horses to native peoples throughout the
region and, still later, the Plains and the Southeast. In the meantime,
some Navajos and Apaches moved near the Rio Grande Valley, strengthening ties with certain pueblos that were reinforced when inhabitants of
those pueblos sought refuge among them in the face or wake of Spanish
entradas.

Yet another variation on the theme of Indian-European contacts in the
sixteenth century was played out in the Northeast, where Iroquoian-
speaking villagers on the Mississippian periphery and Archaic hunter-
gatherers still further removed from developments in the interior met
Europeans of several nationalities. At the outset of the century, Spanish
and Portuguese explorers enslaved several dozen Micmacs and other
Indians from the Nova Scotia-Gulf of St. Lawrence area. Three French
expeditions to the St. Lawrence itself in the 1530s and 1540s followed
the Spanish pattern by alienating most Indians encountered and ending
in futility. Even as these hostile contacts were taking place, fishermen,
whalers, and other Europeans who visited the area regularly had begun
trading with natives. As early as the 1520s, Abenakis on the coast of
Maine and Micmacs were trading the furs of beavers and other animals
for European goods of metal and glass. By the 1540s, specialized fur
traders, mostly French, frequented the coast as far south as the Chesapeake; by the 1550s or soon thereafter, French traders rendezvoused
regularly with Indians along the shores of upper New England, the
Maritimes, and Quebec and at Tadoussac on the St. Lawrence.

What induced Indians to go out of their way to trap beaver and trade the skins for glass beads, mirrors, copper kettles, and other goods? Throughout North America since Paleo-Indian times, exchange in the Northeast was the means by which people maintained and extended their social, cultural, and spiritual horizons as well as acquired items considered supernaturally powerful. Members of some coastal Indian groups later recalled how the first Europeans they saw, with their facial hair and strange clothes and traveling in their strange boats, seemed like supernatural figures. Although soon disabused of such notions, these Indians and many more inland placed special value on the glass beads and other trinkets offered by the newcomers. Recent scholarship on Indians' motives in this earliest stage of the trade indicates that they regarded such objects as the equivalents of the quartz, mica, shell, and other sacred substances that had formed the heart of long-distance exchange in North America for millennia and that they regarded [them] as sources of physical and spiritual wellbeing, on earth and in the afterlife. Indians initially altered and wore many of the utilitarian goods they received, such as iron axe heads and copper pots, rather than use them for their intended purposes. Moreover, even though the new objects might pass through many hands, they more often than not ended up in graves, presumably for their possessors to use in the afterlife. Finally, the archaeological findings make clear that shell and native copper predominated over the new objects in sixteenth-century exchanges, indicating that European trade did not suddenly trigger a massive craving for the objects themselves. While northeastern Indians recognized Europeans as different from themselves, they interacted with them and their materials in ways that were consistent with their own customs and beliefs.

By the late sixteenth century, the effects of European trade began to overlap with the effects of earlier upheavals in the northeastern interior. Sometime between Jacques Cartier's final departure in 1543 and Samuel de Champlain's arrival in 1603, the Iroquoian-speaking inhabitants of Hochelaga and Stadacona (modern Montreal and Quebec City) abandoned their communities. The communities were crushed militarily, and the survivors dispersed among both Iroquois and Hurons. Whether the perpetrators of these dispersals were Iroquois or Huron is a point of controversy, but either way the St. Lawrence communities appear to have been casualties of the rivalry, at least a century old, between the two confederations as each sought to position itself vis-à-vis the French. The effect, if not the cause, of the dispersals was the Iroquois practice of attacking antagonists who denied them direct access to trade goods; this is consistent with Iroquois actions during the preceding two centuries and the century that followed.

The sudden availability of many more European goods, the absorption of many refugees from the St. Lawrence, and the heightening of tensions with the Iroquois help to explain the movement of most outlying Huron communities to what is now the Simcoe Country area of Ontario during the 1580s. This geographic concentration strengthened their confederacy and gave it the form it had when allied with New France during the first half of the seventeenth century. Having formerly existed at the outer margins of an arena of exchange centered in Cahokia, the Hurons and Iroquois now faced a new source of goods and power to the east.

The diverse native societies encountered by Europeans as they began to settle North America permanently during the seventeenth century were not static isolates lying outside the ebb and flow of human history. Rather, they were products of a complex set of historical forces, both local and wide-ranging, both deeply rooted and of recent origin. Although their lives and worldviews were shaped by long-standing traditions of reciprocity and spiritual power, the people in these communities were also accustomed – contrary to popular myths about inflexible Indians – to economic and political flux and to absorbing new peoples (both allies and antagonists), objects, and ideas, including those originating in Europe. Such combinations of tradition and innovation continued to shape Indians' relations with Europeans, even as the latter's visits became permanent.

The establishment of lasting European colonies, beginning with New Mexico in 1598, began a phase in the continent's history that eventually resulted in the displacement of Indians to the economic, political, and cultural margins of a new order. But during the interim natives and colonizers entered into numerous relationships in which they exchanged material goods and often supported one another diplomatically or militarily against common enemies. These relations combined native and European modes of exchange. While much of the scholarly literature emphasizes the subordination and dependence of Indians in these circumstances, Indians as much as Europeans dictated the form and content of their early exchanges and alliances. Much of the protocol and ritual surrounding such intercultural contacts was rooted in indigenous kinship obligations and gift exchanges, and Indian consumers exhibited decided preferences for European commodities that satisfied social, spiritual, and aesthetic values. Similarly, Indians' long-range motives and strategies in their alliances with Europeans were frequently rooted in older patterns of alliance and rivalry with regional neighbors. Such continuities can be glimpsed through a brief consideration of the early colonial-era histories of the Five Nations Iroquois in the

Northeast, the Creeks in the Southeast, and the Rio Grande Pueblos in the Southwest.

Post-Mississippian and sixteenth-century patterns of antagonism between the Iroquois and their neighbors to the north and west persisted, albeit under altered circumstances, during the seventeenth century when France established its colony on the St. Lawrence and allied itself with Hurons and other Indians. France aimed to extract maximum profits from the fur trade, and it immediately recognized the Iroquois as the major threat to that goal. In response, the Iroquois turned to the Dutch in New Netherland for guns and other trade goods while raiding New France's Indian allies for the thicker northern pelts that brought higher prices than those in their own country (which they exhausted by midcentury) and for captives to replace those from their own ranks who had died from epidemics or in wars. During the 1640s, the Iroquois replaced raids with full-scale military assaults (the so-called Beaver Wars) on Iroquoian-speaking communities in the lower Great Lakes, absorbing most of the survivors as refugees or captives. All the while, the Iroquois elaborated a vision of their confederation, which had brought harmony within their own ranks, as bringing peace to all peoples of the region. For the remainder of the century, the Five Nations fought a grueling and costly series of wars against the French and their Indian allies in order to gain access to the pelts and French goods circulating in lands to the north and west.

Meanwhile, the Iroquois were also adapting to the growing presence of English colonists along the Atlantic seaboard. After the English supplanted the Dutch in New York in 1664, Iroquois diplomats established relations with the proprietary governor, Sir Edmund Andros, in a treaty known as the Covenant Chain. The Covenant Chain was an elaboration of the Iroquois' earlier treaty arrangements with the Dutch, but, whereas the Iroquois had termed the Dutch relationship a chain of iron, they referred to the one with the English as a chain of silver. The shift in metaphors was appropriate, for what had been strictly an economic connection was now a political one in which the Iroquois acquired power over other New York Indians. After 1677, the Covenant Chain was expanded to include several English colonies, most notably Massachusetts and Maryland, along with those colonies' subject Indians. The upshot of these arrangements was that the Iroquois cooperated with their colonial partners in subduing and removing subject Indians who impeded settler expansion. The Mohawks in particular played a vital role in the New England colonies' suppression of the Indian uprising known as King Philip's War and in moving the Susquehannocks away from the expanding frontier of settlement in the Chesapeake after Bacon's Rebellion.

For the Iroquois, such a policy helped expand their "Tree of Peace" among Indians while providing them with buffers against settler encroachment around their homelands. The major drawback in the arrangement proved to be the weakness of English military assistance against the French. This inadequacy, and the consequent suffering experienced by the Iroquois during two decades of war after 1680, finally drove the Five Nations to make peace with the French and their Indian allies in the Grand Settlement of 1701. Together, the Grand Settlement and Covenant Chain provided the Iroquois with the peace and security, the access to trade goods, and the dominant role among northeastern Indians they had long sought. That these arrangements in the long run served to reinforce rather than deter English encroachment on Iroquois lands and autonomy should not obscure their pre-European roots and their importance in shaping colonial history in the Northeast.

In the southeastern interior, [the archaeologist] Vernon Knight argues, descendants of refugees from Coosa and neighboring communities regrouped in clusters of Creek *talwas* (villages), each dominated by a large talwa and its "great chief." In the late seventeenth century, these latter-day chiefdom/provinces forged alliances with English traders, first from Virginia and then from Carolina, who sought to trade guns and other manufactured goods for deerskins and Indian slaves. In so doing, the Creeks ensured that they would be regarded by the English as clients rather than as commodities. The deerskin trade proved to be a critical factor in South Carolina's early economic development, and the trade in Indian slaves significantly served England's imperial ambitions vis-à-vis Spain in Florida. After 1715, the several Creek alliances acted in concert as a confederacy – the Creek Nation – on certain occasions. As a result, they achieved a measure of success in playing off these powers and maintaining neutrality in their conflicts with one another. While much differentiates Creek political processes in the colonial period from those of the late Mississippian era, there are strong elements of continuity in the transformation of Mississippian chiefdoms into great Creek talwas.

In the Southwest, the institution of Spanish colonial rule on the Rio Grande after 1598 further affected exchange relations between Pueblo Indians and nearby Apaches and Navajos. By imposing heavy demands for tribute in the form of corn, the Spanish prevented Pueblo peoples from trading surplus produce with their nonfarming neighbors. In order to obtain the produce on which they had come to depend, Apaches and Navajos staged deadly raids on some pueblos, leaving the inhabitants dependent on the Spanish for protection. In retaliation, Spanish soldiers captured Apaches and Navajos whom they sold as slaves to their countrymen to the south. From the beginning, the trading pueblos of Pecos, Picuris, and Taos most resented Spanish control and strongly resisted the proselytizing of Franciscan missionaries. From the late 1660s, drought and disease, intensified Apache and Navajo raids, and the severity of Spanish rule led more and more Indians from all pueblos to question the advantages of Christianity and to renew their ties to their indigenous religious traditions. Spanish persecution of native religious leaders and their backsliding followers precipitated the Pueblo Revolt of 1680, in which the trading Pueblos played a leading role and which was actively supported by some Navajos and Apaches.

When the Spanish reimposed their rule during the 1690s, they tolerated traditional Indian religion rather than trying to extirpate it, and they participated in interregional trade fairs at Taos and other villages. The successful incorporation of Pueblo Indians as loyal subjects proved vital to New Mexico's survival as a colony and, more generally, to Spain's imperial presence in the Southwest during the eighteenth and early nineteenth centuries.

As significant as is the divide separating pre- and post-Columbian North American history, it is not the stark gap suggested by the distinction between prehistory and history. For varying periods of time after their arrival in North America, Europeans adapted to the social and political environments they found, including the fluctuating ties of reciprocity and interdependence as well as rivalry, that characterized those environments. They had little choice but to enter in and participate if they wished to sustain their presence. Eventually, one route to success proved to be their ability to insert themselves as regional powers in new networks of exchange and alliance that arose to supplant those of the Mississippians, Anasazis, and others.

To assert such continuities does not minimize the radical transformations entailed in Europeans' colonization of the continent and its indigenous peoples. Arising in Cahokia's wake, new centers at Montreal, Fort Orange/Albany, Charleston, and elsewhere permanently altered the primary patterns of exchange in eastern North America. The riverine system that channeled exchange in the interior of the continent gave way to one in which growing quantities of goods arrived from, and were directed to, coastal peripheries and ultimately Europe. In the Southwest, the Spanish revived Anasazi links with Mesoamerica at some cost to newer ties between the Rio Grande Pueblos and recently arrived, non-farming Athapaskan speakers. More generally, European colonizers brought a complex of demographic and ecological advantages, most notably epidemic diseases and their own immunity to them, that utterly devastated Indian communities; ideologies and beliefs in their cultural and spiritual superiority to native peoples and their entitlement to natives' lands; and economic, political, and military systems organized for the engrossment of Indian lands and the subordination or suppression of Indian peoples.

Europeans were anything but uniformly successful in realizing their goals, but the combination of demographic and ecological advantages and imperial intentions, along with the Anglo-Iroquois Covenant Chain, enabled land-hungry colonists from New England to the Chesapeake to break entirely free of ties of dependence on Indians before the end of the seventeenth century. Their successes proved to be only the beginning of a new phase of Indian–European relations. By the mid-eighteenth century, the rapid expansion of land-based settlement in the English colonies had sundered older ties of exchange and alliance linking natives and colonizers nearly everywhere east of the Appalachians, driving many Indians west and reducing those who remained to a scattering of politically powerless enclaves in which Indian identities were nurtured in isolation. Meanwhile, the colonizers threatened to extend this new mode of Indian relations across the Appalachians. An old world, rooted in indigenous exchange, was giving way to one in which Native Americans had no certain place.

Notes

1   Robert F. Berkhofer, Jr, *The White Man's Indian: Images of the American Indian from Columbus to the Present* (New York, 1978), p. 3.

2   Charles Hudson et al., "Coosa: A Chiefdom in the Sixteenth-Century Southeastern United States," *American Antiquity*, 50 (1985); David J. Hally, "The Archaeological Reality of de Soto's Coosa," in D. H. Thomas, ed., *Columbian Consequences*, vol. 2: *Archaeological and Historical Perspectives on the Spanish Borderlands East* (Washington, D.C., 1990); Robert L. Blakely, ed., *The King Site: Continuity and Contact in Sixteenth-Century Georgia* (Athens, GA, 1988); Hudson, "A Spanish–Coosa Alliance in Sixteenth-Century Georgia," *Georgia Historical Quarterly*, 72 (1988), 599–626; Hudson, *The Juan Pardo Expeditions: Exploration of the Carolinas and Tennessee, 1566–1568* (Washington, D.C., 1990), 101–9; Hally, "The Chiefdom of Coosa," in Charles Hudson and Carmen Chaves Tesser, eds, *The Forgotten Centuries: Indians and Europeans in the American South, 1525–1704* (Athens, GA, 1994), 227–53.

3   Patricia Galloway, "Confederacy as a Solution to Chiefdom Dissolution: Historical Evidence in the Choctaw Case," in Hudson and Tesser, eds, *Forgotten Centuries*, 393–420.

Documents

H. S. Halbert, a teacher and missionary among the Choctaws in the nineteenth century, collected and later published accounts of Choctaw history and oral traditions. Ordinarily, the work of historians would be considered a secondary source, not a primary document, and indeed Halbert read widely in such primary documents as Spanish explorers' reports on their expeditions through the Southeast. However, Halbert's writings qualify as an original source for several reasons. He conducted oral histories with several Choctaws and recorded valuable firsthand accounts of what nineteenth-century Choctaws knew of Nanih Wayah, a mound in Mississippi which the Choctaws regarded as sacred. Halbert also visited the site of Nanih Wayah and described what the mound looked like in the late nineteenth century.

Since Halbert's main purpose was to study the ancient history of the state of Mississippi, he could also be considered a primary source on how the nineteenth-century American public constructed American history and what role ancient American civilizations were to play in that history. Just a few decades before, American scientists and archaeologists commonly speculated that the thousands of mysterious mounds in Ohio, the Mississippi Valley, and the Southeast were signs of a "civilized," white race having previously occupied North America. In the spirit of Lewis Henry Morgan and Franz Boas, Halbert sought to learn more about Indian cultures and achievements for their own sake. However, also in the spirit of Morgan and Boas, Halbert described Nanih Wayah as an abandoned ruin of a once thriving people, disappearing through the destructive – but also by implication constructive and progressive – actions of the plow.

Nanih Waiya, The Sacred Mound of the Choctaws

H. S. Halbert

As Nanih Waiya is so often referred to in the folklore and traditions of the Choctaws, the writer of this paper has deemed it not amiss to give some account of this noted mound and, in connection therewith, some of the legends with which it is inseparably associated.

Halbert, H. S. 'Nanih Waiya, The Sacred Mound of the Choctaws.' *Publications of the Mississippi Historical Society* 2 (1899): 223–34.

Nanih Waiya is situated on the west side of Nanih Waiya Creek, about fifty yards from it, in the southern part of Winston County, and about four hundred yards from the Neshoba County line. The mound is oblong in shape, lying northwest and southeast, and about forty feet in height. Its base covers about an acre. Its summit, which is flat, has an area of one-fourth of an acre. The mound stands on the southeastern edge of a circular rampart, which is about a mile and a half in circumference. In using the word "circular," reference is made to the original form of the rampart, about one-half of which is utterly obliterated by the plow, leaving only a semi-circle. This rampart is not or rather was not, a continuous circle, so to speak, as it has along at intervals, a number of vacant places or gaps, ranging from twenty to fifty yards wide. According to Indian tradition, there were originally eighteen parts or sections of the rampart, with the same number of gaps. Ten of these sections still remain, ranging from fifty to one hundred and fifty yards in length. All the sections near the mound have long since been leveled by the plow, and in other places some of the sections have been much reduced. But on the north, where the rampart traverses a primeval forest it is still five feet high and twenty feet broad at the base. The process of obliteration has been very great since 1877, when the writer first saw Nanih Waiya. Some of the sections that could then be clearly traced in the field on the west have now utterly disappeared. About two hundred and fifty yards north of Nanih Waiya is a small mound, evidently a burial mound, as can be safely stated from the numerous fragments of human bones that have been exhumed from it by the plow and the hoe. The great number of stone relics, mostly broken, scattered for hundreds of yards around Nanih Waiya, shows that it was the site of pre-historic habitations. In addition to this, the bullets and other relics of European manufacture evidence the continuity of occupancy down within the historic period. The magnitude of these ancient works – the mound and the rampart – together with the legendary traditions connected with them, leads one irresistibly to the conviction that this locality was the great center of the Choctaw population during the pre-historic period. It should here be stated that the symmetry of the mound has been somewhat marred by a tunnel which was cut into it in the summer of 1896 by some *treasure-seekers*, who vainly hoped to unearth some wonderful bonanza from out the deep bosom of Nanih Waiya.

The name Nanih Waiya signifies Bending Hill. *Warrior*, the absurd spelling and pronunciation should be repudiated by the map and the history maker. The adjective *Waiya* signifies "bending, leaning over," but it is difficult to see the appropriateness of the term as applied to the mound. According to the conjecture of the writer, the term was originally applied to the circular rampart, which the Choctaws may have considered a kind of *bending hill*. And in process of time the name could have become so extended as to be applied to the mound and rampart conjointly, and ultimately restricted to the mound alone, as is now the case in popular usage.

According to the classification of the archæologists, Nanih Waiya is a pyramidal mound, which kind of mounds is found almost exclusively in the Gulf States. The chroniclers of De Soto's expedition speak constantly of the mounds, and of these writers, Garcilaso de la Vega tells us exactly how and why they were made. According to his statement, in building a town, the natives first erected a mound two or three pikes in height, the summit of which was made large enough for twelve, fifteen or twenty houses to lodge the cacique and his attendants. At the foot of the mound was laid off the public square, which was proportioned to the size of the town. Around the square the leading men had their houses, whilst the cabins of the common people stood around the other side of the mound. From the "lay" of the land, the writer is satisfied that the public square at Nanih Waiya was on the north, between the mound and the small burial mound. In regard to the rampart, it was, no doubt, surmounted by palisades, as De Soto's writers particularly describe the palisaded walls, which surrounded the Indian towns. As to the gaps in the rampart, the writer is convinced that these gaps were left designedly as places for the erection of wooden forts or towers, as additional protections to the town. The Knight of Elvas describes the town of Pachaha as being "very great, walled, and beset with towers, and many loop-holes were in the towers and the wall." La Vega mentions the towers made at intervals of fifty paces apart in the stockade wall of Maubila, each tower capable of holding eight men. Dupratz describing the circular stockade forts which he had seen among the Southern Indians, expressly states that "at every forty paces a circular tower juts out." Other statements from early writers could be given showing that wooden towers were built along at intervals in the stockade walls that surrounded the ancient towns of the Southern Indians. These statements, no doubt, give us the correct solution to the mystery of the gaps in the earthern rampart at Nanih Waiya.

While there can be no doubt but Nanih Waiya was the residence of the cacique and his attendants, in accordance with the statements of La Vega, other statements induce the belief that the summit of this mound was sometimes used as a place of sun-worship. Sun-worship, it should here be especially noted, was not performed as an isolated ceremony, so to speak, but came in as part of the programme in the transaction of all tribal business, both civil and military. The Choctaws were sun-worshippers, as were all the other branches of the Choctaw-Muscogee family. They regarded the sun as the type or essence of the Great Spirit. And as the Sun, or rather Sun-God, warms, animates and vivifies everything, he is the Master or Father of Life, or, to use the Choctaw expression, *"Aba Inki,"* "the Father above." In like manner, according to their belief, as everything here below came originally from the earth, she is the mother of creation. Sun-worship, it may here be stated, prevailed to some extent, though in a much attenuated form, as late as seventy years ago among the Choctaws, as is evidenced by the actions of the Choctaws of that day during an eclipse of the sun. Even at the present day some faint traces of this sun-worship may be seen in the antics of a Choctaw prophet at a ball play. The chroniclers of De Soto's expedition give us frequent hints as to the prevalence of sun-worship among the Indian tribes of the countries which the Spanish army traversed. Two centuries later, William Bartram, in his description of the Creek rotunda, which was erected upon an artificial mound, gives an elaborate account of the ceremonies in the rotunda connected with partaking of the black drink. He states that the chief first puffed a few whiffs from the sacred pipe, blowing the whiffs ceremoniously upward towards the sun, or, as it was generally supposed, to the Great Spirit, and then puffing the smoke from the pipe towards the four cardinal points. The pipe was then carried to different persons and smoked by them in turn.

Imagination, perhaps, would not err, if going back a few centuries, we could depict scenes similar to this as often enacted upon the flat summit of Nanih Waiya. And, perhaps, the superstitious reverence which the Choctaws have ever manifested towards this mound may be a dim traditionary reminiscence of its once having been a great tribal center of solar worship. The aboriginal mind, in sun-worship, from viewing the sum as the Father of Life, as without the light and warmth of the sun nothing would spring into existence, no doubt instinctively turned to the earth as the Mother of Creation. If there was a father there must be a mother. In the course of time, what more natural that the pre-historic villagers living at the base of Nanih Waiya, with its tremendous pile ever looming up before their eyes, should finally come to regard it as the mother of their race. As far back as history and tradition run, Nanih Waiya has ever thus been regarded by the untutored Choctaws of Mississippi. During the various emigrations from the State, many Choctaws declared that they would never go west and abandon their mother; and that just as long as Nanih Waiya stood, they intended to stay and live in the land of their nativity.

There is another evidence that Nanih Waiya was a great national center during the pre-historic period. The ravages of civilization have still spared some traces of two broad, deeply worn roads or highways connected with the mound, in which now stand large oak trees. The remnant of one of these highways, several hundred yards long, can be seen on the east side of the creek, running toward the southeast. The other is on the west side of the creek, the traces nearest the mound being at the northeastern part of the rampart, thence running towards the north. Many years ago this latter road was traced by an old citizen of Winston county full twenty miles to the north until it was lost in Noxubee swamp, in the northeastern part of Winston County. These are the sole traces of the many highways, that no doubt, in pre-historic times, centered at Nanih Waiya.

Nanih Waiya is a prominent feature in the migration legend of the Choctaws, of which there are several versions. While the versions all agree, to some extent, in their main features, as the immigration from the west or northwest, the prophet and his sacred pole, and the final settlement at Nanih Waiya, there is still much diversity in the respective narratives in regard to the details and other minutiae. The most circumstantial narrative is that of the Rev. Alfred Wright, published in an issue of the *Missionary Herald* of 1828. The version given in Colonel Claiborne's "*Mississippi*," pages 483, 484, is a very unsatisfactory version. The writer of this paper wrote this version in 1877, and sent it to Colonel Claiborne, who inserted it in his history. It was taken down from the lips of Mr. Jack Henry, an old citizen of Okitibbeha County, he stating that he had received it in early life from an Irishman, who had once lived among the Choctaws and who had heard the legend from an old Choctaw woman. As will be seen, the legend was transmitted through several memories and mouths before being finally recorded in printer's ink. It came not direct from Choctaw lips, and no doubt, was unconsciously colored, or its details imperfectly remembered in its transmission through the memories of the two white men. The version which is given below came direct from the lips of the Rev. Peter Folsom, a Choctaw from the nation west, who was employed in 1882 by the Baptists of Mississippi to labor as a missionary among the Mississippi Choctaws. Mr. Folsom stated that soon after finishing his education in Kentucky, one day in 1833, he visited Nanih Waiya with his father and while at the mound his father related to him the migration legend of his people, which according to Mr. Folsom, runs as follows:

In ancient days the ancestors of the Choctaws and the Chickasaws lived in a far western country, under the rule of two brothers, named Chahta and Chikasa. In process of time, their population becoming very numerous, they found it difficult to procure substance in that land. Their prophets thereupon announced that far to the east was a country of fertile soil and full of game, where they could live in ease and plenty. The entire population resolved to make a journey eastward in search of that happy land. In order more easily to procure subsistence on their route, the people marched in several divisions of a day's journey apart. A great prophet marched at their head, bearing a pole, which, on camping at the close of each day, he planted erect in the earth, in front of the camp. Every morning the pole was always seen leaning in the direction they were to travel that day. After the lapse of many moons, they arrived one day at Nanih Waiya. The prophet planted his pole at the base of the mound. The next morning the pole was seen standing erect and stationary. This was interpreted as an omen from the Great Spirit that the long sought-for land was at last found. It so happened, the very day that the party camped at Nanih Waiya that a party under Chikasa crossed the creek and camped on its east side. That night a great rain fell, and it rained several days. In consequence of this all the low lands were inundated, and Nanih Waiya Creek and other tributaries of Pearl River were rendered impassable.

After the subsidence of the waters, messengers were sent across the creek to bid Chikasa's party return, as the oracular pole had proclaimed that the long sought-for land was found and the mound was the center of the land. Chikasa's party, however, regardless of the weather, had proceeded on their journey, and the rain having washed all traces of their march from off the grass, the messengers were unable to follow them up and so returned to camp. Meanwhile, the other divisions in the rear arrived at Nanih Waiya, and learned that here was the center of their new home, their long pilgrimage was at last finished. Chikasa's party, after their separation from their brethren under Chahta, moved on to the Tombigbee, and eventually became a separate nationality. In this way the Choctaws and the Chickasaws became two separate, though kindred nations.

Such is Mr. Folsom's version of the Choctaw migration legend. This national legend is now utterly forgotten by the modern Choctaws living in Mississippi. All, however, look upon Nanih Waiya as the birthplace and cradle of their race. She is "ishki chito," "the great mother." In the very center of the mound, they say, ages ago, the Great Spirit created the first Choctaws, and through a hole or cave, they crawled forth into the light of day. Some say that only one pair was created, but others say that many pairs were created. Old Hopahkitubbe (Hopakitobi), who died several years ago in Neshoba County, was wont to say that after coming forth from the mound, the freshly-made Choctaws were very wet and moist, and that the Great Spirit stacked them along on the rampart, as on a clothes line, so that the sun could dry them.

Soon after the creation, the Great Spirit divided the Choctaws into two "iksa," the "Kashapa Okla," and the "Okla in Holahta," or "Hattak in Holahta." Stationing one iksa on the north and the other on the west side of the sacred mound, the Great Spirit then gave them the law of marriage which they were forever to keep inviolate. This law was that children were to belong to the iksa of their mother, and that one must always marry into the opposite iksa. By this law a man belonging to the

Kashapa Okla must marry a woman of the Okla in Holahta. The children of this marriage belong, of course, to the iksa of their mother, and whenever they marry it must be into the opposite iksa. In like manner a man belonging to the Okla in Holahta must marry a woman of the Kashapa Okla, and the children of this marriage from Kashapa Okla must marry into the Okla in Holahta. Such was the Choctaw law of marriage, given, they say, by Divine authority at Nanih Waiya just after the creation of their race. The iksa lived promiscuously throughout the nation, but as every one knew to which iksa he belonged, no matrimonial mistake could possibly occur. This iksa division of the Choctaws still exists in Mississippi, but is slowly dying out under the influence of Christianity, education, and other results of contact with the white race.

The Choctaws, after their creation lived for a long time upon the spontaneous productions of the earth until at last maize was discovered, as they say, on the south side of Bogue Chito, a few miles distant from Nanih Waiya. There are several versions of the corn-finding myth, in all of which a crow and a child are main factors. Some of the versions state particularly that the crow came from the south, "Oka mahli imma minti tok." Other versions are silent on this point. The version here given is a translation by the writer of a version which was written down for him in the Choctaw language by Ilaishtubbee (Ilaishtobi), a Six Towns Indian. It is as follows:

> A long time ago it thus happened. In the very beginning a crow got a single grain of corn from across the great water, brought it to this country and gave it to an orphan child, who was playing in the yard. The child named it *tauchi*, (corn). He planted it in the yard. When the corn was growing up, the child's elders merely had it swept around. But the child, wishing to have his own way, hoed it hilled it, and laid it by. When this single grain of corn grew up and matured, it made two ears of corn. And in this way the ancestors of the Choctaws discovered corn.

"The great water" referred to in the above myth is the Gulf of Mexico. "Okachito," "great water," is the term invariably applied by the Mississippi Choctaws to the Gulf. If there are any traces of historic truth in the myth, we may infer that it contains a tradition of the introduction of corn into the Choctaw country across the Gulf of Mexico, from South America or from the West Indies. Professor J. W. Harshberger, in his monograph on the nativity and distribution of maize concludes that its earliest home was in Central of America, whence it spread north and south over the continents of America. In his map in which he gives the lines of travel by which maize was distributed, he has two lines in South America. One of these lines extends southward between the Andes and the Pacific as far down as Chili. The second line, after leaving the Isthmus of Panama, goes eastward along the north coast of South America until it enters Venezuela. From Venezuela, it goes to the West Indies and from the West Indies to Florida. This line of maize distribution harmonizes with the Choctaw tradition embodied in the myth that maize came into the Choctaw country from across "the great water," that is, from across the Gulf of Mexico. We learn from the early Spanish writers that there was intercommunication between the natives of Cuba and those of Florida. This being the case, corn could have been introduced among the pre-historic peoples of the Gulf states, across the Gulf, directly or indirectly from South America. To add completeness to the matter, according to Professor Harshberger's map, maize was introduced among the ancient peoples of the States lying north of the Gulf States by a line of distribution running from northern Mexico. It may be still further added that maize was certainly introduced into the Gulf States and into the Mississippi Valley before the beginning of the mound-building era, for only a sedentary agricultural people were capable of building the mounds.

Returning from this digression, the question may be asked, when was Nanih Waiya built, who were its builders, and how long was it in building? As to the last question, it would be a moderate estimate to say that it would take two Irishmen, equipped with spades and wheelbarrows, full ten years of constant toil to build Nanih Waiya and its rampart. The evidence shows that the earth used in making the mound was carried at least one hundred yards – an additional amount of toil that must be taken into consideration in making an estimate of the time consumed in building Nanih Waiya. Furthermore, it can be safely stated that the two supposed Irishmen could accomplish as much in one hour in the way of dirt-piling as three pre-historic natives with their rude tools of wood and stone, and baskets or skins for carrying the earth, could accomplish in one day. Nanih Waiya then must have been a long time in building. There must have been frequent interruptions of work to allow its builders time to raise crops, or in some manner to procure their supplies of food. The probabilities are, that while the work of building the rampart and the towers was carried on continuously until they were completed, so as to have the people of the place well protected from their foes, the work of building the mound was a gradual one. A small or moderate sized mound may first have been built for the cacique and his attendants. In course of time, perhaps by his successor, the mound may have been made larger and higher, each succeeding cacique adding to its size until it attained its present dimensions. In short, the mound may have been the successive work of two or three generations.

As to the builders of Nanih Waiya, all the evidence shows that they were Choctaws. There is no evidence that any race preceded the Choctaws in the occupancy of Central Mississippi. And it is not at all probable that the Choctaws would have held this mound in such excessive reverence if it had been built by an unknown or alien race.

During the decadence of the mound-building custom, the mounds were gradually made smaller and many of these small mounds reveal relics of European manufacture, thus giving indisputable evidence of their modern age. From these facts it can be safely assumed that the larger the mound, the greater, presumably, is its antiquity. Nanih Waiya then, being the largest mound in Central Mississippi, may possibly date back to about fifteen hundred years ago, as the fifth century is given by the archæologists as the beginning of the mound-building age, which age lasted about one thousand years. It may be sufficient to say that Nanih Waiya is very old and was built by the Choctaws themselves, or possibly, granting it a very remote antiquity by the primordial stock, from which, by subsequent differentiation, the various branches of the Choctaw-Muscogee family were formed.

In regard to the modern history of the mound, one event may be placed on record. At some time in 1828, at the instance by Colonel Greenwood Leflore, a great national council of the Choctaws convened at Nanih Waiya. The object of this council was the making of new laws so as to place the Choctaws more in harmony with the requirements of modern civilization. On this occasion severe laws were enacted against drunkenness and against the practice of executing women as witches. This assembly is remarkable as being the only known national Indian council held at Nanih Waiya within the historic period. How many Indian councils similar to this the mound may have witnessed in the pre-historic past can never be known.

This imperfect sketch of the Choctaw sacred mound is brought to a close with a hope, that, as long as Mississippi stands, so long may Nanih Waiya stand, steadfast and immovable, the greatest of Mississippi's pre-historic monuments.

★   ★   ★

An entirely different account of Nanih Wayah appears in this next document, a short story by Muriel Wright (1889–1975), who was a member of the Choctaw Nation of Oklahoma and, by profession, a historian. Best known for an important reference work, A Guide to the Indian Tribes of Oklahoma (1951), Wright also wrote occasional pieces of short fiction, such as this story which uses Nanih Wayah as its setting. The original document, held in the manuscript collections of the Oklahoma Historical Society, is undated, but may have been written sometime in the 1950s or 1960s, when Wright served as editor of the Oklahoma Historical Society's scholarly journal, *The Chronicles of Oklahoma*. Although Wright descended from Choctaws who had removed from Mississippi to Indian Territory, now Oklahoma, in the early nineteenth century, her choosing to write a story with Nanih Wayah at its center is testament to how twentieth-century Oklahoma Choctaws remembered this sacred mound as the heart and spirit of the Choctaw Nation.

Legend of Nanih Wayah

Muriel Hazel Wright

The panther screamed twice this night. Once down the river from afar, came a discordant that rose to the scream of a frightened woman. Unmoved by the wild cry, the Dreamer of the Chahta listened tensely in the darkness by the river. He knew the panther traveled fast. Heavy silence for many minutes forewarned some strange happening. Suddenly, a second scream tore through the night, this time coming from the mountainside a long way up the river. The Dreamer's heart leaped.

"Ah, again! For certain, it is the Big One. My hunt ends at daylight." He almost sang the words, a courage song carrying an ending note of triumph.

This was the third time in the past fortnight the panther had screamed twice in a night – something unusual in one season. During the two weeks, the Dreamer had plotted his hunting, searching out all trails of the mighty beast through the underbrush and the forest, and around the crags of the mountain, even down to the river's edge.

The Dreamer of the Chahta was held in disregard by his people. "The youth only dreams," they said among themselves. "Will he ever become a great warrior?"

But they never taunted him openly, uncertain in their estimate of him, perhaps. It was not necessary for them to tell him their thoughts, and he asked no questions. Sensitive by nature, an inheritance that marked the members of his clan, he reasoned things out for himself. He learned by

Wright, Muriel Hazel. "Legend of Nanih Wayah." In *Native American Writing in the Southeast: An Anthology, 1875–1935*. Eds Daniel F. Littlefield, Jr, and James W. Parins. Jackson: University Press of Mississippi, 1995: 214–20.

observation. He also acquired a knowledge of the woods and streams and of birds and animals that no other Chahta youth had. In fact, it was his appearance, rather than any lack of character, which kept him from sharing the first love of every Chahta youth – that prowess in the ball play. The Dreamer was frail looking, tall and thin, almost to gauntness; his hands and feet were slender and graceful.

For a time after the panther's second scream, the Dreamer sat listening. Finally, since it was some hours before the darkest part of night, he left the river bank and traveled several miles through the forest, on up the mountain to a crag around which the panther's beaten trail led to the river. Selecting a spot that he knew commanded a view of the mountainside, he hid by some high rocks just off the trail, knowing the mighty beast would come along early in the morning after slaking its thirst before going to its lair to sleep through the day.

While the youth waited, he visioned a beautiful mantle from the coat of the panther. Once only, he had glimpsed the animal in the sunlight when, disturbed in its lair, it had moved back into the brush out of sight. In that fleeting moment, the tawny color of its back shone like burnished gold; the grayish tinge of its sides, like silver.

In the dusk of the early day, the young hunter was more alert. He kept a close watch for the slightest movement on the mountainside in the growing light of morning. A rustle in the foliage of a tree by the trail below attracted his attention. His eyes remained riveted on the spot. Gradually, a crouched form was outlined on a large limb marking the edge of a glade in the woods. The panther was waiting, too. In the glance that revealed the crouching animal, the hunter's eye caught another movement beyond the glade. A clump of bushes parted and another form crept out into the grass toward the edge of the glade. The form stopped and half arose, revealing itself – a powerful figure! The son of Talking Warrior!

The Dreamer's blood surged hot, but cool reason served him well. He overcame the word upon his lips that would have broken the silence. Hidden by the rocks on the mountain, he quickly shifted to a better position, at the same time placing an arrow in his bow. Having crept on, Talking Warrior's son was now nearing the tree, unaware of the danger ahead. Steadily, the Dreamer braced one end of the bow between two of his toes and drew back the bowstring –

Twang!

With the arrow through its body, the panther clawed the limb beneath. Suddenly, with a frenzied roar, the huge beast sprang toward the Warrior's son, missed his charge and landed on all four feet. Talking Warrior's son, in the instant of warning, had leaped a few steps backward. Ears flat, open mouth snarling and tail lashing in fury, the panther stood gathering strength for the supreme effort of its life, – all at once, went limp and fell full length upon the ground. The Dreamer's first great kill!

The young hunter came down the trail and stood contemplating the motionless panther. Talking Warrior's son looked from one to the other. Consternation and chagrin mingled in the expression on his face. He had been caught doubly unaware and his resentment doubly flared.

"You bone picker!" he raged. "You steal a prize that rightfully belongs to me – sometime the greatest warrior of the Chahta."

The Dreamer made no reply. He was intent on the beautiful animal stretched at his feet. The other youth divined his thoughts.

"It is well that you admire your kill now," the latter said contemptuously. "Ere the moon passes you will have to adorn the grave of your bone-picker ancestor with the panther's skin to keep the charm. All the good it will do you is lying there.

"Bone picker!" Talking Warrior's son spat out the words. Turning away, he stalked into the forest.

"Bone picker!" The words sank deep in the sensitive soul of the Dreamer. He stooped and felt each one of the panther's feet in turn, – big balls of fur with hidden claws. He lifted the head and looked closely at the massive jaws. He was scarcely able to accomplish his work that day. When at last he spread the panther's skin before him, he marveled at its beauty.

But the Dreamer's heart was heavy. Wearily, he threw himself on the grass. Yet his thoughts gave him no peace. He recalled the contempt and the cold aloofness with which the other Chahta youths had treated him on more than one occasion. Tomorrow he would visit Prophet Chief, the wise old legend keeper of the Chahta. Prophet Chief would be patient with any question and help solve the problem.

The next morning, he found Prophet Chief sitting in the shade of a red elm, scraping and polishing seasoned wood for a bow.

"Do not fret because the Nahullo (One who causes fear)[1] would call us 'bone pickers,'" said Prophet Chief. "Na Foni Aiowah – the Nahullo does not understand, also many of the Chahta who have forgotten the old ways. The thoughts of the ancient Chahta were good.

"Na Foni Aiowah – bone gatherers. They were acquainted with knowledge. Wisely, they gathered up the sacred bones of the dead after the body lying upon its bier – a high scaffold – had been purified by air and wind. Then they washed the bones clean and buried them in the shadow of Nanih Wayah."

Prophet Chief scraped the seasoned wood for his bow with a sharp piece of flint. After a while he stopped and resumed his story.

"The ancient Chahta said that the earth was first a vast plain or quagmire destitute of hills. One time a Superior Being, a Great Red Man, came down from his home in the sky and began to build up a mound which finally rose as high as a mountain in the center of the wide plain. When the mountain was completed, the Great Red Man called forth the Red People from its midst. After the multitude had come forth, he stamped his feet and these people who were just emerging from the mountain into the light of day perished.

"Turning to the Red People who rested in the sunshine, awaiting his command, the Great Red Man delivered a long speech in which he called the mountain 'Nanih Wayah.' During the course of his address, he proclaimed the laws and instructed the people how to live. He also told them they would live forever, but they asked him to repeat this remark, since they had not listened closely to his words. Provoked by their inattentiveness, he at once withdrew his grant of immortality and replied instead, that they should henceforth be subject to death. Then the Red People came down into the plain and dwelt around Nanih Wayah."

Prophet Chief smoothed one side of the seasoned wood with red and yellow sandstone. Presently, he began another story:

"Chahta and Chickasha were two brothers. One day they set forth with all their people from a land in the west – hvshi aiokatulla (the place where the sun falls into the water).[2] They traveled toward the rising sun, in search of a new country in which to live.

"They came to a muddy, slimy river and camped there. The next stop was on the banks of a bloody red stream. They remained by this river and lived on fish for two years. But the springs were low in that region so they followed down the course of the river.

"They heard a noise like thunder. They searched to find whence the noise came. At first they saw a red smoke, then a mountain which thundered. They heard music coming from the mountain. On top of the mountain, they found a whirling pole from which came the music. How could they stop the pole?

"Finally, Chahta took a motherless child and swung it against the pole. The whirling stopped. The child perished. The great Chahta called the pole 'fabussa' and gave it to Isht Ahullo, the wise leader and prophet.

"The Isht Ahullo tied his medicine bag to one end of the pole and planted the other end in the ground, telling the people the 'fabussa' was magic and the standard around which they should pitch their camps at evening. Morning after morning, the pole leaned toward the east, so Isht Ahullo called his followers to arise and march forward again and again.

"The journey continued many years over high mountains, great deserts and wide plains and through deep forests. Enemy tribes they encountered along the way but were overcome by strategy in warfare. Chahta with his men acting as advance guards made a charge. Then the people followed making attacks on the right and on the left, so the enemy was soon in retreat.

"During this time, some of the Isht Ahullos, other than their leader, admonished the people to be strict in observing their ancient customs, especially the sacred duty of caring for the dead. It was thought a sacrilege to leave the remains of those who died along the way to be desecrated by wild beasts in the wilderness. Surely, on account of such treatment at the hands of their children, the grieving spirits of the departed would hover around and bring sorrow to the whole tribe. For that reason, whenever a person died, his bones were carefully preserved, certain ones among the Isht Ahullos having been selected by the wise leader to be Na Foni Aiowah – bone gatherers. Those who were to fill this office were chosen because they were intelligent, trustworthy and had open countenances. Many of them were fine looking and had graceful hands and feet. The wise Isht Ahullo said their descendants through the years to come would also be like them in observing the sacred duties and remembering the lore to the honor of the nation."

Prophet Chief sat for a time, making smooth the other side of the wood for his bow. Then he continued his story.

"When they had traveled many years, however, the people who now called themselves Chahta after the great Chahta himself, began to murmur because the Isht Ahullos continued to advise such rigid respect for the dead. So many Chahta had died that their bones had become a burden.

"Just as they were approaching the banks of a wide river, the Mississippi, they encountered a tribe whose warriors were large and fierce. The Chahta shot over white arrows, the sign of peace. The enemy painted the arrows red and shot them back, a challenge of war. In the battle that followed, the Chahta were held at bay by the side of the mighty stream.

"In a council of war that night, the wise Isht Ahullo called for suggestions in defeating the enemy. The Na Foni Aiowah consulted together. Then their spokesman suggested before the council that stones be cast into the water to bridge the river; that mice be caught and, at the right moment, turned loose among the enemy warriors to gnaw their bowstrings and render them helpless in battle. This suggestion was carried out. The following day, the Chahta marched forward victorious and crossed the mighty river.

"One morning, after crossing to the east side of the Mississippi, the wise Isht Ahullo, who had been the leader during the migration, pointed to the sacred pole standing straight in the midst of the encampment. Surely, this was a sign the Chahta should end their wandering. Having arrived in a fertile country where there were running streams, great forests and little prairies, all teeming with game, the people were delighted to make their homes there.

"Soon after the Chahta had arrived in the new country, the Mi^{n}ko, or Great Chief, ordered the bones of all those who had died during the long journey to be placed together in one spot and covered with moss and bark. To make the pile more secure, men and women worked for many days carrying earth in baskets to cover it until at last a huge mound had been erected.

"Then a great ceremony was held on top of the mound. The sacred emblem of the sun which had been carried from the Far West by the wise Isht Ahullo was set up and the Mi^{n}ko proclaimed the laws to the people, all of whom had gathered for the occasion. During the celebration, the mound was named Nanih Wayah,[3] calling to mind the mountain where the Red People were said first to have seen the light of day. Finally a feast was held at which the Chahta sang these words:

" 'Behold the wonderful work of our hands and let us be glad. Look upon the great mound; its top is above the trees and its black shadow lies on the ground a bowshot. It is surmounted by the golden emblem of the sun; its glitter dazzles the eyes of the multitude. It inhumes the bones of fathers and relatives; they died on our sojourn in the wilderness. They died in a far off wild country; they rest at Nanih Wayah. Our journey lasted many winters; it ends at Nanih Wayah.'

"Thus, the mound became hallowed ground, a place where the cherished bones of our ancestors had been cared for and the people had renewed the life of their nation.

"So, is it strange, oh Chahta youth, that the devoted warriors of our people through the ages have spoken of Nanih Wayah as 'Inholitopa Ishki' (Beloved Mother)? That, in token of their devotion, they often ascend the mound to place on its summit votive offerings – prizes taken in hunting and war?"

Prophet Chief selected a strong length of sinew and fastened it at one end of the seasoned wood which he had polished all day. He made a loop in the other end of the sinew for a bowstring.

"Omeh! Give ear! Oh, Chahta youth," the old man looked straight at the Dreamer. "I behold the fine light in your eyes. I see your graceful hands and feet. I wonder at your intelligence and your ability to attain knowledge. Yet all these attributes are natural, they are yours by inheritance. No one can take them away. The Na Foni Aiowah, our ancestors, held sacred their duties in memory of the dead, preserved the history and the lore of the nation. Remember well, oh youth! You also keep this trust!"

Prophet Chief's work was finished. How gracefully the seasoned wood had sprung in the bow! What power lay within the bowstring!

The Dreamer had arisen. A new strength seemed to have braced his slender figure. A look of joy was on his face.

"Chahta sia hoke! I am a Chahta!" he said proudly.

The next morning when the sun rose on the summit of Nanih Wayah, there lay the beautiful coat of the panther.

Notes

1   "Nahullo" means "white man" in the Chahta (Choctaw) language [Wright's note].
2   The Chahta (Choctaws) still refer to the west as "hvshi aiokatulla," "the place where the sun falls into the water" [Wright's note].
3   The remains of Nanih Wayah, the sacred mound of the Chahta, may still be found in Winston County, Mississippi. The name "Nanih Wayah" means "Mountain that brings forth fruit" or "Fruitful Mountain," also "Productive Mountain" [Wright's note].

Further Reading

Galloway, Patricia. *Choctaw Genesis, 1500–1700*. Lincoln: University of Nebraska Press, 1995.

Josephy, Alvin M., Jr, ed. *America in 1492: The World of the Indian Peoples Before the Arrival of Columbus*. New York: Alfred A. Knopf, 1992.

Shaffer, Lynda Norene. *Native Americans Before 1492: The Moundbuilding Centers of the Eastern Woodlands*. Armonk, NY: M. E. Sharp, 1992.

2

First Encounters

Introduction

Columbus's American venture in 1492 ushered in other Europeans who hoped to find a water passage to India, gold and other commodities such as fish and furs, and territory for the settlement of trading posts, military forts, and colonies. Europeans had had experience with colonial expansion closer to home, and so when they arrived in America, they came equipped not just with large wooden ships and iron weapons but also an ideology that led them to see the people they met as heathen and savage others. Europeans initially viewed Native Americans as potential trading partners, colonial subjects who could be converted to Christianity, or resistant enemies who could then be eliminated in a "just war." Since European explorers created the earliest written accounts of North American Indians, their motives and prejudices are transparent.

A much more difficult task is to read these documents between the lines to arrive at the best understanding of how Indians perceived Europeans. Certainly, curiosity, fear, and suspicion prevailed at their very first meetings. However, most historians working today look for the deeper cultural logic informing Indian actions in their early dealings with Europeans. Once Indians worked past the initial surprise and the puzzle of who these strange people were, they seem to have quickly embraced the benefits of European trade goods such as iron tools, cloth, and glass beads. Europeans also appeared as prospective allies who could add to a Native confederacy's authority in a region or assist one Indian nation in its war against another. Since Europeans proved an unfortunate choice of ally, Indians often had to adopt new strategies to thwart European attempts to control them.

This method of critically reading European documents for Indian perspectives provides the material for Kathleen M. Brown's article, "The Anglo-Algonquian Gender Frontier." Brown explores how English and Algonquian cultural ideas shaped their evolving political and economic relations in the area around Jamestown, Virginia, the first permanent English settlement in America. By analyzing the gender dynamic of English–Algonquian relations, Brown gleans fresh insights into how the English gained control over the Chesapeake region. In this article, she first compares how the English and Virginia Algonquians constructed gender: what were men's and women's social and economic roles, and what were their cultural rules about appropriate behavior for men and women? She then shows how the English took advantage of gender similarities, such as English and Algonquian men's status as warriors, to claim authority over the Powhatan Confederacy. Differences in the gendered division of labor, particularly Indian women's agricultural work and control of the corn supply, meant that English dependence on Indians for corn did little to elevate Algonquian status relative to the English.

Brown coined the telling phrase "gender frontier" to sum up her argument that Europeans and Indians met from gendered perspectives that proved crucially important to subsequent events. She pulled every possible reference to gender out of primary documents, which on the surface do not seem to say much about gender. Particularly valuable sources for her research were Captain John Smith's accounts of the colony in its formative years. This chapter uses comparable records of two other early European colonies: a Spanish *entrada* into what is now the American Southwest, and French settlement of Quebec. The excerpts chosen for inclusion here contain the few instances when women's presence is mentioned, remarks about the gendered division of labor and economic exchanges (trade in food, material goods, sexual favors), and descriptions of military débâcles, all of which constitute moments when ideas about gender influenced Indian and European perceptions of the other. With these documents, can we imaginatively reconstruct, as Brown has done, some sense of how Indians perceived Europeans and the changes in their societies brought about by European contact?

The Anglo-Algonquian Gender Frontier
Kathleen M. Brown

Recent scholarship has improved our understanding of the relationship between English settlers and Indians during the early seventeenth century. We know, for instance, that English expectations about American Indians were conditioned by Spanish conquest literature, their own contact with the Gaelic Irish, elite perceptions of the lower classes, and obligations to bring Christianity to those they believed to be in darkness.

Largely unacknowledged by historians, gender roles and identities also played an important role in shaping English and Indian interactions. Accompanied by few English women, English male adventurers to Roanoake and Jamestown island confronted Indian men and women in their native land. In this cultural encounter, the gender ways, or what some feminist theorists might call the "performances," of Virginia Algonquians challenged English gentlemen's assumptions about the naturalness of their own gender identities. This interaction brought exchanges, new cultural forms, created sites of commonality, painful deceptions, bitter misunderstandings, and bloody conflicts.

Identities as English or Indian were only partially formed at the beginning of this meeting of cultures; it required the daily presence of an "other" to crystallize self-conscious articulations of group identity. In contrast, maleness and femaleness within each culture provided explicit and deep-rooted foundations for individual identity and the organization of social relations. In both Indian and English societies, differences between men and women were critical to social order. Ethnic identities formed along this "gender frontier," the site of creative and destructive processes resulting from the confrontations of culturally-specific manhoods and womanhoods. In the emerging Anglo-Indian struggle, gender symbols and social relations signified claims to power. Never an absolute barrier, however, the gender frontier also produced sources for new identities and social practices.

In this essay, I explore in two ways the gender frontier that evolved between English settlers and the indigenous peoples of Virginia's tidewater. First, I assess how differences in gender roles shaped the perceptions and interactions of both groups. Second, I analyze the "gendering" of the emerging Anglo-Indian power struggle. While the English depicted themselves as warriors dominating a feminized native population, Indian women and men initially refused to acknowledge claims to military supremacy, treating the foreigners as they would subject peoples, cowards, or servants. When English warrior discourse became unavoidable, however, Indian women and men attempted to exploit what they saw as the warrior's obvious dependence upon others for the agricultural and reproductive services that ensured group survival.

The indigenous peoples who engaged in this struggle were residents of Virginia's coastal plain, a region of fields, forests, and winding rivers that extended from the shores of the Chesapeake Bay to the mountains and waterfalls near present-day Richmond. Many were affiliated with Powhatan, the *werowance* [head of the Powhatan Confederacy] who had consolidated several distinct groups under his influence at the time of contact with the English. Most were Algonquian-speakers whose distant cultural roots in the Northeast distinguished them from peoples further south and west where native economies depended more on agriculture and less on hunting and fishing. Although culturally diverse, tidewater inhabitants shared certain features of social organization, commonalities that may have become more pronounced with Powhatan's ambitious chiefdom-building and the arrival of the English.

Of the various relationships constituting social order in England, those between men and women were among the most contested at the time the English set sail for Virginia in 1607. Accompanied by few women before 1620, male settlers left behind a pamphlet debate about the nature of the sexes and a rising concern about the activities of disorderly women. The gender hierarchy the English viewed as "natural" and "God-given" was in fact fraying at the edges. Male pamphleteers argued vigorously for male dominance over women as crucial to maintaining orderly households and communities. The relationship between men and women provided authors with an accessible metaphor with which to communicate the power inequities of abstract political relationships such as that of the monarch to the people, or that of the gentry to the lower orders. By the late sixteenth century, as English attempts to subdue Ireland became increasingly violent and as hopes for a profitable West African trade dimmed, gender figured increasingly in English colonial discourses.

English gender differences manifested themselves in primary responsibilities and arenas of activity, relationships to property, ideals for conduct, and social identities. Using plow agriculture, rural Englishmen cultivated grain while women oversaw household production, including gardening, dairying, brewing, and spinning. Women also constituted a flexible reserve labor force, performing agricultural work when demand for labor was high, as at harvest time. While Englishmen's property ownership formed the basis of their political existence and identity, most women did not own property until they were no longer subject to a father or husband.

By the early seventeenth century, advice-book authors enjoined English women to concern themselves with the conservation of estates rather than with production. Women were also advised to maintain a modest demeanor. Publicly punishing shrewish and sexually aggressive women, communities enforced this standard of wifely submission as ideal and of wifely domination as intolerable. The sexual activity of poor and unmarried women proved particularly threatening to community order; these "nasty wenches" provided pamphleteers with a foil for the "good wives" female readers were urged to emulate.

How did one know an English good wife when one saw one? Her body and head would be modestly covered. The tools of her work, such as the skimming ladle used in dairying, the distaff of the spinning wheel, and the butter churn reflected her domestic production. When affixed to a man, as in community-initiated shaming rituals, these gender symbols communicated his fall from "natural" dominance and his wife's unnatural authority over him.

Advice-book authors described men's "natural" domain as one of authority derived from his primary economic role. A man's economic assertiveness, mirrored in his authority over wife, child and servant, was emblematized by the plow's penetration of the earth, the master craftsman's ability to shape his raw materials, and the rider's ability to subdue his horse. Although hunting and fishing supplemented the incomes of many Englishmen, formal group hunts – occasions in which associations with manual labor and economic gain had been carefully erased – remained the preserve of the aristocracy and upper gentry.

The divide between men's and women's activities described by sixteenth- and seventeenth-century authors did not capture the flexibility of gender relations in most English communities. Beliefs in male authority over women and in the primacy of men's economic activities sustained a perception of social order even as women marketed butter, cheese and ale, and cuckolded unlucky husbands.

Gender roles and identities were also important to the Algonquian speakers whom the English encountered along the three major tributaries of the Chesapeake Bay. Like indigenous peoples throughout the Americas, Virginia Algonquians invoked a divine division of labor to explain and justify differences between men's and women's roles on earth. A virile warrior god and a congenial female hostess provided divine examples for the work appropriate to human men and women. Indian women's labor centered on cultivating and processing corn, which provided up to seventy-five percent of the calories consumed by residents of the coastal plain. Women also grew squash, peas, and beans, fashioned bedding, baskets, and domestic tools, and turned animal skins into clothing and household items. They may even have built the houses of semi-permanent summer villages and itinerant winter camps. Bearing and raising children and mourning the dead rounded out the range of female duties. All were spiritually united by life-giving and its association with earth and agricultural production, sexuality and reproduction. Lineage wealth and political power passed through the female line, perhaps because of women's crucial role in producing and maintaining property. Among certain peoples, women may also have had the power to determine the fate of captives, the nugget of truth in the much-embellished tale of Pocahontas's intervention on behalf of Captain John Smith.

Indian women were responsible not only for reproducing the traditional features of their culture, but for much of its adaptive capacity as well. As agriculturalists, women must have had great influence over decisions to move to new grounds, to leave old grounds fallow, and to initiate planting. As producers and consumers of vital household goods and implements, women may have been among the first to feel the impact of new technologies, commodities, and trade. And as accumulators of lineage property, Indian women may have been forced to change strategies as subsistence opportunities shifted.

Indian men assumed a range of responsibilities that complemented those of women. Men cleared new planting grounds by cutting trees and burning stumps. They fished and hunted for game, providing highly valued protein. After the last corn harvest, whole villages traveled with their hunters to provide support services throughout the winter. Men's pursuit of game shaped the rhythms of village life during these cold months, just as women's cultivation of crops determined feasts and the allocation of labor during the late spring and summer. By ritually separating themselves from women through sexual abstinence, hunters periodically became warriors, taking revenge for killings or initiating their own raids. This adult leave-taking rearticulated the *huskanaw*, the coming of age ritual in which young boys left their mother's homes to become men.

Men's hunting and fighting roles were associated with life-taking, with its ironic relationship to the life-sustaining acts of procreation, protection and provision. Earth and corn symbolized women, but the weapons of the hunt, the trophies taken from the hunted, and the predators of the animal world represented men. The ritual use of *pocones*, a red dye, also reflected this gender division. Women anointed their bodies with *pocones* before sexual encounters and ceremonies celebrating the harvest, while men wore it during hunting, warfare, or at the ritual celebrations of successes in these endeavors.

The exigencies of the winter hunt, the value placed on meat, and intermittent warfare among native peoples may have been the foundation of male dominance in politics and religious matters. Women were not without their bases of power in Algonquian society, however; their important roles as agriculturalists, reproducers of Indian culture, and caretakers of lineage property kept gender relations in rough balance. Indian women's ability to choose spouses motivated men to be "paynefull" in their hunting and fishing. These same men warily avoided female spaces the English labeled "gynaeceum," in which menstruating women may have gathered. By no means equal to men, whose political and religious decisions directed village life, Indian women were perhaps more powerful in their subordination than English women.

Even before the English sailed up the river they renamed the James, however, Indian women's power may have been waning, eroded by Powhatan's chiefdom-building tactics. During the last quarter of the sixteenth century, perhaps as a consequence of early Spanish forays into the region, he began to add to his inherited chiefdom, coercing and manipulating other coastal residents into economic and military alliances. Powhatan also subverted the matrilineal transmission of political power by appointing his kinsmen to be *werowances* of villages recently consolidated into his chiefdom. The central military force under his command created opportunities for male recognition in which acts of bravery, rather than matrilineal property or political inheritance, determined privileges. Traditions of gift-giving to cement alliances became exchanges of tribute for promises of protection or non-aggression. Powhatan thus appropriated corn, the product of women's labor, from the villages he dominated. He also communicated power and wealth through conspicuous displays of young wives. Through marriages to women drawn from villages throughout his chiefdom, Powhatan emblematized his dominance over the margins of his domain and created kinship ties to strengthen his influence over these villages. With the arrival of the English, the value of male warfare and the symbolism of corn as tribute only intensified, further strengthening the patriarchal tendencies of Powhatan's people.

Almost every writer described the land west and south of Chesapeake Bay as an unspoiled "New World." Small plots of cultivated land, burned forest undergrowth, and seasonal residence patterns often escaped the notice of English travelers habituated to landscapes shaped by plow agriculture and permanent settlement. Many writers believed the English had "chanced in a lande, even as God made it," which indigenous peoples had failed to exploit.

Conquest seemed justifiable to many English because Native Americans had failed to tame the wilderness according to English standards. Writers claimed they found "only an idle, improvident, scattered people ... carelesse of anything but from hand to mouth." Most authors compounded impressions of sparse indigenous populations by listing only numbers of fighting men, whom they derided as impotent for their failure to exploit the virgin resources of the "bowells and womb of their Land." The seasonal migration of native groups and the corresponding shift in diet indicated to the English a lack of mastery over the environment, reminding them of animals. John Smith commented, "It is strange to see how their bodies alter with their diet; even as the deare and wild beastes, they seem fat and leane, strong and weak."[1]

The English derision of Indian dependence on the environment and the comparison to animals, while redolent with allusions to England's own poor and to the hierarchy of God's creation, also contained implicit gender meanings. Women's bodies, for example, showed great alteration during pregnancy from fat to lean, strong to weak. English authors often compared female sexual appetites and insubordination to those of wild animals in need of taming. Implicit in all these commentaries was a critique of indigenous men for failing to fulfill the responsibility of economic provision with which the English believed all men to be charged. Lacking private property in the English sense, Indian men, like the Gaelic Irish before them, appeared to the English to be feminine and not yet civilized to manliness.

For many English observers, natives' "failure" to develop an agricultural economy or dense population was rooted in their gender division of labor. Women's primary responsibility for agriculture merely confirmed the abdication by men of their proper role and explained the "inferiority" of native economies in a land of plenty. Smith commented that "the land is not populous, for the men be fewe; their far greater number is of women and children," a pattern he attributed to inadequate cultivation. Of the significance of women's work and Indian agriculture, he concluded, "When all their fruits be gathered, little els they plant, and this is done by their women and children; neither doth this long suffice them, for neere 3 parts of the yeare, they only observe times and seasons, and live of what the Country naturally affordeth from hand to mouth." In Smith's convoluted analysis, the "failure" of Indian agriculture, implicitly associated in other parts of his text with the "idleness" of men and the reliance upon female labor, had a gendered consequence; native populations became vulnerable and feminized, consisting of many more women and children than of "able men fitt for their warres."

English commentators reacted with disapproval to seeing women perform work relegated to laboring men in England while Indian men pursued activities associated with the English aristocracy. Indian women, George Percy claimed, "doe all their drugerie. The men takes their pleasure in hunting and their warres, which they are in continually." Observing that the women were heavily burdened and the men only lightly so, John Smith similarly noted "the men bestowe their times in fishing, hunting, wars and such manlike exercises, scorning to be seene in any woman like exercise," while the "women and children do the rest of the worke." Smith's account revealed his discomfort with women's performance of work he considered the most valuable.

The English were hard pressed to explain other Indian behavior without contradicting their own beliefs in the natural and divinely-sanctioned characteristics of men and women. Such was the case with discussions of Indian women's pain during childbirth. In judgements reminiscent of their descriptions of Irish women, many English writers claimed that Indian women gave birth with little or no pain. English readers may have found this observation difficult to reconcile with Christian views of labor pains as the source of maternal love and as punishment for the sins of Eve. Belief in indigenous women's closer proximity to nature – an interpretive stance that required an uncomfortable degree of criticism of civilization – allowed the English to finesse Indian women's seeming exemption from Eve's curse. This is also why the association of Native American gender norms with animals proved so powerful for the English; it left intact the idea of English gender roles as "natural," in the sense of fulfilling God's destiny for civilized peoples, while providing a similarly "natural" explanation for English dominance over indigenous peoples.

The English were both fascinated and disturbed by other aspects of Native American society through which gender identities were communicated, including hairstyle, dress and make-up. The native male fashion of going clean-shaven, for example, clashed with English associations of beards with male maturity, perhaps diminishing Indian men's claims to manhood in the eyes of the English. Upon seeing an Indian with a full "blacke bush beard," Smith concluded that the individual must be the son of a European as "the Salvages seldome hav any at all." It probably did not enhance English respect for Indian manhood that female barbers sheared men's facial hair.

Most English writers found it difficult to distinguish between the sexual behavior of Chesapeake dwellers and what they viewed as sexual potency conveyed through dress and ritual. English male explorers were particularly fascinated by indigenous women's attire, which seemed scanty and immodest compared to English women's multiple layers and wraps. John Smith described an entertainment arranged for him in which "30 young women came naked out of the woods (only covered behind and before with a few greene leaves), their bodies al painted." Several other writers commented that Native Americans "goe altogether naked," or had "scarce to cover their nakednesse." Smith claimed, however, that the women were "alwaies covered about their midles with a skin and very shamefast to be seene bare." Yet he noted, as did several other English travelers, the body adornments, including beads, paintings, and tattoos, that were visible on Indian women's legs, hands, breasts, and faces. Perhaps some of the "shamefastness" reported by Smith resulted from Englishmen's close scrutiny of Indian women's bodies.

For most English writers, Indian manners and customs reinforced an impression of sexual passion. Hospitality that included sexual privileges, for instance sending "a woman fresh painted red with *Pocones* and oile" to be the "bedfellow" of a guest, may have confirmed in the minds of English men the reading of Indian folkways as sexually provocative. Smith's experience with the thirty women, clad in leaves, body paint, and buck's horns and emitting "hellish cries and shouts," undoubtedly strengthened the English association of Indian culture with unbridled passion:

> ... they solemnly invited Smith to their lodging, but no sooner was hee within the house, but all these Nimphes more tormented him than ever, with crowding, and pressing, and hanging upon him, most tediously crying, *love you not mee.*

These and other Indian gender ways left the English with a vivid impression of unconstrained sexuality that in their own culture could mean only promiscuity.

The stark contrast between Indian military techniques and formal European land stratagems reinforced English judgements that indigenous peoples were animalistic by nature. George Percy's description of one skirmish invoked a comparison to the movement of animals: "At night, when we were going aboard, there came the Savages creeping upon all foure, from the Hills, like Beares, with their Bowes in their mouthes." While writers regaled English readers with tales of Indian men in hasty retreat from English guns, thus reconfirming for the reader the female vulnerability of Indians and the superior weaponry of the English, they also recounted terrifying battle scenes such as the mock war staged for the entertainment of John Smith, which included "horrible shouts and screeches, as though so many infernall helhounds could not have made them more terrible." Englishmen were perhaps most frightened, however, by reports of Caribbean Indians that echoed accounts of Irish cannibalism; George Percy claimed that Carib men scalped their victims, or worse still, that certain tribes "will eate their enemies when they kill them, or any stranger if they take them." Stories like these may have led Smith to believe he was being "fattened" for a sacrifice during his captivity in December 1607.

Although the dominant strand of English discourse about Indian men denounced them for being savage and failed providers, not all Englishmen shared these assessments of the meaning of cultural differences. Throughout the early years of settlement, male laborers deserted military compounds to escape puny rations, disease and harsh discipline, preferring to take their chances with local Indians whom they knew had food aplenty. Young boys like Henry Spelman, moreover, had nearly as much to fear from the English, who used him as a hostage, as he did from his Indian hosts. Spelman witnessed and participated in Indian culture from a very different perspective than most Virginia chroniclers. While George Percy and John Smith described Indian entertainments as horrible antics, Spelman coolly noted that Patawomeck dances bore a remarkable resemblance to the Darbyshire hornpipe.

Even among men more elite and cosmopolitan than Spelman, a lurking and disquieting suspicion that Indian men were like the English disrupted discourses about natural savagery and inferiority. John Smith often explained Indian complexions and resistance to the elements as a result of conditioning and daily practice rather than of nature. Smith also created areas of commonality with Algonquians through exchanges of gifts, shared entertainments, and feasts. Drawn into Indian cultural expressions despite himself, Smith gave gifts when he would have preferred to barter and concocted Indian explanations for English behavior. Despite the flamboyant rhetoric about savage warriors lurking in the forests like animals, Smith soon had Englishmen learning to fight in the woods. He clearly thought his manly English, many of whom could barely shoot a gun, had much to learn from their Indian opponents.

Most English did not dwell on these areas of similarity and exchange, however, but emphasized the "wild" and animalistic qualities of tidewater peoples. English claims to dominance and superiority rested upon constructions of Indian behavior as barbaric. Much as animals fell below humans in the hierarchy of the natural world, so the Indians of English chronicles inhabited a place that was technologically, socially, and morally below the level of the civilized English. Anglo-Indian gender differences similarly provided the English with cultural grist for the mill of conquest. Through depictions of feminized male "naturalls," Englishmen reworked Anglo-Indian relations to fit the "natural" dominance of men in gender relations. In the process, they contributed to an emerging male colonial identity that was deeply rooted in English gender discourses.

The gendering of Anglo-Indian relations in English writing was not without contest and contradiction, however, nor did it lead inevitably to easy conclusions of English dominance. Englishmen incorporated Indian ways into their diets and military tactics, and Indian women into their sexual lives. Some formed close bonds with Indian companions, while others lived to father their own "naturall" progeny. As John Rolfe's anguish over his marriage to Pocahontas attested, colonial domination was a complex process involving sexual intimacy, cultural incorporation and self-scrutiny.

The Englishmen who landed on the shores of Chesapeake Bay and the James River were not the first European men that Virginia Algonquians had seen. During the 1570s, Spanish Jesuits established a short-lived mission near the James River tributary that folded with the murder of the clerics. The Spaniards who revenged the Jesuit deaths left an unfavorable impression upon local Chickahominy, Paspegh, and Kecoughtan Indians. At least one English ship also pre-empted the 1607 arrival of the Jamestown settlers; its captain was long remembered for killing a Rappahanock river *werowance*.

The maleness of English explorers' parties and early settlements undoubtedly raised Indian suspicions of bellicose motives. Interrogating Smith at their first meeting about the purpose of the English voyage, Powhatan was apparently satisfied with Smith's answer that the English presence was temporary. Smith claimed his men sought passage to "the backe Sea," the ever-elusive water route to India which they believed lay beyond the falls of the Chesapeake river system. Quick to exploit native assumptions that they were warriors, Smith also cited revenge against Powhatan's own mortal enemies, the Monacans, for their murder of an Englishman as a reason for their western explorations. The explanation may have initially seemed credible to Powhatan because the English expedition consisted only of men and boys. Frequent English military drills in the woods and the construction of a fort at Jamestown, however, may have aroused his suspicions that the English strangers planned a longer and more violent stay.

Equipped with impressive blasting guns, the English may have found it easy to perpetuate the warrior image from afar; up close was a different matter, however. English men were pale, hairy, and awkward compared to Indian men. They also had the dirty habit of letting facial hair grow so that it obscured the bottom part of their faces where it collected food and other debris. Their clumsy stomping through the woods announced their presence to friends, enemies, and wildlife alike and they were forced, on at least one very public occasion, to ask for Indian assistance when their boats became mired in river ooze. Perhaps worst of all from the perspective of Indian people who valued a warrior's stoicism in the face of death, the Englishmen they captured and killed died screaming and whimpering. William Strachey recorded the mocking song sung by Indian men sometime in 1611, in which they ridiculed "what lamentation our people made when they kild him, namely saying how they [the Englishmen] would cry whe, whe."

Indian assumptions about masculinity may have led Powhatan to overestimate the vulnerability of Smith's men. The gentlemen and artisans who were the first to arrive in Virginia proved to be dismal farmers, remaining wholly dependent upon native corn stores during their first three years and partially dependent thereafter. They tried, futilely, to persuade Indians to grow more corn to meet their needs, but their requests were greeted with scorn by Indian men who found no glory in the "woman-like exercise" of farming. Perhaps believing that the male settlement would always require another population to supply it, Powhatan tried to use the threat of starvation to level the playing field with the English. During trade negotiations with Smith in January 1609, Powhatan held out for guns and swords, claiming disingenuously that corn was more valuable to him than copper trinkets because he could eat it.

When Powhatan and other Indian peoples reminded Smith of his dependence upon Indian food supplies, Smith reacted with anger. In his first account of Virginia, he recalled with bitterness the scorn of the Kecoughtan Indians for "a famished man": they "would in derision offer him a handfull of Corne, a peece of bread." Such treatment signified both indigence and female vulnerability to the English, made worse by the fact that the crops they needed were grown by women. At Kecoughtan, Smith responded by "let[ting] fly his muskets" to provoke a Kecoughtan retreat and then killing several men at close range. The survivors fell back in confusion, allowing the image of their god Okeus to fall into English hands. After this display of force, he found the Kecoughtan "content" to let the English dictate the terms of trade: Kecoughtan corn in exchange for copper, beads, hatchets, and the return of Okeus. The English thus used their superior weaponry to transform themselves from scorned men into respected warriors and to recast the relationship: humble agriculturists became duty-bound to produce for those who spared their lives.

Powhatan's interactions with Englishmen may also have been guided by his assessment of the gender imbalance among them. His provision of women to entertain English male guests was a political gesture whose message seems to have been misunderstood as sexual license by the English. Smith, for example, believed the generosity stemmed from Powhatan's having "as many women as he will," and thereby growing occasionally "weary of his women." By voluntarily sharing his wealth in women and thus communicating his benign intent, Powhatan invoked what he may have believed to be a transcendent male political bond, defined by men's common relationship to women. Powhatan may also have believed that by encouraging English warriors' sexual activity, he might diminish their military potency. It was the fear of this loss of power, after all, that motivated Indian warriors' ritual abstinence before combat. Ultimately, Powhatan may have hoped that intimacy between native women and English men would lead to an integration of the foreigners and a diffusion of the threat they presented. Lacking women with whom to reciprocate and unfettered by matrilineage ties, the English, Powhatan may have reasoned, might be rapidly brought into alliance. Powhatan's gesture, however, only reinforced the English rationale for subjugating the "uncivilized" and offered English men an opportunity to express the Anglo-Indian power relationship sexually with native women.

Indian women were often more successful than Powhatan in manipulating Englishmen's desires for sexual intimacy. At the James River village of Appocant in late 1607, the unfortunate George Cawson met his death when village women "enticed [him] up from the barge into their howses." Oppossunoquonuske, a clever *werowansqua* of another village, similarly led fourteen Englishmen to their demise. Inviting the unwary men to come "up into her Towne, to feast and make Merry," she convinced them to "leave their Armes in their boat, because they said how their women would be afrayd ells of their pieces."

Although both of these accounts are cautionary tales that represent Indians literally as feminine seducers capable of entrapping Englishmen in the web of their own sexual desires, the incidents suggest Indian women's canny assessment of the men who would be colonial conquerors. Exploiting Englishmen's hopes for colonial pleasures, Indian women dangled before them the opportunity for sexual intimacy, turning a female tradition of sexual hospitality into a weapon of war. Acknowledging the capacity of English "pieces" to terrorize Indian women, Oppossunoquonuske tacitly recognized Englishmen's dependence on their guns to construct self-images of bold and masculine conquerors. Her genius lay in convincing them to rely on other masculine "pieces." When she succeeded in getting Englishmen to set aside one colonial masculine identity – the warrior – for another – the lover of native women – the men were easily killed.

Feigned sexual interest in Englishmen was not the only tactic available to Indian women. Some women clearly wanted nothing to do with the English strangers and avoided all contact with them. When John Smith traveled to Tappahannock in late 1607, for example, Indian women fled their homes in fear. Other Indian women treated the English not as revered guests, to be gently wooed into Indian ways or seduced into fatal traps, but as lowly servants. Young Henry Spelman recorded such an incident during his stay at the house of a Patawomeck *werowance*. While the *werowance* was gone, his first wife requested that Spelman travel with her and carry her child on the long journey to her father's house. When Spelman refused, she struck him, provoking the boy to return the blows. A second wife then joined in the fray against Spelman, who continued to refuse to do their bidding. Upon the *werowance*'s return, Spelman related the afternoon's events and was horrified to see the offending wife brutally punished. In this Patawomeck household, women's and men's ideas about the proper treatment of English hostages differed dramatically.

In addition to violence and manipulations of economic dependence and sexual desire, Algonquians tried to maneuver the English into positions of political subordination. Smith's account of his captivity, near-execution, and rescue by Pocahontas was undoubtedly part of an adoption ritual in which Powhatan defined his relationship to Smith as one of patriarchal dominance. Smith became Powhatan's prisoner after warriors easily slew his English companions and then "missed" with nearly all of the twenty or thirty arrows they aimed at Smith himself. Clearly, Powhatan wanted Smith brought to him alive. Smith reported that during his captivity he was offered "life, libertie, land and women," prizes Powhatan must have believed to be very attractive to Englishmen, in exchange for information about how best to capture Jamestown. After ceremonies and consultations with priests, Powhatan brought Smith before an assembly where, according to Smith, Pocahontas risked her own life to prevent him from being clubbed to death by executioners. It seems that Smith understood neither the ritual adoption taking place nor the significance of Powhatan's promise to make him a *werowance* and to "for ever esteeme him as [he did] his son Nantaquoud."

Powhatan subsequently repeated his offer to Smith, urging the adoptive relationship on him. Pronouncing him "a werowance of Powhatan, and that all his subjects should so esteeme us," Powhatan integrated Smith and his men into his chieftancy, declaring that "no man account us strangers nor Paspaheghans, but Powhatans, and that the Corne, weomen and Country, should be to us as to his owne people."

Over the next weeks and months the two men wrangled over the construction of their short-lived alliance and the meaning of Powhatan's promises to supply the English with corn. In a long exchange of bitter words, the two men sidestepped each other's readings of their friendship as distortions and misperceptions. Smith claimed he had "neglected all, to satisfie your desire," to which Powhatan responded with a plain-spoken charge of bad faith: "some doubt I have of your comming hither, that makes me not so kindly seeke to relieve you ... for many do informe me, your comming is not for trade, but to invade my people and possesse my Country."

Smith and Powhatan continued to do a subtle two-step over the meaning of the corn. Was it tribute coerced by the militarily superior English? Or was it a sign of a father's compassion for a subordinate *werowance* and his hungry people? Powhatan made clear to Smith that he understood the extent of the English dependence upon his people for corn. "What will it availe you, to take that perforce, you may quietly have with love, or to destroy them that provide you food?" he asked Smith. "What can you get by war, when we can hide our provision and flie to the woodes, whereby you must famish by wronging us your friends." He also appreciated the degree to which the English could make him miserable if they did not get what they wanted:

> think you I am so simple not to knowe, it is better to eate good meate, lie well, and sleepe quietly with my women and children, laugh and be merrie with you, have copper, hatchets, or what I want, being your friend; then bee forced to flie from al, to lie cold in the woods, feed upon acorns, roots, and such trash, and be so hunted by you, that I can neither rest, eat, nor sleepe; but my tired men must watch, and if a twig but breake, everie one crie there comes Captaine Smith, then I must flie I knowe not whether, and thus with miserable feare end my miserable life.

Ultimately, Powhatan attempted to represent his conflict with Smith as the clash of an older, wiser authority with a young upstart. "I knowe the difference of peace and warre, better then any in my Countrie," he reminded Smith, his paternal self-depiction contrasting sharply with what he labeled Smith's youthful and "rash unadvisednesse." Dis-pleased with this rendering of their relationship with its suggestion of childish inexperience, Smith reasserted the English warrior personae with a vengeance. He informed Powhatan that "for your sake only, wee have curbed our thirsting desire of revenge," reminding him that the "advantage we have by our armes" would have allowed the English easily to overpower Powhatan's men "had wee intended you anie hurt."

Although we can never know with any certainty what the all-male band of English settlers signified to indigenous peoples, their own organization of gender roles seems to have shaped their responses to the English. Using sexual hospitality to "disarm" the strangers and exploiting English needs for food, Algonquians were drawn into a female role as suppliers of English sexual and subsistence needs. Although Indian women were occasionally successful in manipulating English desires for sexual intimacy and dominance, the English cast these triumphs as the consequence of female seduction, an interpretation that only reinforced discourses about feminized Algonquians. Dependence upon indigenous peoples for corn was potentially emasculating for the English; they thus redefined corn as tribute or booty resulting from English military dominance.

The encounter of English and Indian peoples wrought changes in the gender relations of both societies. Contact bred trade, political reshuffling, sexual intimacy and warfare. On both sides, male roles intensified in ways that appear to have reinforced the patriarchal tendencies of each culture. The very process of confrontation between two groups with male-dominated political and religious systems may initially have strengthened the value of patriarchy for each.

The rapid change in Indian life and culture had a particularly devastating impact upon women. Many women, whose office it was to bury and mourn the dead, may have been relegated to perpetual grieving. Corn was also uniquely the provenance of women; economically it was the source of female authority, and religiously and symbolically they were identified with it. The wanton burning and pillaging of corn supplies, through which the English transformed their dependence into domination, may have represented to tidewater residents an egregious violation of women. Maneuvering to retain patriarchal dominance over the English and invoking cultural roles in which women exercised power, Algonquian Indians may have presented their best defense against the "feminization" of their relationship to the English. But as in Indian society itself, warriors ultimately had the upper hand over agriculturists.

English dominance in the region ultimately led to the decline of the native population and its way of life. As a consequence of war, nutritional deprivation, and disease, Virginia Indians were reduced in numbers from the approximately 14,000 inhabitants of the Chesapeake Bay and tidewater in 1607 to less than 3,000 by the early eighteenth century. White settlement forced tidewater dwellers further west, rupturing the connections between ritual activity, lineage, and geographic place. Priests lost credibility as traditional medicines failed to cure new diseases while confederacies such as Powhatan's declined and disappeared. Uprooted tidewater peoples also encountered opposition from piedmont inhabitants upon whose territory they encroached. The erosion of traditionally male-dominated Indian political institutions eventually created new opportunities for individual women to assume positions of leadership over tribal remnants.

The English, meanwhile, emerged from these early years of settlement with gender roles more explicitly defined in English, Christian, and "middling order" terms. This core of English identity proved remarkably resilient, persisting through seventy years of wars with neighboring Indians and continuing to evolve as English settlers imported Africans to work the colony's tobacco fields. Initially serving to legitimate the destruction of traditional Indian ways of life, this concept of Englishness ultimately constituted one of the most powerful legacies of the Anglo-Indian gender frontier.

Note

1 Sources for the quotations: John Smith, *The Proceedings of the English Colonies in Virginia* [London, 1612] and "Description of Virginia" [London, 1612], and George Percy, "Observations by Master George Percy, 1607," all in Lyon Gardiner Tyler, ed., *Narratives of Early Virginia 1606–1625* (New York: Barnes and Noble, 1907); Karen Kupperman, ed., *Captain John Smith: A Select Edition of His Writings* (Chapel Hill: University of North Carolina Press, 1988); Philip Barbour, ed., *The Complete Works of Captain John Smith* (Chapel Hill: University of North Carolina Press, 1986); Henry Spelman, "Relation of Virginia," in E. Arber and A. G. Bradley, eds, *Travels and Works of Captain John Smith* (Edinburgh: John Grant, 1910); William Strachey, *The Historie of Travell into Virginia Britania* (London, 1612).

Documents

In the tradition of the Spanish *conquistadores* who had conquered Mexico for Spain, Francisco Vásquez de Coronado headed north in 1540 to claim the gold and treasure rumored to belong to the Indians of Cíbola. Better known today as Zuni Pueblo, Cíbola had no gold and few other prospects to reward ambitious adventurers seeking wealth and glory. With a large army of Native allies from Mexico and vast herds of livestock and horses, Coronado's expedition traversed its way east, camping during the winter of 1540–1 near Tiguex Province, a collection of 12 Southern Tiwa Pueblos straddling the Rio Grande River, located north of what is today Albuquerque, New Mexico. "Pueblo," the Spanish word for "town," became an overarching label encompassing different southwestern peoples who shared some cultural traits, most visibly their densely settled villages. The following account, written after the fact by expedition member Pedro de Castañeda, tells of the Spaniards' resort to force while at Tiguex. As winter settled in, Coronado's men became desperate for more clothes. Their demands diminished Pueblo tolerance of the Spanish to the point of war. Castañeda's ethnographic overview of Pueblo architecture, foodways, and economy illuminates how the war over clothing may have had a deeper gendered significance.

Castañeda's History of the Expedition

Pedro de Castañeda of Náxera

Chapter XV: Why Tiguex Revolted, and the Punishment Inflicted Upon Its people Without Any One of Them Being to Blame

We have already told how the general [Coronado] arrived at Tiguex, where he found Don García López de Cárdenas and Hernando de Alvarado; how he sent the latter back to Cicuye, and how Alvarado brought Captain Bigotes and the governor of the pueblo as prisoners. The latter was an old man. The people at Tiguex did not feel well about these arrests. This ill feeling was aggravated by the general's desire to gather some clothing to distribute among the soldiers. For this purpose he sent for an Indian chief of Tiguex with whom we were already acquainted and with whom we were on good terms. Our men named him Juan Alemán because they said he had some resemblance to a certain Juan Alemán living in Mexico. The general spoke with him, asking him to furnish three hundred or more pieces of clothing which he needed to distribute to his men. He replied that it was not in his power to do this, but in that of the governors'; that they had to discuss the matter among the pueblos; and that the Spaniards had to ask this individually from each pueblo. The general ordered it thus and provided that certain chosen men who were with him should go to ask for it. As there were twelve pueblos, some were to go on one side of the river and some on the other. As all this was unexpected, the natives were not given time to discuss or consult about the matter. As soon as a Spaniard came to the pueblo, he demanded the supplies at once, and they had to give them, because he had to go on to the next one. With all this there was

Excerpts from Pedro de Castañeda of Náxera, "Castañeda's History of the Expedition." In *Narratives of the Coronado Expedition, 1540–1542*. Eds George P. Hammond and Agapito Rey. Albuquerque, NM: University of New Mexico Press, 1940: 223–56.

nothing the natives could do except take off their own cloaks and hand them over until the number that the Spaniards asked for was reached. Some of the soldiers who went along with these collectors, when the latter gave them some blankets or skins that they did not consider good enough, if they saw an Indian with a better one, they exchanged it with him without any consideration or respect, and without inquiring about the importance of the person they despoiled. The Indians resented this very much.

In addition to what has been narrated, an outstanding person, whose name I shall omit to spare his honor, left the pueblo where the camp was and went to another one a league distant, and on seeing a beautiful woman in the pueblo, he called her husband down below and asked him to hold his horse by the bridle while he went up; and, as the pueblo was entered from the top, the Indian thought that he was going to some other place. While the native was detained there, some commotion took place, the man came back, took his horse, and rode away. When the Indian climbed to the upper part, he learned that he had ravished or had attempted to ravish his wife. Accompanied by other prominent persons in the pueblo, he came to complain, saying a man had outraged his wife, and told them how it had taken place. The general ordered all the soldiers and persons in his company to appear before him, but the Indian could not identify the man, either because he had changed clothes or for some other reason. But he said he would recognize the horse because he had held it by the rein. He was led through the stalls, and when he saw a blossom-colored horse covered with a blanket, he said that the owner of that horse was the man. The owner denied it, saying that the Indian had not recognized him, and perhaps he was mistaken also in the horse. In the end he went away without getting any redress for what he had demanded.

On another day an Indian from [our] army who was guarding the horses came bleeding and wounded, saying that the Indians of the land had killed one companion and were driving the horses before them to their pueblos. The soldiers went to round up the horses, many of which were found missing, including seven mules belonging to the general.

One day Don García López de Cárdenas went to visit the pueblos and to get an interpreter from them. He found the pueblos inclosed by a palisade and heard a great shouting inside, with horses running around as in a bull ring and the Indians shooting arrows at them. The natives were all up in arms. Cárdenas could do nothing because they refused to come out into the field, and as the pueblos are strong they could not be harmed. The general ordered Don García López de Cárdenas to go at once with the rest of the force and surround a pueblo. This was the pueblo where the greatest damage had been done and where the incident of the Indian woman had taken place.

The general went ahead, accompanied by many captains, such as Juan de Zaldívar, Barrionuevo, Diego López, and Melgosa. They caught the Indians so unawares that they soon took possession of the high terraces, but at great risk because the defenders wounded many of our men with arrows which they shot from the inside of their houses. In much danger our men remained on the top during the day, the night, and part of the following day, taking good shots with crossbows and harquebuses. Down on the ground the mounted men, together with many Indian allies from New Spain, built some heavy smudge fires in the basements, into which they had broken holes, so that the Indians were forced to sue for peace. Pablo de Melgosa and Diego López, the alderman from Seville, happened to be in that place and they answered their signs for peace by similar ones, which consisted of making a cross. The natives soon laid down their arms and surrendered at their mercy. They were taken to the tent of Don García, who, as was affirmed, did not know of the peace and thought that they were surrendering of their own accord, as defeated men.

As the general had ordered them not to take any one alive, in order to impose a punishment that would intimidate the others, Don García at once ordered that two hundred stakes be driven into the ground to burn them alive. There was no one who could tell him of the peace which had been agreed upon, as the soldiers did not know about it either, and those who had arranged the terms of peace kept silent, believing it was none of their business. Thus when the enemies saw that their comrades were being tied and that the Spaniards had started to burn them, about one hundred who were in the tent began to offer resistance and defend themselves with what they found about them and with stakes which they rushed out to seize. Our footmen rushed the tent on all sides with sword thrusts that forced the natives to abandon it, and then the mounted men fell upon them; as the ground was level, none escaped alive except a few who had remained concealed in the pueblo and who fled that night. These spread the news throughout the land, telling how the peace that was granted them had not been kept. This resulted in great harm later. After this incident, and as it snowed on them, the Spaniards abandoned the pueblo and returned to their quarters at the time when the army arrived from Cíbola.

Chapter XVI: How Tiguex Was Besieged and Taken, and What Else Happened During the Siege

As I have said already, when they had just conquered that pueblo it began to snow in that land, and it snowed so much for two months that the Spaniards could do nothing except go over the trials and tell the natives to come peacefully and that they would be pardoned, giving them all sorts of assurances. To this the Indians replied that they would not trust those who did not know how to keep the word they had pledged and reminded them that they were still holding Bigotes a prisoner and that, at the burned pueblo, they had not kept the peace. [...]

Don García López de Cárdenas went with a part of the force to another pueblo located one-half league farther on, because most of the people of these pueblos had taken refuge in these two places. But they paid no attention to the requisitions for peace made upon them, nor would they grant it; on the contrary, they shot arrows from the terraces with much shouting. Don García López returned to the company that had remained to oppose the pueblo of Tiguex.

Then the warriors of the pueblo came out in large numbers. Our men, half checking the horses, pretended that they were running away, and as a result they drew the enemy into the plain, where they turned upon them in such a way that they struck down some of the most prominent among them. The others took shelter in the pueblo, at the top of it. Thus the captain returned to quarters.

Immediately after this the general gave the order to lay siege to the pueblo. He set out one day with his men, in good array and with a few hand-ladders. Upon his arrival he established camp close to the pueblo, and shortly afterward attacked; but the enemy had been getting ready for many days and had so many stones to hurl on our men that they stretched many on the ground. They wounded close to one hundred men with arrows, of whom some died later because of the inefficient care of a poor surgeon who was with the army. The siege lasted fifty days. During this time the Spaniards attacked several times. What troubled the Indians most was their lack of water. Within the pueblo they dug a very deep well, but they were unable to obtain water; on the contrary, it caved in while they were digging, killing thirty persons. Of the besieged, two hundred men died in the various attacks. One day when there was a vigorous fight they killed Francisco de Ovando on our side, captain and maestre de campo during the time when Don García López was away on his explorations, and a certain Francisco de Pobares, a fine gentleman. They dragged Francisco de Ovando into the pueblo, as our men were unable to rescue him. This was very much regretted, as he was a distinguished person and besides very honorable, gracious, and unusually well liked.

One day, before the pueblo was finally taken, the Indians asked for a conference. When their request became known, they said that as they had learned that we did not harm women and children, they wanted to give us theirs, because they were exhausting their water. We were unable to induce them to make peace. They insisted that we would not keep our word. So they delivered about one hundred persons, consisting of women and children, as no more would leave the pueblo. While they delivered them, our men remained on their horses in formation before the pueblo. Don Lope de Urrea was on horseback, without helmet, receiving the boys and girls in his arms. When they ceased bringing more, Don Lope urged them to make peace, offering them all sorts of promises of security. They warned him to draw back, for they did not want to trust people who did not keep their friendship or the word they gave. As he would not withdraw, an Indian came out armed with a bow and arrow and threatened to kill him, saying that he would shoot if he did not go away. However much the other Spaniards shouted for Don Lope to put on his head armor, he refused, saying that the natives would not harm him while he remained there. When the Indian saw that he would not go away, he shot an arrow, which landed at the foot of Don Lope's horse. Putting another arrow in his bow, he told him to leave or he would shoot to kill. Don Lope put on his helmet and slowly rejoined the other riders without being harmed by the Indians. When they saw he was in a safe place they began to shout and howl and to send a shower of arrows. The general did not wish to fight them on that day because he wanted to see if he could find a way to make peace with them, to which they never consented.

Fifteen days later the Indians decided to abandon the pueblo during the night, and they did so. Placing their women in the middle they set out during the first quarter of the watch. During that quarter forty mounted men were on guard. When the men in the barracks of Don Rodrigo Maldonado sounded the alarm, the enemy fell upon them, killing a Spaniard and a horse and wounding others. However, they were repulsed, a good many of them being killed. They fell back to the river, which was high and extremely cold, and as the men from the camp quickly rushed to attack, few of the enemy escaped death or injury. In the morning the army crossed the river and found many wounded Indians who had collapsed because of the intense cold. They brought them back to heal them and make servants of them. Thus ended the siege, and the pueblo was conquered, although there were a few who had remained in the pueblo and who resisted in one of the sections, but they were overcome in a few days. [...]

Chapter IV: How the People of Tiguex Live, As Well As Those of The Province of Tiguex and Its Environs

Tiguex is a province of twelve pueblos, on the banks of a large and mighty river. Some pueblos are on one bank, some on the other. It is a spacious valley two leagues wide. To the east there is a snow-covered sierra, very high and rough. At its foot, on the other side, there are seven pueblos, four in the plain and three sheltered on the slope of the sierra.

Seven leagues to the north there is Quirix, with seven pueblos. Forty leagues to the northeast there is the province of Hemes, with seven pueblos. To the north or east, four leagues away, is found Acha. To the southeast there is Tutahaco, a province comprising eight pueblos. All these pueblos have, in general, the same ceremonies and customs, although some have practices among them not observed elsewhere. They are governed by the counsel of their elders. They build their pueblo houses in common. The women mix the plaster and erect the walls; the men bring the timbers and set them in place. They have no lime, but they mix a mortar made with charcoal ash and dirt, which is almost as good as if it were made with lime. For although the houses are four stories high, their walls are built only half a yard thick. The people gather large amounts of brush and reeds, set fire to it, and when it is between charcoal and ash, they throw in a large amount of water and dirt and mix it, then make round balls with it, which they use as stones when dry. They set them with this same mixture, so that it becomes like a mortar.

The unmarried young men serve the pueblo in general. They bring the firewood that is needed and stack it up in the patios of the pueblos, from where the women take it to their homes. These young men live in the estufas, which are located in the patios of the pueblo. They are built underground, either square or round, with pine columns. Some have been seen having twelve pillars, four to the cell, two fathoms thick; the common ones had three or four columns. The floors are paved with large smooth slabs like the baths in Europe. In the interior there is a fireplace like the binnacle of a boat where they burn a handful of brush with which they keep up the heat. They can remain inside the estufa as in a bath. The top is even with the ground. We saw some so large that they could be used for a game of ball.

When some one wishes to marry he must have the permission of the rulers. The man must spin and weave a blanket and place it before the woman. She covers herself with it and becomes his wife. The houses are for the women, the estufas for the men. If a man repudiates his wife he must come to the estufa. It is punishable for the women to sleep in the estufas or to enter them for any other purpose than to bring food to their husbands or sons. The men spin and weave; the women take care of the children and prepare the food. The land is so fertile that they need to cultivate only once a year, just for planting, for the snow falls and covers the fields, and the maize grows under the snow. In one year they harvest enough for seven years. There are numerous cranes, geese, crows, and thrushes which feed on the planted fields. With all this, when, in the following year, they proceed to plant again, they find the fields covered with maize, which they had not been able to gather fully.

There were in these provinces large numbers of native hens and cocks with gills. These, if not dressed or cut open, could be kept for sixty days after death without giving any smell. This was true also of human beings. And they could be kept even longer during the winter. The towns are free from filth because the inhabitants go outside to discharge excrement, and they urinate in earthen jars, which they empty outside the pueblo.

Their houses are well separated and extremely clean in the places where they cook and where they grind flour. They do this in a separate place or room in which there is a grinding place with three stones set in mortar. Three women come in, each going to her stone. One crushes the maize, the next grinds it, and the third grinds it finer. Before they come inside the door they remove their shoes, tie up their hair and cover it, and shake their clothes. While they are grinding, a man sits at the door playing a flageolet, and the women move their stones, keeping time with the music, and all three sing together. They grind a large amount at one time. All their bread is made with flour, mixed with hot water, in the shape of wafers. They gather large quantities of herbs, which they dry and keep for their cooking throughout the year. There are no edible fruits in this land, except pine nuts. The natives have their own preachers. No sodomy was observed among them nor the sacrificing or eating of human flesh. They are not a cruel people, as was shown at Tiguex, where Francisco de Ovando remained dead for some forty days. When the pueblo was at last taken the Spaniards found his body whole, among the native dead, without any other injury than the wound from which he died. He was as white as snow, without any bad smell.

From one of our Indians who had been a captive among these people for a year, I learned some details of their customs. In particular I asked him why the young women went about naked in that province when it was so cold; he answered that the maidens had to go about that way until they took a husband and that as soon as they had relations with a man they covered themselves. In that region the men wore jackets of dressed deerskin and over them their robes. Throughout these provinces one finds pottery glazed with alcohol, and jugs of such elaborate designs and shapes that it was surprising.

★   ★   ★

Sixteenth-century French explorations of the St Lawrence River in Canada led eventually to a permanent French colony at Quebec, a fur trading post founded by Samuel de Champlain in 1608. The Native people in the area –

the Algonquins, Montagnais, and Hurons – saw in Champlain's small band of men useful allies in their war against the Iroquois to the south. ("Algonquian" refers to the language spoken by many eastern Indian peoples; Champlain's "Algonquin" allies were an Algonquian-speaking nation in Canada.) Champlain and his men, with their inefficient but impressively noisy muskets, joined their new-found Indian allies in battle. What follows are excerpts from Champlain's account of the Quebec settlement and the origins of the Indian–French alliance. Clearly, Champlain relished the role of military hero. At least, that is how he presented himself to his readers. However, since we see these events through his eyes only, we cannot be sure that the Indians were as impressed with Champlain as he was with himself. In his descriptions of Indians or "savages" (the French typically called Indians *sauvages*), Champlain claims a superiority over them, which from Champlain's perspective was then reinforced by his assuming the role of military commander, or captain, in their joint military ventures.

Voyages of Samuel de Champlain, 1604–1618

Samuel de Champlain, ed. W. L. Grant

[...] While the carpenters, sawers of boards, and other workmen were employed on our quarters, I set all the others to work clearing up around our place of abode, in preparation for gardens in which to plant grain and seeds, that we might see how they would flourish, as the soil seemed to be very good.

Meanwhile, a large number of savages were encamped in cabins near us, engaged in fishing for eels, which begin to come about the 15th of September, and go away on the 15th of October. During this time, all the savages subsist on this food, and dry enough of it for the winter to last until the month of February, when there are about two and a half, or at most three, feet of snow; and, when their eels and other things which they dry have been prepared, they go to hunt the beaver until the beginning of January. At their departure for this purpose, they intrusted to us all their eels and other things, until their return, which was on the 15th of December. But they did not have great success in the beaver-hunt, as the amount of water was too great, the rivers having overrun

W. L. Grant, ed. *Voyages of Samuel de Champlain, 1604–1618*. New York: Charles Scribner's Sons, 1907: 140–66.

their banks, as they told us. I returned to them all their supplies, which lasted them only until the 20th of January. When their supply of eels gave out, they hunted the elk and such other wild beasts as they could find until spring, when I was able to supply them with various things. I paid especial attention to their customs.

These people suffer so much from lack of food that they are sometimes obliged to live on certain shell-fish, and eat their dogs and the skins with which they clothe themselves against the cold. I am of opinion that, if one were to show them how to live, and teach them the cultivation of the soil and other things, they would learn very aptly. For many of them possess good sense, and answer properly questions put to them. They have a bad habit of taking vengeance, and are great liars, and you must not put much reliance on them, except judiciously, and with force at hand. They make promises readily, but keep their word poorly. The most of them observe no law at all, so far as I have been able to see, and are, besides, full of superstitions. I asked them with what ceremonies they were accustomed to pray to their God, when they replied that they had none, but that each prayed to him in his heart, as he wished. That is why there is no law among them, and they do not know what it is to worship and pray to God, living as they do like brute beasts. But I think that they would soon become good Christians, if people would come and inhabit their country, which they are for the most part desirous of. There are some savages among them, called by them Pilotois, whom they believe to have intercourse with the devil face to face, who tells them what they must do in regard to war and other things; and, if he should order them to execute any undertaking, they would obey at once. So, also, they believe that all their dreams are true; and, in fact, there are many who say that they have had visions and dreams about matters which actually come to pass or will do so. But, to tell the truth, these are diabolical visions, through which they are deceived and misled. This is all I have been able to learn about their brutish faith. All these people are well proportioned in body, without deformity, and are agile. The women, also, are well-formed, plump, and of a swarthy color, in consequence of certain pigments with which they rub themselves, and which give them a permanent olive color. They are dressed in skins: a part only of the body is covered. But in winter they are covered throughout, in good furs of elk, otter, beaver, bear, seals, deer, and roe, of which they have large quantities. In winter, when the snow is deep, they make a sort of snow-shoe of large size, two or three times as large as that used in France, which they attach to their feet, thus going over the snow without sinking in; otherwise, they could not hunt or walk in many places. They have a sort of marriage, which is as follows: When a girl is fourteen or fifteen years old, and has several suitors, she may keep company with all she likes. At the end of five or six years, she takes the one that pleases her for her husband, and they live together to the end of their lives. But if, after living some time together, they have no children, the man can disunite himself and take another woman, alleging that his own is good for nothing. Hence, the girls have greater freedom than the married women.

After marriage, the women are chaste, and their husbands generally jealous. They give presents to the fathers or relatives of the girls they have wedded. These are the ceremonies and forms observed in their marriages. In regard to their burials: When a man or a woman dies, they dig a pit, in which they put all their property, as kettles, furs, axes, bows, arrows, robes, and other things. Then they place the body in the pit and cover it with earth, putting on top many large pieces of wood, and another piece upright, painted red on the upper part. They believe in the immortality of the soul, and say that they shall be happy in other lands with their relatives and friends who are dead. In the case of captains or others of some distinction, they celebrate a banquet three times a year after their death, singing and dancing about the grave.

All the time they were with us, which was the most secure place for them, they did not cease to fear their enemies to such an extent that they often at night became alarmed while dreaming, and sent their wives and children to our fort, the gates of which I had opened to them, allowing the men to remain about the fort, but not permitting them to enter, for their persons were thus as much in security as if they had been inside. I also had five or six of our men go out to reassure them, and to go and ascertain whether they could see anything in the woods, in order to quiet them. They are very timid and in great dread of their enemies, scarcely ever sleeping in repose in whatever place they may be, although I constantly reassured them, so far as I could, urging them to do as we did; namely, that they should have a portion watch while the others slept, that each one should have his arms in readiness like him who was keeping watch, and that they should not regard dreams as the actual truth to be relied upon, since they are mostly only false, to which I also added other words on the same subject. But these remonstrances were of little avail with them, and they said that we knew better than they how to keep guard against all things; and that they, in course of time, if we continued to stay with them, would be able to learn it. [...]

Immediately upon my arrival, Pont Gravé and I had a conference in regard to some explorations which I was to make in the interior, where the savages had promised to guide us. We determined that I should go in a shallop with twenty men, and that Pont Gravé should stay at Tadoussac to arrange the affairs of our settlement; and this determination was carried out, he spending the winter there. This arrangement was especially desirable, since I was to return to France, according to the orders sent out by Sieur de Monts, in order to inform him of what I had done and the explorations I had made in the country.

After this decision, I set out at once from Tadoussac, and returned to Quebec, where I had a shallop fitted out with all that was necessary for making explorations in the country of the Iroquois, where I was to go with our allies, the Montagnais. [. . .]

Pursuing our route, I met some two or three hundred savages, who were encamped in huts near a little island called St. Éloi, a league and a half distant from St. Mary. We made a reconnoissance, and found that they were tribes of savages, called Ochateguins [Hurons] and Algonquins, on their way to Quebec, to assist us in exploring the territory of the Iroquois, with whom they are in deadly hostility, sparing nothing belonging to their enemies.

After reconnoitring, I went on shore to see them, and inquired who their chief was. They told me there were two, one named Yroquet, and the other Ochasteguin, whom they pointed out to me. I went to their cabin, where they gave me a cordial reception, as is their custom.

I proceeded to inform them of the object of my voyage, with which they were greatly pleased. After some talk, I withdrew. Some time after, they came to my shallop, and presented me with some peltry, exhibiting many tokens of pleasure. Then they returned to the shore.

The next day, the two chiefs came to see me, when they remained some time without saying a word, meditating and smoking all the while. After due reflection, they began to harangue in a loud voice all their companions who were on the bank of the river, with their arms in their hands, and listening very attentively to what their chiefs said to them, which was as follows: that nearly ten moons ago, according to their mode of reckoning, the son of Yroquet had seen me, and that I had given him a good reception, and declared that Pont Gravé and I desired to assist them against their enemies, with whom they had for a long time been at warfare, on account of many cruel acts committed by them against their tribe, under color of friendship; that, having ever since longed for vengeance, they had solicited all the savages, whom I saw on the bank of the river, to come and make an alliance with us, and that their never having seen Christians also impelled them to come and visit us; that I should do with them and their companions as I wished; that they had no children with them, but men versed in war and full of courage, acquainted with the country and rivers in the land of the Iroquois; that now they entreated me to return to our settlement, that they might see our houses, and that, after three days, we should all together come back to engage in the war; that, as a token of firm friendship and joy, I should have muskets and arquebuses fired, at which they would be greatly pleased. This I did, when they uttered great cries of astonishment, especially those who had never heard nor seen the like. [. . .]

Now, as we began to approach within two or three days' journey of the abode of their enemies, we advanced only at night, resting during the day. But they did not fail to practise constantly their accustomed superstitions, in order to ascertain what was to be the result of their undertaking; and they often asked me if I had had a dream, and seen their enemies, to which I replied in the negative. Yet I did not cease to encourage them, and inspire in them hope. When night came, we set out on the journey until the next day, when we withdrew into the interior of the forest, and spent the rest of the day there. About ten or eleven o'clock, after taking a little walk about our encampment, I retired. While sleeping, I dreamed that I saw our enemies, the Iroquois, drowning in the lake near a mountain, within sight. When I expressed a wish to help them, our allies, the savages, told me we must let them all die, and that they were of no importance. When I awoke, they did not fail to ask me, as usual, if I had had a dream. I told them that I had, in fact, had a dream. This, upon being related, gave them so much confidence that they did not doubt any longer that good was to happen to them.

When it was evening, we embarked in our canoes to continue our course; and, as we advanced very quietly and without making any noise, we met on the 29th of the month the Iroquois, about ten o'clock at evening, at the extremity of a cape which extends into the lake on the western bank. They had come to fight. We both began to utter loud cries, all getting their arms in readiness. We withdrew out on the water, and the Iroquois went on shore, where they drew up all their canoes close to each other and began to fell trees with poor axes, which they acquire in war sometimes, using also others of stone. Thus they barricaded themselves very well.

Our forces also passed the entire night, their canoes being drawn up close to each other, and fastened to poles, so that they might not get separated, and that they might be all in readiness to fight, if occasion required. We were out upon the water, within arrow range of their barricades. When they were armed and in array, they despatched two canoes by themselves to the enemy to inquire if they wished to fight, to which the latter replied that they wanted nothing else: but they said that, at present, there was not much light, and that it would be necessary to wait for daylight, so as to be able to recognize each other; and that, as soon as the sun rose, they would offer us battle. This was agreed to by our side. Meanwhile, the entire night was spent in dancing and singing, on both sides, with endless insults and other talk; as, how little courage we had, how feeble a resistance we should make against their arms, and that, when day came, we should realize it to our ruin. Ours also were not

slow in retorting, telling them they would see such execution of arms as
never before, together with an abundance of such talk as is not unusual
in the siege of a town. After this singing, dancing, and bandying words
on both sides to the fill, when day came, my companions and myself
continued under cover, for fear that the enemy would see us. We
arranged our arms in the best manner possible, being, however, separated, each in one of the canoes of the savage Montagnais. After arming
ourselves with light armor, we each took an arquebuse, and went on
shore. I saw the enemy go out of their barricade, nearly two hundred in
number, stout and rugged in appearance. They came at a slow pace
towards us, with a dignity and assurance which greatly amused me,
having three chiefs at their head. Our men also advanced in the same
order, telling me that those who had three large plumes were the chiefs,
and that they had only these three, and that they could be distinguished
by these plumes, which were much larger than those of their companions, and that I should do what I could to kill them. I promised to do all
in my power, and said that I was very sorry they could not understand
me, so that I might give order and shape to their mode of attacking their
enemies, and then we should, without doubt, defeat them all; but that
this could not now be obviated, and that I should be very glad to show
them my courage and good-will when we should engage in the fight.

As soon as we had landed, they began to run for some two hundred
paces towards their enemies, who stood firmly, not having as yet noticed
my companions, who went into the woods with some savages. Our men
began to call me with loud cries; and, in order to give me a passage-way,
they opened in two parts, and put me at their head, where I marched
some twenty paces in advance of the rest, until I was within about thirty
paces of the enemy, who at once noticed me, and, halting, gazed at me,
as I did also at them. When I saw them making a move to fire at us, I
rested my musket against my cheek, and aimed directly at one of the
three chiefs. With the same shot, two fell to the ground; and one of their
men was so wounded that he died some time after. I had loaded my
musket with four balls. When our side saw this shot so favorable for
them, they began to raise such loud cries that one could not have heard it
thunder. Meanwhile, the arrows flew on both sides. The Iroquois were
greatly astonished that two men had been so quickly killed, although
they were equipped with armor woven from cotton thread, and with
wood which was proof against their arrows. This caused great alarm
among them. As I was loading again, one of my companions fired a shot
from the woods, which astonished them anew to such a degree that,
seeing their chiefs dead, they lost courage, and took to flight, abandon-
ing their camp and fort, and fleeing into the woods, whither I pursued
them, killing still more of them. Our savages also killed several of them,

and took ten or twelve prisoners. The remainder escaped with the wounded. Fifteen or sixteen were wounded on our side with arrow-shots; but they were soon healed.

After gaining the victory, our men amused themselves by taking a great quantity of Indian corn and some meal from their enemies, also their armor, which they had left behind that they might run better. After feasting sumptuously, dancing and singing, we returned three hours after, with the prisoners. The spot where this attack took place is in latitude 43° and some minutes, and the lake was called Lake Champlain.

Further Reading

Barbour, Philip L., ed. *The Complete Works of Captain John Smith (1580–1631)*. 3 vols. Chapel Hill: University of North Carolina Press for the Institute of Early American History and Culture, 1986.

Gleach, Frederic W. *Powhatan's World and Colonial Virginia: A Conflict of Cultures*. Lincoln: University of Nebraska Press, 1997.

Jaenen, Cornelius J. *Friend and Foe: Aspects of French–Amerindian Cultural Contact in the Sixteenth and Seventeenth Centuries*. New York: Columbia University Press, 1976.

Kupperman, Karen, *Settling with the Indians: The Meeting of English and Indian Cultures in America, 1580–1640*. Totowa, NJ: Rowman and Littlefield, 1980.

Perdue, Theda. *Cherokee Women: Gender and Culture Change, 1700–1835*. Lincoln: University of Nebraska Press, 1998.

Sando, Joe S. *Pueblo Nations: Eight Centuries of Pueblo Indian History*. Santa Fe, NM: Clear Light, 1992.

Weber, David J. *The Spanish Frontier in North America*. New Haven: Yale University Press, 1992.

3

International Diplomacy and Cultural Exchange

Introduction

An active area of scholarly research in recent years has been the "middle ground," to borrow the phrase popularized by Richard White's important book *The Middle Ground: Indians, Empires, and Republics in the Great Lakes Region, 1650–1815* (New York, 1991). White and a host of other historians have closely examined how Indians and Europeans communicated their diplomatic objectives across the cultural divide. White used the term "middle ground" to mean a particular moment in the evolving relations between nations, when neither Indians nor Europeans had the upper hand in the balance of power. They communicated through cultural compromises. By adopting elements of each other's rituals and rhetoric, they formed a "middle ground" of symbols and meanings upon which they built shared objectives.

Timothy J. Shannon's article "Dressing for Success on the Mohawk Frontier: Hendrick, William Johnson, and the Indian Fashion" argues that Iroquois–English councils on the colonial New York frontier took place on a "middle ground." Shannon focuses on clothing as a medium of cultural exchange and a tool for political maneuvering. Instead of assuming that Indians who wore European clothing were assimilating European culture, Shannon puts forth a more complex interpretation of clothing as a constantly shifting symbol of cultural identity, social class or status, friendship, and political alliance. Indian preferences for certain items, colors, and quality of manufacture led them to selectively incorporate European material culture into their own. At the same time, clothing's symbolic meanings lent it flexibility in self-presentation. Clothing was as powerful a language as the words exchanged at councils.

Shannon's unique contribution to the study of Indian–European diplomacy lies in his analysis of paintings as documents of their times. Other valuable sources are the transcripts of Indian councils kept by European scribes, who over the years recorded hundreds, perhaps thousands, of Indian speeches. The two documents accompanying Shannon's article are written accounts, one from the official record and the other an unofficial memoir, of a council held at Lancaster, Pennsylvania in 1744. Indians and Europeans met in council to hammer out political disagreements and plan an amicable future, but as Shannon's article shows and as council records further demonstrate, cultural differences had to be transcended if political objectives were to be met.

Dressing for Success on the Mohawk Frontier: Hendrick, William Johnson, and the Indian Fashion

Timothy J. Shannon

In the mid-eighteenth century, colonist William Johnson and Mohawk leader Hendrick forged a partnership that dominated European–Indian relations in the Mohawk Valley of New York. Johnson, an Irish fur trader and merchant who settled in the region in 1738, served as New York's Indian agent from 1746 to 1751 and in 1755 became the British crown's first Superintendent of Indian Affairs. Hendrick, a Mohawk from the village of Canajoharie, had been active in European–Indian diplomacy since the late 1690s; by the 1740s he was the most widely recognized Indian leader in the northern colonies. Together, Johnson and Hendrick exerted a tremendous influence on the Covenant Chain, an alliance governing economic and diplomatic relations between the Iroquois confederacy and Great Britain's North American colonies.

Visual images of Johnson and Hendrick provide insight into the roles they played within the Covenant Chain. In an early portrait, Johnson appears in a fine scarlet coat, green vest, and cravat – dress that declared his status as a colonial merchant and militia officer (figure 1). This portrait contrasts with another recorded by Cadwallader Colden, a

Shannon, Timothy J. "Dressing for Success on the Mohawk Frontier: Hendrick, William Johnson, and the Indian Fashion." *The William and Mary Quarterly*, 3rd series, 53 (January 1996): 13–42.

Figure 1   Sir William Johnson (1715–1774) by John Wollaston, c. 1750, oil on canvas. Collection of the Albany Institute of History and Art. Gift of Laura Munsell Tremaine.

New York councillor and contemporary of Johnson's. Colden attended a Covenant Chain treaty conference in Albany in August 1746, where he saw Johnson enter the city gates, "riding at the head of the *Mohawks*, dressed and painted after the manner of an *Indian* War Captain," followed by Indians "likewise dressed and painted, as is usual when they set out in War." Such a dramatic scene offers a striking juxtaposition to the portrait of a staid, well-dressed colonial gentleman.

An impressive portrait of Hendrick dates to a visit he made to London in 1740, when he was about sixty years old (figure 2). Hendrick appears in costume appropriate for the royal court: blue suit and cocked hat trimmed in lace, a ruffled shirt with long cuffs, and cravat. Tradition has it that King George II presented this outfit to him. Hendrick holds a tomahawk in one hand and a string of wampum in the other, combining the attire of eighteenth-century English gentry with symbolic props of North American Indian diplomacy. Four years later, Dr. Alexander Hamilton, an Annapolis physician touring the northern colonies, provided a verbal description of Hendrick to complement this visual one. In Boston, Hamilton observed a procession of Indians attending a treaty conference. He noted that Hendrick and the other Indian leaders "had all laced hats, and some of them laced matchcoats and ruffled shirts."

Scholars of material culture have long noted the importance of clothing in self-presentation. Costume and fashion provide what one cultural anthropologist has called "an expressive medium" through which individuals communicate with others. Such factors as the color, fabric, and fit of the clothing, along with posture and manners, tell us about the wearer's social position, occupation, and elements of personal identity from religious beliefs to sexual preferences. In addition to keeping the body warm and dry, clothing may denote status, signify a rite of passage, or even convey spiritual powers. The importance of clothing to material culture therefore extends far beyond its utility to include a variety of expressive properties that may be manipulated by its wearer.

Historians of the British-Atlantic world have applied these insights in studying the eighteenth-century consumer revolution. In England, the expansion of markets and consumer choices profoundly affected clothing fashion and the public's buying habits. In North America, consumption of British manufactures increased dramatically after 1740, altering colonists' everyday activities and reshaping their notions of taste and refinement. Through goods and styles imported from England, provincial Americans imitated British consumers and cultivated new standards of gentility based on self-presentation.

For the Indians of northeastern America, this consumer revolution had been underway since European contact. They too encountered expanding markets and new choices as they became increasingly dependent on European weapons, tools, and clothing. Indians adopted these goods when they found them technologically advantageous but valued them also for aesthetic properties, such as color and shape, and for ceremonial uses, such as mourning the dead, that Europeans were slow

Figure 2 "The brave old Hendrick," anonymous engraving, 1755. Courtesy of the John Carter Brown Library at Brown University.

to comprehend. Indian consumers were selective and demanding, often haggling over prices and refusing inferior goods. In short, they engaged wholeheartedly in the consumer revolution, but on their own terms and in ways shaped by their cultural values and practices.

Within this consumer revolution, both Europeans and Indians found uses for the expressive properties of clothing. As the portraits of Johnson and Hendrick indicate, costume played an important role in intercultural contact and exchange. The Mohawk Valley in which Johnson and Hendrick lived was a jumble of differing ethnicities and languages. Clothing helped the Valley's inhabitants communicate in ways other than the written or spoken word. Apparel had been a popular trade good in the Mohawk Valley since the early seventeenth century. Under the Covenant Chain alliance, it acquired considerable importance as a tool of diplomacy. Indians and colonists gathered periodically in Albany to make speeches and renew the alliance that preserved peace and trade between them. Treaty participants exchanged presents, usually bundles of furs from the Indians and manufactured items from the colonists. Over the course of the eighteenth century, the Indians' presents remained small and symbolic, but the colonists' grew into substantial donations of material goods. Clothing included in such grants ranged from cheap woolens to fine linens, from such necessaries as shirts and blankets to ornamental ribbons, earrings, and beads. Europeans also presented Indians with weapons, liquor, tools, food, and even cash, but none of these items had the universal appeal and diversity of choice that clothing offered to Indian men, women, and children.

Clothing helped the Mohawk Valley's inhabitants establish what Richard White calls a "middle ground" of cultural mediation. In White's study, middle ground both refers to a geographic region between the Mississippi River and the Appalachian Mountains and describes a culturally constructed space shaped by the rituals and customs that governed the fur trade and European-Indian diplomacy.[1] Clothing helped establish such a space in the Mohawk Valley. Through their participation in the consumer revolution, Indians and colonists there did more than simply imitate the fashions of English gentlefolk. They used trade goods to invent new appearances, new ceremonies, and a new, visual language by which they communicated in a diverse and contentious world.

Clothing provided an important means of cultural mediation in the Mohawk Valley because it endowed its possessor with a capacity for self-fashioning. Other assets, such as multilingual fluency and political connections, certainly helped overcome cultural differences, but the careers of Johnson and Hendrick prove the importance of looking the part as well. Costume, when used correctly, increased the cultural mobility of its wearer. Clothing was acquired more easily than a foreign language and changed more readily than a native accent. It provided people with constant opportunity to re-invent themselves from one audience to the next, to create new appearances, and to gain influence through participation in trade. In the Mohawk Valley, no one manipulated these opportunities more skillfully than Hendrick and Johnson.

From the perspective of London or Paris in the mid-eighteenth century, the Mohawk Valley divided North America into three distinct units: British to the east, Indian to the west, French to the north. In actuality, colonial and native populations did not neatly arrange themselves *in partes tres*. Albany, its population still predominantly Dutch, served as an eastern gateway to the region from the Hudson River. It was also a trading center for Indians who carried furs and goods between Canada and New York by way of Lake Champlain. The Mohawks inhabited two villages west of Albany: Tiononderoge, which Europeans called the "lower castle," and Canajoharie, the "upper castle." German, Irish, and Scots-Irish colonists lived near Tiononderoge, where the Schoharie River met the Mohawk; many of them were tenants of William Johnson and his uncle Peter Warren. Mount Johnson, Johnson's diplomatic and mercantile headquarters, stood north of the Mohawk between the two Indian villages. Moving farther upstream, a traveler entered German Flats, settled by German Palatines in the 1720s. More Germans and Scots-Irish lived south of this region in Cherry Valley, near the headwaters of the Susquehanna River. Farther west, on the southeastern shore of Lake Ontario, a handful of British soldiers garrisoned Oswego, a post that attracted Indian and colonial traders throughout the Great Lakes region to its summer markets.

Although far inland from major seaports, the Mohawk Valley's inhabitants actively engaged in the British-Atlantic economy. Indians and colonists ferried goods along the Mohawk River between Albany and Oswego. Johnson lived in the middle of this trade. To agents in New York City and London, he sent furs, along with wheat and peas grown by local farmers and ginseng gathered by Indians. He imported clothing, tools, weapons, and liquor for his storehouse, which he located to intercept Indians and colonists headed downstream to Albany.

The goods that flowed into the Mohawk Valley had a pervasive effect on cultural identities there, allowing inhabitants to engage in behaviors and habits not normally associated with colonial frontier life. Johnson himself is an excellent example. By 1749, he had amassed a fortune large enough to live in the style of an English gentleman. On the Mohawk River, forty miles removed from the nearest colonial population center, he built a home "60 foot long, by 32 Wide two Story High, all Stone." He purchased household slaves and servants and imported the luxuries that defined colonial gentility: books and newspapers, the *Gentleman's Magazine* from London, fine writing paper and sealing wax, musical instruments, and prints. In 1763, Johnson built his own Georgian-style mansion, Johnson Hall, to complement the baronetcy the crown awarded him during the Seven Years' War.

Johnson was not the only Mohawk Valley inhabitant to indulge in imported goods. Traveling in the region in 1748–1749, Swedish naturalist Peter Kalm encountered a world shaped by consumerism. While he found Albany overwhelmingly Dutch in character – its citizens spoke Dutch, had Dutch manners, and practiced Dutch religion – he qualified this observation with one telling remark: "Their dress is however like that of the English." English clothing had managed to penetrate the insular world of Dutch Albany well in advance of English language or politics. Even more noteworthy are Kalm's observations on tea drinking, a practice he found almost universal among colonists. In the Mohawk Valley, he saw Indian women enjoying this new luxury as well. Johnson, recorded Kalm, said that "several of the Indians who lived close to the European settlements had learned to drink tea." Kalm, who criticized colonial women for drinking tea as hot as possible, added that "Indian women in imitation of them, swallowed the tea in the same manner." Johnson included tea, sugar, and teapots for "Chief Familys" among his Indian presents. Tea drinking, a consumer activity by which colonial Americans commonly expressed their gentility, became an agent of cultural assimilation between Europeans and Indians in the Mohawk Valley.

Clothing exchanged in the Mohawk Valley trade also challenged traditional cultural differences. Indians wore European clothing, but they did so in a distinctive way that contemporaries recognized as the "Indian Fashion." Indian consumers rarely adopted European costume from head to foot, and they expressed strong distaste for tight-fitting clothing such as breeches and shoes. Instead, they traded for European cloth cut from the bolt, which they put to any number of uses. The coarse woolen blankets, strouds, duffels, and half-thicks that made up the bulk of this trade they arranged around their bodies as shirts, skirts, robes, and coats. Indian men also favored long linen hunting shirts, which they wore draped over the waist. On the lower body, Indians used European cloth as loincloths, leggings, and moccasins that left more skin exposed than Europeans considered proper. The Indian fashion favored certain colors and fabrics, and European traders adjusted their stock accordingly. Johnson provided woolens in shades of blue, red, and black as well as flowered serge and striped calicoes in "lively Colours."

The Indian fashion also adopted European goods for bodily decoration. Indians painted and tattooed their bodies with such traditional materials as bear's grease and natural dyes; they added to this mix with imported verdigris, which has a green pigment, and vermillion, which has a red. Objects of European origin became jewelry for the hair, nose, ears, and arms. Johnson listed glass beads, silver armbands, brass wire, and medals embossed with the British arms among his trade goods as well as buttons, buckles, lace, and brightly colored ribbons. Indians could incorporate these items into their dress with cloth-working tools provided by European traders: scissors, needles, thread, pen knives, and awl blades. Items for personal grooming included buckling combs and looking glasses.

Indians of both sexes valued these European goods, but contemporaries noted gender differences in their tastes and habits. Kalm observed that women were not as quick to "clothe themselves according to the new styles," although he occasionally saw some wearing caps of homespun or "coarse blue broad-cloth" in imitation of colonial women. Men frequently examined their decorations in mirrors and "upon the whole, [were] more fond of dressing than the women." Another indication of male immersion in fashion in Johnson's inclusion of ribbons, combs, razors, and looking glasses among the presents he made to warriors. Johnson gave women and children blankets, shirts, and stockings earmarked in special sizes for them, and women adopted European items as jewelry. Richard Smith, a land speculator visiting the Mohawk Valley in 1769, recalled that some women wore "Silver Broaches each of which passes for a Shilling and are as current among the Indians as Money," while "the younger sort" of both sexes used "Bobs and Trinkets in their Ears and Noses, Bracelets on their Arms and Rings on their Fingers."

A further distinction within the Indian fashion arose between the costumes of sachems [leaders] and warriors. Johnson's account for presents he distributed during King George's War gives detailed portraits of the well-dressed sachem and the well-dressed warrior. For example, on May 11, 1747, ten Senecas appeared at Johnson's home with news about Indian affairs. To nine of them Johnson gave a shirt, paint, and knives. To the tenth, whom he identified as "the Capt[ain]," he also gave paint and knives, along with "A Shirt very fine with Ruffles & ribon" and "A fine lac'd Hatt...with a Cockade." The same account shows that Johnson distributed shirts, blankets, stockings, laps, ribbons, paint, combs, scissors, razors, and looking glasses to warriors, along with weapons and provisions. Sachems received many of these goods, but their presents always included a ruffled shirt, laced hat, silver medal, or fine coat. Presents for warriors – paint, razors, combs, ribbons, mirrors – emphasized bodily decoration for battle. Presents for sachems featured clothing – fine shirts, hats, and coats – appropriate for diplomacy.

Judging from contemporary reports, Indians attending treaty conferences with Europeans observed this fashion distinction between sachems and warriors. Visitors in the Mohawk Valley recognized a visual difference between "the common sort" of Indians, who generally wore clothing limited to "a Shirt or Shift with a Blanket or Coat," and their leaders, who were more likely to "imitate the English Mode" and appear in hats, coats, and ruffled shirts. Europeans viewed Indian costume in the same way that they looked at their own – as an indication of the wearer's place within a hierarchical social order. Coming from a culture that regulated colors and fabrics worn by different classes, Europeans interpreted the Indian fashion as a similar means of establishing social distinctions. A sachem who appeared at a public treaty meeting wearing a ruffled shirt, fine coat, and laced hat became the visual counterpart of the colonial gentlemen across the council fire. Even such novices to Indian affairs as Dr. Hamilton could readily distinguish sachems from "a multitude of the plebs of their own complexion" by analyzing their dress.

Indians attached their own meaning to the European clothing they wore. Ethnohistorians and anthropologists have argued that Indians invested presents they received from Europeans with ideological value that often outweighed their utilitarian value. Beads and cloth of a certain color or shape, for example, represented physical or emotional well-being and gave spiritual wealth to their possessor. Presents received at a treaty council symbolized friendship between the giver and recipient, and Indians perceived them as material evidence of peace and goodwill. The context in which Indians acquired European clothing thus shaped the way they used it: they might invest clothing presented to them at a treaty conference with a ceremonial significance that would merit saving and wearing it again on similar occasions. Such ideological value helps explain why Indian men were more likely than Indian women to dress in a distinctive fashion when among Europeans. Johnson's accounts reveal that he distributed clothing to sachems and warriors personally – often in one-to-one encounters – when going to war, honoring the dead, or entertaining friends. When he gave clothing to Indian women and children, he distributed it in much greater quantities and for more utilitarian reasons: on May 24, 1747, for example, he entered a debit in his accounts of £49.17.0 for "Cloathing for their [Indian warriors'] Women and Children being naked." Under such circumstances, men were more likely than women or children to attach ideological value to their presents; warriors and sachems more often received clothing as a result of diplomatic ceremony than of simple need.

Europeans and Indians recognized the peculiar type of costume known as the Indian fashion, but for entirely different reasons. Europeans distributed clothing in ways that allowed them to construct a visual sense of social difference and hierarchy among Indians. Indians incorporated this clothing into their dress for the decorative, ideological, and utilitarian value they attached to it. This blending of European goods with Indian custom enabled each side to interpret the clothing from its own perspective yet still use it as an agent of cultural exchange and mediation. The Indian fashion became part of the middle ground between Europeans and Indians in the Mohawk Valley. Because this fashion relied on the acquisition and distribution of material goods, individuals involved in European–Indian trade and diplomacy could manipulate it to their advantage. Johnson's and Hendrick's attention to self-presentation thus contributed to their power. Realizing that an impressive outfit, a well-orchestrated entrance, or a ceremonial presentation of a gift could speak volumes, Johnson and Hendrick used the nonverbal language of appearance to negotiate cultural borders.

Hendrick's life blended European and Indian experiences on the Mohawk Valley's middle ground. Born a Mahican sometime around 1680, he was adopted by the Mohawks as a child and converted to Christianity as a young man. The various names he used throughout his life attest to his cultural mobility. At an Albany conference in 1701, Hendrick signed his mark to the proceedings, and the colonial secretary penned "Teoniahigarawe alias Hendrik" alongside it. When he visited the court of Queen Anne nine years later, Englishmen rendered his Indian name as "Tee Yee Neen Ho Ga Row" an attached to it the title, "Emperour of the Six Nations." British records also identify him as King Hendrick and Hendrick Peters. Pennsylvania Indian interpreter Conrad Weiser knew him as "Henery Dyionoagon." Each of these names reveals a different facet of Hendrick's reputation. "Tee Yee Neen Ho Ga Row" and "Dyionoagon" obviously had Indian origins. "Hendrick Peters," a name he most likely acquired at the time of his baptism, reflected his interaction with the local Dutch. "King Hendrick" carried the authority of an ambassador to royal courts and colonial governments.

Englishmen often called Hendrick "king" or "emperour," but his interests and concerns were rooted in a much smaller world than such a title would indicate. He was one of the headmen of Canajoharie, the "upper castle" of Mohawks, located about sixty miles west of Albany. As a representative of Canajoharie at treaty conferences, he conducted land sales, presented grievances against trade and land frauds, and negotiated terms of war, alliance, and peace with European neighbors. Although his reputation reached throughout the northern colonies and across the Atlantic, Hendrick's perspective on European–Indian relations remained local, and his constituency rarely stretched beyond the perimeter of his village.

Hendrick had a reputation for pride and stubborn independence that often frustrated colonial officials. European contemporaries called him a "politician," a term that implied opportunism, intrigue, and deceit in the eighteenth century, as it often does today. Johnson referred to him as "the Politician Hendrick." Peter Wraxall, Johnson's secretary, noted "the great Hendricks Political Talents." Thomas Pownall called Hendrick "a bold artfull intriguing fellow [who] has learnt no small share of European politics." Weiser, who grew up in Mohawk country, expressed a similar sentiment. He lamented that the Indians had become "apostates as to their Old Natural Principle of Honesty" and in the same sentence vented his distaste for "that Proud and Impudent Henery Dyionoagon." Even Dr. Hamilton, the touring physician from Annapolis, knew enough of Hendrick's reputation to call him "a bold, intrepid fellow."

Hendrick's appearance blended European and Indian identities in a way that created a special category of Indian: the intercultural diplomat who learned European politics but remained independent of European control. Consider the earliest portrait of Hendrick, painted in 1710 when he and three other Indians visited Queen Anne's court. Two leading New Yorkers, Peter Schuyler and Francis Nicholson, sponsored this trip in an effort to win royal support for an expedition against Canada. Styling their native ambassadors "the Four Indian Kings," they introduced Hendrick as Tee Yee Neen Ho Ga Row, "the Emperour of the Six Nations." So that the Indians would make an appearance befitting their titles, Schuyler and Nicholson provided them with new clothing, including scarlet mantles trimmed in gold. At court, the Indians made a speech, most likely spoken by Hendrick, and the queen responded with presents including cottons, woolens, necklaces, combs, scissors, mirrors, tobacco boxes, and a sword and pair of pistols for each king. She also commissioned John Verelst to paint their full-length likenesses.

Comparison of two of these portraits (figures 3, 4) reveals Hendrick's emerging role as an intercultural diplomat. Both Indians appear in standard poses, wearing scarlet mantles. Each stands before a wooded background that includes an animal denoting his clanship (wolf, bear, or turtle). Several important differences set Hendrick, or Tee Yee Neen Ho Ga Row, apart from the others. Each king holds a weapon – gun, club, or bow – except Hendrick, who displays a wampum belt, a tool of diplomacy. Hendrick is the only king wearing the genteel costume of breeches and buckled shoes; the others wear hunting shirts draped over bare legs and moccasined feet. The portraits indicate that Hendrick's power is derived from his political skills rather than his martial talents. These paintings were reproduced as prints and widely circulated in England and the colonies, making Hendrick's visage one of the most common images of an Indian in the British empire.

Figure 3 "Tee Yee Neen Ho Ga Row Emperour of the Six Nations," engraving by J. Simon after John Verelst, 1710. Courtesy of the John Carter Brown Library at Brown University.

Figure 4 "Sa Ga Yeath Qua Pieth Tow King of the Maquas," engraving by J. Simon after John Verelst, 1710. Courtesy of the John Carter Brown Library at Brown University.

The elements of an Indian diplomat's appearance are confirmed in the portrait done when Hendrick returned to London in 1740 (figure 2). In this work Hendrick is the well-dressed sachem described in Johnson's accounts, wearing a laced hat, fine coat, and ruffled shirt. The influence of native custom on the Indian fashion is apparent in the tattooing on Hendrick's face. The wampum belt so prominently displayed in the 1710 portrait has been reduced to a single string held at the waist, and he now flourishes an impressive tomahawk in his right hand. While this portrait is more militant than the previous one, the most important element remains consistent: Hendrick's fine court dress.

Hendrick's costume added to his prestige and influence among Indians as well. Much of his power as a sachem rested on his ability to funnel goods from his European counterparts to his fellow villagers. In this capacity, the people of Canajoharie could not have asked for a more productive emissary. From 1701, when his name first appears in English records, until his death in 1755, Hendrick regularly attended treaty conferences and received presents from colonial and royal officials. His diplomacy played an important role in his village's livelihood. By the 1730s, Canajoharie faced a precarious existence: the fur trade had bypassed the village in the late 1720s with the construction of Oswego. At about the same time, the Albany magistrates who administered New York's Indian affairs turned their attention from the Mohawks to the Canadian Indians who carried furs south from Montreal. Missionaries in the region reported that Canajoharie's population declined as families "have gone over to the french Interest & settled in their Territories." In this context of shrinking population and eroding economic independence, Hendrick's diplomacy helped sustain the village.

Hendrick's influence peaked between 1744 and 1755, precisely at the time when Canajoharie – because of a decreasing land base, warfare, and disrupted trade – was losing other means of support. In his own brand of shuttle diplomacy, Hendrick traveled beyond the Mohawk Valley to attend European–Indian councils in Montreal, Boston, New York City, and Philadelphia. These missions enabled him to tap into the flow of goods in the British-Atlantic economy and divert a larger share of them to his village. Before European audiences, he followed the Indian fashion. Costume enabled Hendrick to gain further access to European presents, which, when redistributed at Canajoharie, increased his standing among the villagers. Dress, in short, helped preserve Hendrick's reputation abroad and at home, among Indians and Europeans.

Europeans who observed Hendrick's activities in the 1740s and 1750s often accused him of greed and extortion. Pownall, reporting on New York Indian affairs in 1753, believed Hendrick made himself rich through presents, taking "at different times above six hundred dollars of

[New York governor] Mr. Clinton." In 1745, New York Indian interpreter Arent Stevens warned that Hendrick would not do business
without "a promise of a handsom present" and advised his superiors
always to provide the Mohawk sachem with more "than you gave him
hopes of." Weiser, conducting diplomacy in the Mohawk Valley in 1750,
claimed that Hendrick offered assistance if Weiser would make him "a
handsome Present." The New York Assembly, aware of Hendrick's
reputation for avarice, recommended that Governor Clinton privately
present him with twenty Spanish dollars before ending an Indian conference in 1753.

Hendrick, it seems, had become almost too European. When Weiser
and Pownall complained of his familiarity with "European politics,"
they lamented the loss of honesty they associated with Indians they
met in public councils. William Smith, the eighteenth-century New
York historian, referred to sachems as blanket-clad republicans gathered
in outdoor assemblies, like "the ancient orators of Greece and Rome."
Hendrick's willingness, and that of other sachems, to dress in genteel
finery called to mind instead images associated with European courtiers.
Such sachems might say one thing and mean another; they might
deceive to further private ambition. These Indians wore clothing that
reflected power rather than humility, intrigue rather than honesty. The
Indian diplomat enjoyed greater mobility because his costume helped
him move beyond his village into colonial council chambers and royal
courts. Hendrick, like any other participant in the eighteenth-century
consumer revolution, adapted himself to a changing world by taking part
in it, and the goods he acquired expanded rather than limited his choices
in presenting himself to others.

Hendrick's wide-ranging influence in the 1740s and 1750s represented a moment in European–Indian affairs in the Mohawk Valley
when British goods had penetrated the region, but colonists and soldiers
did not yet control it. During this time of mediation, the well-dressed
sachem emerged as a model of Indian leadership. His dress incorporated
European elements but did not symbolize submission to European
authority. Once this period of accommodation passed, however, so too
did this image of intercultural diplomacy.

The transition is evident in portraits of Hendrick published after his
death. In them, he has lost his genteel costume and donned clothing and
accoutrements that European artists more commonly attributed to
Indians. A print published in London in 1756 presents him as one of
the blanket-clad sachems William Smith likened to the orators of
antiquity (figure 5). The transformation is complete in an 1847 lithograph entitled "Soi-En-Ga-Rah-Ta, or King Hendrick" (figure 6). Here
the facial scarring and tattoos visible in the 1740 portrait (figure 2) have

been grafted onto a much younger Indian warrior draped in an animal robe and bareheaded except for a scalplock decorated with feathers. Gone are the wampum, scarlet mantle, breeches, buckled shoes, cocked hat, ruffled shirt, and fine coat that Hendrick wore or carried in portraits completed during his lifetime. Gone, in short, is Hendrick the well-dressed intercultural diplomat, replaced by a nineteenth-century artist's stereotypical depiction of the nearly naked, noble savage.

Hendrick's cooperation with William Johnson in European–Indian diplomacy began during King George's War (1744–1748). In 1746, Governor George Clinton appointed Johnson New York's Indian agent. By distributing presents and supplies, Johnson sponsored Mohawk raids on French colonists and their Indian allies. In his expense account between December 1746 and November 1747 he identified by name more than thirty Indians with whom he conducted this business. Hendrick's name appears in thirteen entries, eight more than any other. He received from Johnson a pair of boots, a laced coat, medicine, cash, and an unspecified "private present" as well as provisions, transportation, and entertainments for his friends, warriors, and dependents.

After the war ended, Johnson and Hendrick continued their diplomatic partnership. In this Irish trader Hendrick found a supplier of goods for his village to replace the Albany Dutch, who now curried the favor of Canadian Indians. Johnson's mercantile business and political reputation profited from the relationship. As a merchant supplying the western fur trade at Oswego, he needed to preserve friendly relations with his Indian neighbors, and his success in this regard made him a favorite of Clinton and other royal officials. Indian diplomacy also provided Johnson with constant demand for his goods. The presents he distributed among Indians came from his own stock, and he charged the expense to the colonial treasury.

By the early 1750s, Johnson and Hendrick had become indispensable to New York's Indian relations. Johnson provided the Mohawks with goods, and they refused to treat with any New York official except him. His influence was obvious at a treaty conference convened in 1751. Johnson, who had recently resigned as the colony's Indian agent because the assembly refused to pay his expenses, declined the governor's invitation to the meeting. In Albany, Hendrick told Clinton "one half of Collo. Johnson belonged to his Excellency [Clinton], and the other to them [the Mohawks]." He then asked permission to send a messenger to Johnson, who attended after receiving the Indians' request. At another conference three years later, Johnson and Hendrick reversed these roles. This time the Mohawks failed to show for an Albany conference called to address their grievances. They finally arrived after the governor prevailed

Hendrick the Sachem, or Chief of the Mohawks.
Etched from an Original Drawing.

Publifh'd according to the Act.March 31.1756. by T.Jefferys at Charing Crofs.

Figure 5 "Hendrick the Sachem, or Chief of the Mohawks," etching published by T. Jefferys, 1756. © Collection of The New-York Historical Society.

on Johnson to secure their attendance. In December 1754, Pennsylvania's colonial secretary Richard Peters enlisted Johnson's help in convincing the Mohawks to confirm a land deed in Philadelphia. Hendrick was reluctant to go at first, but he agreed after Johnson promised to "join, & back him here among the Six Nations." Cooperation between Hendrick and Johnson enabled both to extend their reputations and cement their hold over Covenant Chain proceedings.

Sarony & Major Lith.

117 Fulto St. New York.

SOI-EN-GA-RAH-TA, OR KING HENDRICK.

1740 See P.413.

Figure 6 "Soi-En-Ga-Rah-Ta, or King Hendrick," colored lithograph by Sarony and Major, from Henry R. Schoolcraft, *Notes on the Iroquois* (Albany, 1847), frontispiece. Photograph courtesy of Syracuse University Library, Department of Special Collections.

Through his involvement with Indian trade and diplomacy Johnson became interested in the Indians' material culture. Like many eighteenth-century gentlemen, he collected and displayed within his home "curiosities," objects he valued for beauty, craftsmanship, or rarity. These included wampum, bows and arrows, calumets, and Indian clothing. Other gentleman-collectors requested Johnson's assistance in procuring such items of Indian dress as beaver coats, moccasins, and belts. A Continental army officer visiting Johnson Hall in 1776 noted many such artifacts, including "Trappings of Indian Finery" and "good old King Hendrick's Picture."

Johnson's curiosities attested to his acquaintance with and influence among the Indians. Colden believed Johnson owed this influence to his "compliance with their humours in his dress & conversation." Johnson's secretary, Wraxall, noted that the Indians looked on his boss "as their Cheif, their Patron & their Brother." Johnson himself wrote of his relationship with the Indians, "I am no Stranger to their Customs & Manners." Red Head, an Onondaga sachem, thanked Johnson at a 1753 conference for speaking to the Indians "in our own way, which is more Intelligable to us, because more conformable to the Customs and Manners of our Fore Fathers."

Johnson spoke to the Indians in their own way in actions and appearances as well as words. He made a constant effort to transact his business in the Indians' cultural context. No colonial agent was more successful in presenting himself in a pleasing and impressive manner. This ability extended far beyond Johnson's willingness to don Indian dress and war paint: he cultivated the art of self-presentation in various forms adapted to Covenant Chain treaty making. In staging entrances, conducting negotiations, and distributing presents, Johnson used material goods to create appearances that advanced his reputation among Indians and Europeans.

Johnson's success as an Indian agent began with his work as a merchant. Johnson, the primary supplier of manufactured goods between Albany and Oswego, commanded considerable business and dominated the Mohawk Valley trade. Two lists of presents he distributed among the Indians illustrate the types of goods that flowed along this route. They fall into six broad categories. The first is weapons and ammunition – rifles, pistols, hatchets, knives, swords, powder, shot, and flints – to assist the Indians in hunting and warfare. Second, the Indians received tools and wares for everyday tasks: kettles, frying pans, scissors, needles, awls, pen knives, fire tongs. Toys and novelties such as jews harps, hawks bells, looking glasses, liquor, tobacco, pipes, tea, and sugar make up a third category. In times of war and famine, Johnson provided a fourth category: grants of food, including cows, corn, bread, and peas. Fifth, he made occasional cash grants for influential sachems. Clothing, the sixth category, is the most diverse, comprising the manufactured items that shaped the Indian fashion, from such staple products as blankets and strouds to such finery as laced hats, ribbons, buttons, and beads.

Table 1 offers a closer look at some goods Johnson purchased for a treaty conference at his home in June 1755. All of the categories described above are represented except food, which Johnson distributed along with numerous other incidental gifts once the meeting convened. As the table indicates, clothing made up by far the largest part of the purchase. It accounted for fifteen kinds of items and approximately 66.5 percent of the total value of the presents.

The sheer amount of goods supplied by Johnson could be misleading: quantity was not the only factor that contributed to his success. Indeed, any agent with resources from a colonial or royal treasury could dump goods in Indian laps. Critics of Albany's Commissioners of Indian Affairs often complained of just that: colonial officials saddled visiting Indians with wagon loads of goods, caring little for how the goods were presented or how the Indians got them home. Local merchants then traded rum to the Indians for their presents as they left the city, only to sell the goods back to them at "a dear rate" later. Such conduct on the part of colonial officials indicated either stubborn ignorance or callous disregard for the ceremonial nature of gift giving.

Johnson, by contrast, exhibited a keen appreciation for the cultural dynamics of this practice. An account he kept during King George's War illustrates how he went about distributing presents. In table 2, all the presents of clothing Johnson made between December 1746 and November 1747 are classified by recipient. Warriors received items necessary to outfit war parties: paint, shirts, ribbon, gimps, caps, laps, hides, and snowshoes. Sachems received finery associated with the Indian fashion: laced hats, fine coats, ruffled shirts, and silver medals. Johnson gave strouds, hose, shirts, and other necessaries to the women and children of Indian men who went to war. Lastly, he clothed the dead by presenting black burial strouds to their relatives.

Women and children received most of the clothing Johnson distributed: they accounted for almost 69 percent of his total expenditure on clothing during this period. Outfitting warriors and sachems accounted for 16.3 percent and 12.5 percent respectively and outfitting the dead only 2.6 percent. Johnson distributed presents to warriors and sachems in small quantities, usually valued at no more than £1 or £2 at a time, when they visited his home to share news or hold councils. The presents he gave to women and children involved much larger donations. Of the twenty-four entries for presents of this type, fourteen were for disbursements valued at £10 or more, and two top £100. By comparison, only

Table 1 Goods distributed by William Johnson at a Treaty Conference, June 1755

Item	Quantity	Value ($\pounds$)
Weapons and ammunition:		
Long knives, sheathed	10 dozen	6.0.0
Large pistols	10 dozen	5.0.0
Gun flints	3,000	5.5.0
Holland gun powder	9 kegs	8.0.0
Lead in small bars	2,000 lb.	45.0.0
Subtotal:		69.5.0
Tools and wares:		
Brass kettles	400	60.0.0
Frying pans	50	12.10.0
Razors	10 dozen	7.10.0
Awl blades	4 gross	2.0.0
Cups: 1 gill	1 dozen	
1/2 gill	2 dozen	8.10.0
Brass wire	20 lb.	4.10.0
Subtotal:		95.0.0
Toys and novelties:		
Looking glasses	8 dozen	12.0.0
Jews harps	24 dozen	3.0.0
Fine wrought pens	30 dozen	12.0.0
Hawks bells	38 dozen	4.15.0
Buckling combs	20 dozen	5.0.0
Pipes	1 case	
Tobacco	1,000 lb.	21.12.4
Subtotal:		58.7.4
Cash:		
Private grants to sachems		107.4.0
Subtotal:		107.4.0
Clothing and bodily decoration:		
Strouds	16 pieces	144.0.0
Blankets	8 pieces	72.0.0
Penniston	3 pieces	39.17.4
Garlix	6 pieces	40.0.0
Calico	8 pieces	26.0.0
Callamancoe	16 pieces	24.0.0
French blankets	40	32.0.0
French blankets, second size	40	20.0.0
French blankets, third size	40	16.0.0
Flowered serge	4 pieces	20.0.0
Gartering	20 rolls	7.0.0
Gimps	40 pieces	12.0.0
Vermillion	40 lb.	28.0.0
Worsted clocked hose	8 dozen	11.4.0
Worsted clocked hose, small	10 dozen	9.10.0
Private presents – stroud,		
shirt, and lap to each sachem	97	155.4.0
Subtotal:		656.18.4
Total:		$\pounds$986.11.8

Source: *Johnson Paper*, 2:570–71

Table 2 Clothing distributed by William Johnson as Indian presents, December 1746–November 1747

	Number of account entries	Value	Number of entries greater than £10	Percent of total expense
Clothing for warriors (shirts, paint, ribbon, caps, laps, snowshoes, hides)	25	£149.8.7	3	16.3
Clothing for sachems (laced hats, fine coats, ruffled shirts, silver medals)	15	114.11.0	2	12.5
Clothing for families (blankets, strouds, hose, caps, laps, shirts, deerskins)	24	629.5.2	14	68.6
Clothing for the dead (black burial strouds)	5	24.8.0	0	2.6
Total:	69	£917.12.9	19	100.0

Source: *Johnson Papers*, 9:15–31.

three entries for warriors' presents and two for sachems' presents top £10. Presents made for outfitting the dead seem to have involved the most personal contact between Johnson and the recipient. Of five entries, none exceeded £10, and in two of them Johnson mentions the living recipient by name.

Johnson selected his gifts according to the intended recipient, and he often presented these goods in person. In this sense, he owed his influence to his role as a distributor of Indian goods rather than as a mere supplier of them. Indians treated presents as tangible symbols of reciprocity and friendship; to them, peace and alliance could not be purchased by large, one-time donations of goods. Rather, they needed to be continually renewed and strengthened by the periodic exchange of presents. As Johnson explained it, in addition to large presents made at treaty conferences, the Indians "expect to be indulged with constant little Presents, this from the Nature of the Indians cannot be avoided & must be complied with."

A large proportion of the goods Johnson distributed fell into the category of "constant little Presents." The expense was staggering. By his own account, Johnson spent £7,177 on Indian presents during King

George's War. Between March 1755 and October 1756, early in the Seven Years' War, he expended a total of £17,446. His liberality caused friction with the New York assembly, which refused to reimburse him fully for outlays during King George's War. Johnson blasted the assembly for failing to help "defray from time to time the expences I am dayly obliged to be at in treating with all sorts of Indians – The well ordering of whom is of much more importance to the Welfare of His Ma[jes]tys Government than the whole act of governing the unruly Inhabitants [of New York]." On the eve of renewed Anglo-French hostilities in 1754, Johnson predicted disaster for New York because of the assembly's parsimony, noting that it had appropriated only "the miserable pittance of £170 [New] York Curr[en]cy P[er] Annum" for Indian presents.

Johnson knew that the practice of gift giving required more than deep pockets. His greatest asset as an Indian agent was his penchant for ceremonial presentations of both himself and the goods he distributed. He had a flair for the theatrical that suited the pageantry of treaty making, as evidenced in his taste for spectacular entrances. His arrival at Albany in 1746 dressed as a Mohawk war captain is one example. Two years later, he staged another grand entrance, this time at Onondaga, the seat of the Iroquois confederacy. Johnson arrived at this treaty conference with a party of Indian and European attendants. On entering Onondaga, he found "all the Sachims & Warriours . . . stood in order with rested arms and fired a Volley, after which my Party returned the Compliment." That evening, he provided two feasts, one for the village's sachems and one for "the Warriours & dancers who I hope will be merry which is my greatest pleasure to make & see them so."

In such instances, Johnson imitated, not Albany's Indian commissioners, but French Indian agents, whom he praised for always putting on a good show. Unlike the Albany Dutch, Johnson explained to Clinton in 1749, the French "observe a quite different conduct, much to their own advantage. . . . They never employ a Trader to negotiate any matters with the Indians but a Kings officer, who in whatever Rank or capacity is attended by a Retinue of Soldiers accordingly to denote his consequence[.] If he be but a Lieutenant or Ensign it is sufficient to command Respect from the Savages, who tho' somewhat warlike are actuated by their Fears at *a small appearance of Power.*" Johnson cultivated this small appearance of power in his Indian negotiations not only through his dress but also through warriors and sachems who accompanied him and served as visual testimony of his influence. Such a retinue could not be secured or maintained without the liberal distribution of personal presents detailed in Johnson's accounts.

Johnson paid attention to the ceremonial nature of gift giving and particularly honored the Indians' condolence rituals. When a treaty conference began, Europeans and Indians usually exchanged condolence speeches to honor each side's recent dead. The Indians also expected and customarily received a present of black burial strouds. When colonial agents omitted these presents, Indians might delay negotiations or express anger that the proper ceremony had not been observed. Johnson regularly complained that the Albany magistrates ignored this custom in treating with the Indians. "This ceremony is also attended with a great deal of form," he explained to Clinton in 1749. "It was always neglected in the late [Albany Indian] Commiss[ione]rs time, which gave the French an opportunity of doing it." To Weiser, Johnson wrote that the condolence ceremony was "always expected by the five Nations to be performed by Us, and [is] what th[e]y look much upon." As the evidence in table 2 indicates, Johnson also made private condolence presents to Indians when requested.

In distributing goods, Johnson never lost the opportunity to enhance his appearance as the Indians' friend and benefactor. At a conference in June 1755, Indians from several nations approached Johnson with three young men they claimed worthy to be sachems and asked him to "distinguish them with the usual cloathing." Johnson readily complied. His accounts show an entry from the same day for "3 Ruffled Shirts for 3 young Sachems." Through such presentations, Johnson moved beyond merely supplying the Indians with goods to inserting himself into their rituals and identities. The Indians' consumer revolution redefined how a sachem was supposed to dress, and Johnson, through the manipulation of material goods, made himself a pivotal figure in those changing definitions.

Just as Hendrick appreciated the importance his European contemporaries attached to clothing, so Johnson understood the Indians' interpretation of presents. When Europeans bestowed presents, they believed the goods symbolized the recipients' submission to and dependence on a crown or colonial government. The Indians, on their part, perceived these presents as evidence of mutual regard between treaty participants. By making "constant little Presents" and observing ceremonial detail, Johnson recognized the important role goods played in the Indians' view of the Covenant Chain. The Indians acknowledged his incorporation of their values by accepting him into their councils and naming him "Warraghiyagey," doer of great business.

Between 1744 and 1755, Hendrick and Johnson became the two most influential figures in the Covenant Chain. Their participation in treaty conferences was essential for preserving peace between New Yorkers and Indians. Each one, however, continued to operate independently of the other and for different reasons. Johnson pursued political influence and royal favor. Hendrick's perspective remained local, as he employed his diplomatic skills to acquire presents and restore Canajoharie's prominence in New York's Indian relations. Both men made masterly use of the material culture of the other, manipulating goods associated with the Indian fashion to extend and preserve their influence on the Mohawk frontier.

Close examination of the careers of Johnson and Hendrick suggests the great potential of material culture methods to enlighten us about European–Indian relations. The Indian trade was not simply a matter of economics, of European supply versus Indian demand. Participants attached meaning to these goods beyond the utilitarian value of a new gun, a shirt, or a knife. The goods that passed between Europeans and Indians, like the rituals involved in their exchange, created a language of speech, deportment, and appearance that crossed cultural barriers. Today, Iroquois nations in western New York continue to receive bolts of cloth from the United States according to eighteenth-century treaty obligations. The federal government has offered to convert these grants into monetary payments, but the Iroquois have declined, explaining that the cloth's value as a symbol of their territorial and political sovereignty cannot be rendered in a cash equivalent. Johnson's and Hendrick's use of clothing illustrated the ideological element in the material culture of European–Indian relations, which allowed both sides to express themselves in ways not typically recorded in treaty minutes.

Note

1 Richard White, *The Middle Ground: Indians, Empires, and Republics in the Great Lakes Region, 1650–1815* (Cambridge, 1991), 50–93.

Documents

The 1744 Council of Lancaster was a major event. Representatives from the powerful Six Nations (Iroquois) Confederacy and other, less powerful Indian nations in the northeast attended and met with delegates from the colonies of Pennsylvania, Virginia, and Maryland. For several weeks, they discussed trade, unresolved acts of violence between their respective peoples, and most importantly land. These excerpts, focusing on a land dispute between the Iroquois and the colony of Maryland, illustrate how much of council diplomacy was taken up by ceremony: kinship terms as forms of address, the granting of special names, the exchange of wampum (white and purple beads strung into strings or belts), drinking, shouting, signing and affixing seals to written deeds, and giftgiving, including gifts of clothing. Is it easy to tell whose customs are whose? Do they understand and willingly participate in each other's rituals? We join the council towards its conclusion, on a day when Canassatego, an Onondaga man renowned for his oratorical ability, served as speaker for the Six Nations.

Excerpts from the Treaty of Lancaster, 1744

In the Court House at Lancaster, June 26th, 1744.

PRESENT:

The Honourable GEORGE THOMAS, Esqr., Lieutenant Governor, &^{ca} [Pennsylvania].
The Honourable Commissioners of Virginia.
The Honourable Commissioners of Maryland.
The Deputies of the Six Nations.
Conrad Weiser, Interpreter.

Canassatego Spoke as follows:
"Brother, the Governor of Maryland –
"When you invited us to kindle a Council Fire with you, Conedogwainet was the place agreed upon, but afterwards you by Brother Onas [Pennsylvania], upon second thoughts, considering that it would be difficult to get Provisions and other accommodations where there were but few houses or Inhabitants, desired we should meet Our Brother at Lancaster, and at his instance we very readily agreed to meet you here, and are glad of the Change, for we have found plenty of every thing, and as yesterday you bid us Welcome, and told us you were glad to see us, we likewise assure you we are as glad to see you, and in token of our Satisfaction we present you with this String of Wampum."
Which was received with the usual Ceremony.
"Brother, the Governor of Maryland:
"You tell us that when about seven years ago you heard by Our Brother Onas of our Claim to some Lands in your Province, you took no notice of it, believing, as you say, that when we should come to

Excerpts from Treaty of Lancaster, 1744. [Hazard, Samuel, ed.], *Minutes of the Provincial Council of Pennsylvania*, vol. 4. Harrisburg: Theo. Fenn & Co., 1851 (reprint edition, New York. AMS Press, 1968): 705–37.

reconsider that matter we should find that we had no Right to make any Complaint of the Governor of Maryland, and would drop our demand. And that when about two years ago we mentioned it again to our Brother Onas, you say We did it in such Terms as looked like a design to Terrify you; and you tell us further, that we must be beside ourselves in using such a rash expression as to tell you we know how to do ourselves Justice if you should still refuse. It is true we did say so, but without any ill design – for we must inform you that when we first desired Our Brother Onas to use his influence with you to procure us satisfaction for Our Lands, We at the same time desired him, in case you should disregaird our Demand, to write to the Great King beyond the Seas, who would own Us for his Children as well as you, to compel you to do us Justice. And two years ago, when we found that you paid no regaird to Our Just demand, nor that Brother Onas had convey'd our Complaint to the Great King over the Seas, we were resolved to use such Expressions as would make the greatest Impressions on your minds, and we find it had its effect, for you tell us 'That your Wise men held a Council together and agreed to Invite us, and to enquire of Our Right to any of your Lands; and if it should be found that we had a Right we were to have a Compensation made for them;' and, likewise, you tell us that our Brother, the Governor of Maryland, by the Advice of these wise men has sent you to brighten the Chain, and to assure us of his willingness to remove whatsoever impedes a good understanding between us. This shews that your wise men understand our Expressions in their true Sense. We had no design to Terrify you, but to put you on doing us the Justice you had so long delayed. Your wise men have done well; and as there is no obstacle to a Good understanding between us, except this affair of the Land, we on our Parts do give you the Strongest assurances of our Good Dispositions towards you, and that we are as desirous as you to Brighten the Chain and to put away all hindrances to a perfect good understanding; and in token of our sincerity we give you this Belt of Wampum."

Which was received, & the Interp^r ordered to give the Jo-hah.

"Brother, the Governor of Maryland:

"When you mentioned the affair of the Land Yesterday, you went back to old Times, and told us you had been in posession of the Province of Maryland above One hundred Years; but what is one hundred years in comparison to the length of Time since our Claim began? – Since we came out of this Ground? For we must tell you that long before One hundred years Our ancestors came out of this very Ground, and their Children have remained here ever since. You came out of the Ground in a Country that lyes beyond Seas, there you may have a just Claim, but here you must allow Us to be your elder Brethren, and the Lands to belong to us long before you know anything of them. It is true that above

One hundred years ago the Dutch came here in a Ship and brought with them several Goods, such as Awls, Knives, Hatchets, Guns, and many other particulars, which they gave us, and when they had taught us how to use their things, and we saw what sort of People they were, we were so well pleased with them that we tyed their Ship to the Bushes on the Shoar, and afterwards liking them still better the longer they stayed with us, and thinking the Bushes to slender, we removed the Rope and tyed it to the trees, and as the Trees were lyable to be blown down by high Winds, or to decay of themselves, We, from the affection We bore them, again removed the Rope, and tyed it to a Strong and big Rock (Here the Interpreter said they mean the Oneida Country), and not content with this, for its further security We removed the Rope to the Big-Mountain (Here the Interpreter says they mean the Onondaga Country), and there we tyed it very fast and rowled Wampum about it, and to make it still more Secure we stood upon the Wampum, and sat down upon it to defend it, and did our Best endeavours that it might remain uninjured for ever During all this Time; the Newcomers, the Dutch, acknowledged Our Rights to the Lands, and solicited us from time to time to grant them Parts of Our Country, and to enter into League and Covenant with us, and to become one People with us.

"After this the English came into the Country, and, as we were told, became one People with the Dutch; about two years after the Arrival of the English, an English Governor came to Albany, and finding what great friendship subsisted between us and the Dutch, he approved it mightly, and desired to make as Strong a league and to be upon as good Terms with us as the Dutch were, with whom he was united, and to become one People with Us, and by his further care in looking what had passed between us he found that the Rope which tyed the Ship to the Great mountain was only fastened with Wampum, which was liable to break and rot, and to perish in a course of years, he therefore told us that he would give us a silver Chain, which would be much stronger and last for Ever. This we accepted, and fastened the Ship with it, and it has lasted ever since. Indeed, we have had some small Differences with the English, and during these misunderstandings some of their young men would, by way of Reproach, be every now and then telling us that we should have perished if they had not come into the Country and furnished us with Strowds [cloth] and Hatchets and Guns and other things necessary for the Support of Life. But we always gave them to understand that they were mistaken, that we lived before they came amongst us, and as well or better, if we may believe what our Forefathers have told Us. We had then room enough and Plenty of Deer, which was easily caught, and tho' we had not Knives, Hatchets, or Guns, such as we have now, yet we had Knives of Stone and Hatchets of Stone, and Bows and

Arrows, and these Served Our Uses as well then as the English ones do now. We are now Straitned and sometimes in want of Deer, and lyable to many other Inconveniences since the English came among Us, and particularly from that Pen and Ink work that is going on at the Table (pointing to the Secretarys), and we will give you an Instance of this. Our Brother Onas, a great while ago, came to Albany to Buy the Sasquehannah Lands of Us, but our Brother, the Governor of New York, who, as we suppose, had not a Good understanding with Our Brother Onas, advised us not to Sell him any Lands, for he would make an ill use of it, and Pretending to be Our Good friend, he advised us, in order to prevent Onas's or any other persons imposing upon us, and that we might always have Our Land when we should want it, to put it into his Hands, and told us he would keep it for Our use, and never open his Hands, but keep them close shut, and not part with any of it but Our request. Accordingly we Trusted him, and put Our Land into his Hands, and Charged him to keep it safe for Our Use; but some time after he went away to England and carryed Our Land with him, and there Sold it to Our Brother Onas for a Large Sum of money; and when, at the Instance of Our Brother Onas, we were minded to sell him some Lands, He told us that we had sold the Sasquehannah Lands already to the Governor of New York, and that he had bought them from him in England, tho' when he came to Understand how the Governor of New York had deceived Us, he very generously paid Us for our Lands over again.

"Tho' we mention this Instance of an Imposition put upon us by the Governor of New York, yet we must do the English the Justice to say, we have had their hearty Assistances in Our Wars with the French, who were no sooner arrived amongst us than they began to render us uneasy and to provoke us to War, and we have had several Wars with them, during all which we constantly received assistance from the English, and by their Means we have alwise been able to keep up Our Heads against their Attacks.

"We now come nearer home. We have had your Deeds Interpreted to Us, and we acknowledge them to be good and valid, and that the Conestogoe or Sasquehannah Indians had a Right to sell those Lands unto you, for they were then their's; but since that time We have Conquered them, and their Country now belongs to Us, and the Lands we demanded satisfaction for are no part of the Lands comprized in those Deeds – they are the Cohongoroutas Lands. Those we are sure you have not possessed One hundred Years; No, nor above Ten years. And we made our Demand so soon as we knew your People were Settled in those Parts. These have never been sold, but remain still to be disposed of; And we are well pleased to hear you are Provided with Goods, and do assure you of Our Willingness to Treat with You for those unpurchased

Lands, In confirmation whereof We present you with this Belt of Wampum."

Which was received with the usual Ceremony.

Canassatego added:

"That as the Three Governors of Virginia, Maryland, and Pennsylvania, had divided the Lands among, they could not for this Reason tell how much each had got, nor were they concerned about it, so that they were paid by all the Governors for the Several Parts each Possessed; and this they left to their Honour and Justice."

In the Court House Chamber at Lancaster, June the 29th 1744, A.M.

PRESENT:

The Honourable the Commissioners of Maryland.
The Deputies of the Six Nations.
Conrad Weiser, Interpreter.

Mr. Weiser informed the Honourable Commissioners the Indians were ready to give their answer to the Speech made to them here yesterday Morning by the Commissioners. Whereupon Canassatego spoke as follows, looking on a Deal Board where were some black lines describing the Courses of Potowmack and Sasquehanna:

"Brethren –

"Yesterday you Spoke to Us concerning the Lands on this side Potowmack River, and as we have deliberately considered of what you said to us on that matter, we are now very ready to settle the Bounds of such Lands, and Release our Right and Claim thereto.

"We are willing to renounce all Right to Lord Baltimore of all those Lands lying two Miles above the uppermost Fork of Patowmack or Cohongoruton River, near which Thomas Cressap has a Hunting or Trading Cabbin, by a North Line to the Bounds of Pennsylvania. But in case such Limits shall not include every Settlement or Inhabitant of Maryland, then such other Lines and Courses from the said two Miles above the Forks to the outermost Inhabitants or Settlements as shall include every Settlement and Inhabitant in Maryland, and from thence by a North Line to the Bounds of Pennsylvania, shall be the Limits. And further, if any People already have or shall settle beyond the Lands now described and Bounded, they shall enjoy the same free from any Disturbance of us in any manner whatsoever, and we do and shall accept those People for our Brethren, and as such always Treat them.

"We earnestly desire to live with you as Brethren, and hope you will shew us all Brotherly kindness; In token whereof We present you with a Belt of Wampum."

Which was received with the usual Ceremony.

Soon after the Commissioners and Indians departed the Court House Chamber.

In the Court House at Lancaster, June the 30th, 1744.

The Honourable GEORGE THOMAS, Esquire, Governor.
The Honourable the Commissioners of Virginia.
The Honourable the Commissioners of Maryland.
The Deputies of the Six Nations.
Conrad Weiser, Interpreter.

The three Governments Entertained the Indians and all the Gentlemen in town with a handsome Dinner; the Six Nations in their order having returned thanks with the usual Solemnity of Jo-ha-han, the Interpreter informed the Governor and the Commissioners that as the Lord Proprietor and Governor of Maryland was not known to the Indians by any particular Name, they had agreed in Council to take the first opportunity of a large company to present him with one, and as this with them is deemed a matter of great Consequence, and attended with abundance of Forme, the several Nations had drawn Lots for the performance of the Ceremony, and the Lot falling on the Cayogo Nation, they had chosen Gachradodow, one of their Chiefs, to be their Speaker, and he desired leave to begin, which being given, he on an elevated part of the Court House, with all the dignity of a Warrior, the Gesture of an Orator, and in a very gracefull Posture, spoke as follows:

"As the Governor of Maryland had Invited them here to Treat about their Lands and brighten the Chain of Friendship, the United Nations thought themselves so much obliged to him that they had come to a Resolution in Council to give to the Great man who is Proprietor of Maryland a particular Name, by which they might hereafter correspond with him, and as it had fallen to the Cayogo's Lot in Council to consider of a proper name for that Chief Man, they had agreed to give him the Name of Tocarry-ho-gan, denoting Precedency, Excellency, or living in middle or Honourable Place betwixt Assaraquoa [Virginia] and their Brother Onas, by whom their Treaties might be better carryd on." And then addressing himself to his Honour, the Governour of Pennsylvania, The Honourable the Commissioners of Virginia and Maryland, and to the Gentlemen then present, he Proceeded:

"As there is a Company of Great Men now Assembled, We take this Time and opportunity to Publish this Matter, That it may be known Tocarry-ho-gan is Our Friend, and that we are ready to Honour him, and that by such Name he may be always called and known among Us. And We hope he will ever Act towards us according to the Excellency of the Name we have now Given him, and enjoy a long and happy life."

The Honourable the Governor and Commissioners, and all the Company present, returned the Compliment with three Huzza's, and after drinking Healths to Our gracious King and Six Nations, the Commissioners of Maryland proceeded to Bussiness in the Court House Chamber with the Indians, where Conrad Weiser the Interpreter was present.

The Honourable the Commissioners order'd Mr. Weiser to tell the Indians that a Deed, releasing all their Claim and Title to certain Lands lying in the Province of Maryland, which by them was agreed to be given and executed for the use of the Lord Baron of Baltimore, Lord Proprietary of that Province, was now on the Table and Seals ready fixed thereto. The Interpreter acquainted them therewith as desired, and then gave the Deed to Canassatego the Speaker, who made his Mark and put his Seal and Delivered it, after which thirteen other Chiefs or Sachims of the Six Nations Executed it in the same manner in the Presence of the Honourable the Commissioners of Virginia and divers other Gentlemen of that Colony, and of the Provinces of Pennsylvania and Maryland.

At the House of Mr. George Sanderson in Lancaster, 2d July, 1744, A. M.

PRESENT:

The Honourable the Commissioners of Maryland.
Several of the Chiefs of the Indians of the Six Nations.
Conrad Weiser, Interpreter.

The several Chiefs of the Indians of the Six Nations who had not Signed the Deed of Release of their Claim to some Land in Maryland, tender'd to them on Saturday last in the Chamber of the Court House in this Town, did now readily Execute the same, and caused Mr. Weiser likewise to sign it, as well with his Indian as with his own proper Name of Weiser, as a Witness and Interpreter.

In the Court House at Lancaster, July the 4th, 1744, A.M.

[Speaker: Canassatego]

"Brother Tocarry-hogan:

"You told us yesterday that since there was now nothing in Controversie between us, and the Affair of the Land was Settled to your satisfaction, you would now brighten the Chain of Friendship which hath Subsisted between you and us ever since we became Brethren. We are well pleased with the Proposition, and we thank you for it. We also are inclined to renew all Treaties and keep a good Correspondence with you. You told us further, if ever we should perceive the Chain had Contracted any Rust to let you know and you would take care to take the Rust out, and preserve it bright. We agree with you in this, and shall, on our Parts, do every thing to preserve a good Understanding, and to live in the same Friendship with you as with our Brothers Onas and Assaraquoa; in Confirmation whereof we give you this Belt of Wampum."

On which the usual Cry of Yo-hah was given.

"Brethren:

"We have now finished our Answer to what you said to us Yesterday, and shall now proceed to Indian Affairs that are not of so General a Concern.

"Brother Assaraquoa:

"There lives a Nation of Indians on the other side of your Country, the Tuscaroraes, who are our Friends, and with whom we hold Correspondence; but the Road between us and them has been stopped for some time on Account of the Misbehaviour of some of Our Warriors. We have open'd a New Road for our Warriors and they shall keep to that; but as that would be inconvenient for Messengers going to the Tuscaroraes we desire they may go the old Road. We frequently send Messengers to one another, and shall have more Occasion to do so now that we have concluded a Peace with the Cherikees. To enforce our Request we give you this String of Wampum."

Which was received with the usual Cry of Approbation.

"Brother Assaraquoa:

"Among these Tuscaroraes there live a few families of the Conoy Indians who are desirous to leave them and to remove to the rest of their Nation among us, and the Straight Road from them to Us lyes through the Middle of your Country. We desire you will give them free passage through Virginia, and furnish them with Passes; and to enforce our Request we give you this String of Wampum."

Which was received with the usual Cry of Approbation.

"Brother Onas, Assaraquoa, and Tocarry-hogan:

"At the close of your respective Speeches Yesterday you made us very handsome Presents, and we should return you something suitable to your Generosity; but, alas, we are poor, and shall ever remain so long as there are so many Indian Traders among us. Their's and the white People's Cattle have eat up all the Grass and made Deer Scarce. However, we have Provided a Small Present for you, and tho' some of you gave us more than others, yet as you are all equally Our Brethren, we shall leave it to you to divide it as you Please." And then presented Three Bundles of Skins which were received with the usual Ceremony from the three Governments.

"We have one thing further to say, and that is We heartily recommend Union and a Good Agreement between you our Brethren. Never disagree, but preserve a strict Friendship for one another, and thereby you as well as we will become the Stronger.

"Our wise Forefathers established Union and Amity between the Five Nations; this has made us formidable, this has given us great weight and Authority with our Neighboring Nations.

"We are a Powerfull confederacy, and by your observing the same Methods our wise Forefathers have taken, you will acquire fresh Strength and Power; therefore, whatever befalls you, never fall out with one another."

The Governor replied:

"The Honourable Commissioners of Virginia and Maryland have desired me to Speak for them, therefore I, in behalf of those Governments as well as of the Province of Pennsylvania, return you thanks for the many Proofs you have given in your Speeches of your Zeal for the Service of your Brethren the English, and in particular for your having so Early engaged in a Neutrality the Several Tribes of Indians in the French Alliance. We do not Doubt but you will faithfully Discharge your Promises. As to your Presents, we never estimate these things by their Real Worth, but by the Disposition of the Giver. In this Light we accept them with Great Pleasure, and put a high value upon them. We are obliged to you for Recommending Peace and Good Agreement amongst ourselves. We are all Subjects as well as you of the Great King beyond the Water, and in Duty to his Majesty and from the good Affection we bear to each other, as well as from a regard to our Interests, we shall always be inclined to live in Friendship."

Then the Commissioners of Virginia presented the Hundred Pounds in Gold, together with a Paper containing a Promise to recommend the Six Nations for further favor to the King, which they received with Yohah, and the Paper was given by them to Conrad Weiser to keep for them. The Commissioners likewise Promised that their publick Messengers should not be Molested in their Passage through Virginia, and that they would prepare Passes for such of the Conoy Indians as were willing to remove to the Northward.

Then the Commissioners of Maryland presented their Hundred pounds in Gold, Which was likewise received with the Yo-hah.

Canassatego said, "We mentioned to You Yesterday the Booty you had taken from the French, and asked you for some of the Rum, which we supposed to be part of it, and you gave us some, but it turned out unfortunately that you gave us it in French Glasses, we desire now You will give us some in English Glasses."

The Governor made answer, "We are glad to hear you have such a Dislike for what is French. They cheat you in your Glasses as well as in every thing else. You must Consider we are at a Distance from Williamsburg, Annapolis, and Philadelphia, where our Rum Stores are, and that altho' we brought up a good quantity with us, you have almost drank it out; but notwithstanding this, we have enough left to fill our English Glasses, and will Shew the Difference between the Narrowness of the French and the Generosity of the English towards you."

The Indians gave in their Order five Yo-hahs, and the Honourable Governor and Commissioners calling for some Rum and some middle-Sized Wine Glasses drank Health to the Great King of England and the Six Nations, and put an End to the Treaty by three loud Huzza's, in which all the Company Joined.

In the Evening the Governor went to take his leave of the Indians, and presenting them with a String of Wampum he told them that was in return for one he had received of them, with a Message to desire the Governor of Virginia to suffer their Warriors to go through Virginia unmolested, which was rendred unnecessary by the Present Treaty. [. . .]

The Indians received these two Strings of Wampum with the usual Yo-hah.

The Governor then asked them what was the reason that more of the Shawanaes from their Town on Hohio, were not at the Treaty? But seeing that it would require a Council in Form, and perhaps another day to give an answer, he desired they would give answer to Conrad Weiser upon the Road on their Return Home, for he was to Set out to Philadelphia the next Morning.

Canassatego in Conclusion spoke as follows:

"We have been hindred by a great deal of Bussiness from waiting on you to have some private Conversation with you, chiefly to enquire after the Health of Onas beyond the Water; we desire you will tell them we have a grateful Sense of all their Kindness for the Indians. Brother Onas told us when he went away he would not stay long from us; we think it is a great while, and want to know when we may expect him, and desire when You write You will recommend us heartily to him;" which the Governor promised to do, and then took his leave of them.

The Commissioners of Virginia gave Canassatego a Scarlet Camblet Coat, and took their leave of them in form, and at the same time delivered their Passes to them, according to their Request.

The Commissioners of Maryland presented Gachradodow with a Broad Gold laced Hat, and took their leave of them in the same manner.

★　★　★

Witham Marshe attended the 1744 Council at Lancaster as secretary for the Maryland treaty commissioners. Marshe kept a journal of the council, probably for his own amusement and as a record of what was for him an exciting adventure. Marshe would have been sitting at or near the same table as the clerk for Pennsylvania, who wrote the version of the council proceedings reprinted above. Marshe's private journal describes the same events but admits to more tension and dissent than the official record reveals.

Witham Marshe's Journal of the Treaty Held with the Six Nations by the Commissioners of Maryland, and other Provinces, at Lancaster, in Pennsylvania, June, 1744

[...] *Thursday, [June 21st, 1744], P. M.* Arrived at Lancaster town about two o'clock, and put up our horses at Peter Worrall's, who here keeps an inn. Here I bespoke a dinner for our commissioners, and the Maryland gentlemen, which was soon got ready, to our great comfort. Procured a room and two beds, in Worrall's house, for our chaplain and myself.

Neither the governor of Pennsylvania, nor the Virginia commissioners, were arrived at the time when we did; but about six in the evening they came hither, attended by several Virginia gentlemen, and some from the city of Philadelphia.

Here we were informed that the Indians would not arrive till to-morrow, they marching very slow, occasioned by their having a great many small children and old men.

Messrs. Calvert, Craddock and myself went into, and viewed the court-house of this town. It is a pretty large brick building, two stories high. The ground room, where the justices of this county hold their court, is very spacious. There is a handsome bench, and railed in, whereon they sit, and a chair in the midst of it, which is filled by the judge. Below this bench, is a large table, of half oval form; round this, and under their Worships, sit the county clerk, and the several attornies

Marshe, Witham. "Witham Marshe's Journal of the Treaty Held with the Six Nations by the Commissioners of Maryland, and Other Provinces, at Lancaster, in Pennsylvania, June, 1744." *Collections of the Massachusetts Historical Society, for the Year MDCCC.* Vol. 7, 1st series, 171–201 (reprint edition, New York: Johnson Reprint Corp., 1968).

of the court, who, here, as well as in most other courts of the plantations, plead as counsellors. There are particular seats and places allotted to the sheriff, crier, &c.

Fronting the justices' bench, and on each side of it, are several long steps, or stairs, raised each above the other, like the steps leading into the north door of St. Paul's. On these steps, stand the several auditors and spectators, when a court is held here. It was on these, that the Indian chiefs sat, when they treated with the several governments. This court-house is capable to contain above 800 persons, without incommoding each other.

When we had surveyed this room, we went up stairs, into one over head. This is a good room, and has a large chimney. In this the justices sit in the month of February, for the convenience of the fire. Adjoining to this room, is a smaller one, where the juries are kept to agree on their verdict.

On the top of the court-house is a kind of cupola. We ascended a ladder, and got into it. From hence we had a complete view of the whole town, and the country several miles round, and likewise of part of Susquehannah river, at twelve miles distance.

This town has not been begun to be built above sixteen years. It is conveniently laid out into sundry streets, and one main street, in the midst of which stands the court-house and market. Through this runs the road to the back country, on Susquehannah. There are several cross streets on each side of the main street, which are indifferently well built, as to quantity of houses.

The inhabitants are chiefly High-Dutch, Scotch-Irish, some few English families, and unbelieving Israelites, who deal very considerably in this place.

The spirit of cleanliness has not as yet in the least troubled the major part of the inhabitants; for, in general, they are very great sluts and slovens. When they clean their houses, which, by the bye, is very seldom, they are unwilling to remove the filth far from themselves, for they place it close to their doors, which, in the summer time, breeds an innumerable quantity of bugs, fleas, and vermin. [...]

The houses, for the most part, are built and covered with wood, except some few, which are built of brick and stone. They are generally low, seldom exceeding two stories. All the owners of lots and houses, here, pay a ground rent, greater or less, according to the grant of them by James Hamilton, Esq. who is the proprietor of the town.

There are hills which environ Lancaster, as likewise some thick woods, which, in the summer, render it very hot, especially in the afternoon. The soil is then dry and very sandy, which, when a fresh wind blows, almost choak the inhabitants.

The water here is very bad, occasioned by their springs, and even wells, being stored with lime-stones. This gave me a looseness, and palled my appetite; but soon left me, after I refrained drinking the water by itself.

They have a very good market in this town, well filled with provisions of all kinds, and prodigiously cheap.

Our commissioners and company supped at Worrall's, and passed away an hour or two very agreeably; after which I retired to bed; but had not long reposed myself, when I was most fiercely attacked by the neighbouring Dutch fleas and bugs, which were ready to devour both me and the minister: however, after killing great quantities of my nimble enemies, I got about two hours sleep.

Mr. Calvert was more inhumanly used by them than myself, as was likewise Mr. Craddock. On the next night, Mr. Calvert left our lodgings, and laid in the court-house chamber, among the young gentlemen from Virginia, who there had beds made on the floor for that purpose.

Friday, June 22d, 1744.

Rose betwixt 4 and 5. Breakfasted with Mr. commissioner Thomas, Colonels Colvill and King, at Worrall's.

The Indian chiefs not being yet come, we had no business to do.

The honourable the commissioners of Virginia gave our commissioners, and the several Maryland gentlemen, an invitation to dine with them in the court-house, which we did, betwixt one and two. During our dinner, the deputies of the Six Nations, with their followers and attendants, to the number of 252, arrived in town. Several of their squaws, or wives, with some small children, rode on horseback, which is very unusual with them. They brought their fire-arms and bows and arrows, as well as tomahawks. A great concourse of people followed them. They marched in very good order, with *Cannasateego*, one of the Onondago chiefs, at their head; who, when he came near to the court-house wherein we were dining, sung, in the Indian language, a song, inviting us to a renewal of all treaties heretofore made, and that now to be made.

Mr. Weiser, the interpreter, who is highly esteemed by the Indians, and is one of their council of state, (though a German by birth) conducted them to some vacant lots in the back part of the town, where sundry poles and boards were placed. Of these, and some boughs of trees from the woods, the Indians made *wigwams*, or cabins, wherein they resided during the treaty. They will not, on any occasion whatsoever, dwell, or even stay, in houses built by white people.

They placed their cabins according to the rank each nation of them holds in their grand council. The *Onondagoes* nation was placed on the right hand and upper end; then the others, according to their several dignities.

After dining, and drinking the loyal healths, all the younger gentlemen of Virginia, Maryland, and Pennsylvania, went with Mr. Conrad Weiser to the Indian camp, where they had erected their several cabins. We viewed them all, and heartily welcomed *Cannasateego*, and *Tachanuntie*, (alias the Black Prince) two chiefs of the Onondagoes, to town. They shaked us by the hands, and seemed very well pleased with us. I gave them some snuff, for which they returned me thanks in their language.

The first of these sachems (or chiefs) was a tall, well-made man; had a very full chest, and brawny limbs. He had a manly countenance, mixed with a good-natured smile. He was about 60 years of age; very active, strong, and had a surprising liveliness in his speech, which I observed in the discourse betwixt him, Mr. Weiser, and some of the sachems.

Tachanuntie, another sachem, or chief of the same nation, was a tall, thin man; old, and not so well featured as Cannasateego: I believe he may be near the same age with him. He is one of the greatest warriors that ever the Five Nations produced, and has been a great war-captain for many years past.

He is also called *the Black Prince*, because, as I was informed, he was either begotten on an Indian woman by a negro, or by an Indian chief on some negro woman; but by which of the two, I could not be well assured.

The Governor of Canada, (whom these Indians call *Onantio*) will not treat with any of the Six Nations of Indians, unless *Tachanuntie* is personally present, he having a great sway in all the Indian councils.

Our interpreter, Mr. Weiser, desired us, whilst we were here, not to talk much of the Indians, nor laugh at their dress, or make any remarks on their behaviour: if we did, it would be very much resented by them, and might cause some differences to arise betwixt the white people and them. Besides, most of them understood English, though they will not speak it when they are in treaty.

The Indians, in general, were poorly dressed, having old match-coats, and those ragged; few, or no shirts, and those they had, as black as the Scotchman made the *Jamaicans*, when he wrote in his letter they were as black as that ● blot.

When they had rested some little space of time, several of them began to paint themselves with divers sorts of colours, which rendered them frightful. Some of the others rubbed bear's grease on their faces, and then laid upon that a white paint. When we had made a sufficient survey of them and their cabins, we went to the court-house, where the Indians were expected to meet the Governor of Pennsylvania, the Hon. GEORGE THOMAS, Esq. and to be by him congratulated on their arrival at this town.

Friday, P. M. Between 5 and 6 o'clock, Mr. Weiser accompanied the several Indian chiefs from their camp up to the court-house, which they entered and seated themselves after their own manner. Soon after, his Honour the Governor, the honourable the commissioners of Virginia, the honourable the commissioners of Maryland, and the young gentlemen from the three governments, went into the court-house to the Indians. There the Governor, and all the commissioners, severally welcomed the Indians to Lancaster, and shaked hands with the sachems.

Then his Honour seated himself in the chair on the bench, the Virginia commissioners placed themselves, *to wit*, the Hon. Col. Thomas Lee, and Col. William Beverly, on his right hand, and our honourable commissioners on his left. William Peters, Esq. secretary of Pennsylvania, sat in the middle of the table, under the Governor, and Mr. William Black, secretary to the Virginia commissioners, on his right hand, and myself, as secretary to the commissioners of Maryland, on his left hand.

The Governor desired the interpreter to tell the Indians. "He was very glad to see them here, and should not trouble them with business this day, but desired they would rest themselves, after their great journey." This, Mr. Weiser interpreted to them, whereat they seemed well enough pleased, and made the Governor a suitable answer.

When this was done, a good quantity of punch, wine, and pipes and tobacco, were given to the sachems, and the Governor and all the commissioners drank to them, whom they pledged. When they had smoked some small time, and each drank a glass or two of wine and punch, they retired to their cabins.

Our landlord shewed me the book, wherein he keeps the account of the expenses of ours and the Virginia commissioners, and which was ordered to be produced every morning to me, to know exactly the amount of each day's expense.

Saturday, June 23d, 1744, at Lancaster.

This day I was seized with a lax, and small fever, occasioned by drinking the water of this town. [...]

All this day the Indians staid in their wigwams; and it is usual for them to rest two days after their journey before they treat, or do business with the English.

After supper, this evening, I went with Mr. President Logan's son, and divers other young gentlemen, to the Indians' camp, they being then dancing one of their lighter war dances.

They performed it after this manner: Thirty or forty of the younger men formed themselves into a ring, a fire being lighted (notwithstanding the excessive heat) and burning clear in the midst of them. Near this, sat three elderly Indians, who beat a drum to the time of the others' dancing. Then the dancers hopped round the ring, after a frantic fashion, not unlike the priests of Bacchus in old times, and repeated, sundry times, these sounds, *Yohoh! Bugh!* Soon after this, the major part of the dancers (or rather hoppers) set up a horrid shriek or halloo!

They continued dancing and hopping, after this manner, several hours, and rested very seldom. Once, whilst I staid with them, they did rest themselves; immediately thereupon, the three old men began to sing an Indian song, the tune of which was not disagreeable to the white by-standers. Upon this, the young warriors renewed their terrible shriek and halloo, and formed themselves into a ring, environing the three old ones, and danced as before. Mr. Calvert, myself, and some others slipped through the dancers, and stood near the fire; and when the drum-beaters ceased their noise, we shaked them by the hand. Here we presented some clean pipes to them, which were very acceptable, most of the Indians being great smokers of tobacco. A *Conestogoe*, or *Susquehannah* Indian, stood without the circle, and importuned the white by-standers to give money to the young children, which was done. Whilst this diversion happened, some High-Dutch, belonging to the town, brought their guns with them to the camp; which being perceived by the *Conestogoe*, he informed us, it would be very displeasing to the Indians, who would resent it, though brought thither with ever so innocent an intent; therefore desired us to tell the Germans to withdraw, and leave their musquets out of their sight, otherwise some bad consequences might ensue. We complied with his request, and made the Germans retire.

From the camp I went to Worrall's, and sat up till eleven o'clock; to whose house I heard the Indian drum, and the warriors repeating their terrible noise and dancing; and at this sport of theirs, they continued till near one in the morning.

These young men are surprisingly agile, strong, and straight limbed. They shoot, both with the gun and bow and arrow, most dexterously. They likewise throw their tomahawk (or little hatchet) with great certainty, at an indifferent large object, for twenty or thirty yards distance. This weapon they use against their enemies, when they have spent their powder and ball, and destroy many of them with it.

The chiefs, who were deputed to treat with the English by their different nations, were very sober men, which is rare for an Indian to be so, if he can get liquor. They behaved very well, during our stay amongst them, and sundry times refused drinking in a moderate way. When ever they renew old treaties of friendship, or make any bargain about lands they sell to the English, they take great care to abstain from intoxicating drink, for fear of being over-reached; but when they have finished their business, then some of them will drink without measure. [...]

Monday morning, 25th June, 1744.

At 10 o'clock, the Indian sachems met the Governor, the honourable commissioners of Virginia, and those of this province, when his Honour made them a speech, to which Cannasateego returned an answer in behalf of all the others present.

The Indians staid in the court-house about two hours; and were regaled with some bumbo and sangree.

The honourable commissioners from Virginia and Maryland dined in the court-house, as did the gentlemen of both governments; we had two tables, and a great variety of victuals; our company being about thirty in number.

In the court-house, Monday, P. M.

The Governor, and all the honourable commissioners, resumed their several seats here; and then the chiefs came in, and took their places.

Edmund Jenings, Esq. as first commissioner for Maryland, made a speech to the Six Nations, which was interpreted to them by Mr. Weiser. Whilst Mr. Jenings delivered his speech, he gave the interpreter a string and two belts of wampum, which were by him presented to the sachem Cannasateego; and the Indians thereupon gave the cry of approbation; by this we were sure the speech was well approved by the Indians. This cry is usually made on presenting wampum to the Indians in a treaty, and is performed thus: The grand chief and speaker amongst them pronounces the word *jo-hah!* with a loud voice, singly; then all the others join in this sound, *woh!* dwelling some little while upon it, and keeping exact time with each other, and immediately, with a sharp noise and force, utter this sound, *wugh!* This is performed in great order, and with the utmost ceremony and decorum; and with the Indians is like our English huzza!

Monday evening, in the court-house chamber.

I supped with the Governor, the honourable commissioners, and the gentlemen of Philadelphia, who attended his Honour to this town. We had an elegant entertainment; and after supper the Governor was extremely merry, and thereby set an example of agreeable mirth, which ran through the whole company. During this merriment, two Germans happened to pass by the court-house with a harp and fiddle, and played some tunes under the window of our room: upon that, they were ordered to come up stairs, where the Governor required them to divert us, which they did, but not with the harmony of their music, (for that was very uncouth and displeasing to us, who had heard some of the best hands in England) but by playing a tune, of some sort, to a young Indian, who danced a jig with Mr. Andrew Hamilton, in a most surprising manner. At nine o'clock, the Governor and commissioners left us; and then the younger persons raised their jollity by dancing in the Indian dress, and after their manner.

Tuesday, 26th June.

Copied fair the proceedings of yesterday with the Indians, as also Gov. Thomas's speech to them, which were transmitted to his Excellency Thomas Bladen, Esq. Governor of Maryland, by Mr. Commissioner Jenings.

We dined in the court-house; and soon after I received orders from the above commissioner, to acquaint all the Maryland gentlemen, "That they should desist going into the court-house this afternoon, during our treaty with the Six Nations." Pursuant to which order, I informed the gentlemen of our commissioners' pleasure, at which the first were much disgusted, as were the Virginia gentlemen, who had the same commands laid on them by the secretary of their commissioners.

Five o'clock, P. M. His Honour the Governor of Pennsylvania, and the honourable the commissioners of Virginia and Maryland, met the Indian chiefs in the court-house, when Cannasateego answered our speech of yesterday, and presented a string and two belts of wampum: which being done, the further execution of the treaty was adjourned until the next day.

By order of our commissioners, and at the request of Mr. Weiser, the interpreter, I bought half a gross of tobacco pipes, to be presented to the Indians at their camp; which was accordingly done, and they seemed well pleased at the gift, such pipes being scarce with them. [. . .]

Thursday, 28th of June, 1744, A. M.

At 9 this morning, the commissioners of Maryland and the Six Nations met in the court-house chamber, according to agreement of yesterday.

Here we opened the several bales and boxes of goods, to be presented the Indians, they having been bought at Philadelphia, and sent hither for that end.

Before the chiefs viewed and handled the several goods, Mr. Commissioner Jenings made them a speech in the name of the Governor of Maryland, with which, after it was interpreted to them by Mr. Weiser, they seemed well pleased.

The chiefs turned over, and narrowly inspected the goods, and asked the prices of them; which being told them, they seemed somewhat dissatisfied; and desired to go down into the court-house, to consult among themselves, (which is their usual method, if it concerns any matter of importance, as this was, for they must give a particular account of their whole negotiation to their several tribes, when they return) with their interpreter. They did so; and after some time came up again, and agreed with our commissioners to release their claim and right to any lands now held by the inhabitants of Maryland, and for which the said Indians were not heretofore satisfied, in consideration of the following goods, viz.

	£.	s.	d.
4 pieces of strouds, at £.7	£.28	0	0
2 pieces ditto, £.5,	10	0	0
200 shirts,	63	12	0
3 pieces half thicks,	11	0	0
3 ditto duffle blankets, at £.7,	21	0	0
1 ditto, ditto,	6	10	0
47 guns, at £.1–6–0,	61	2	0
1lb. vermilion,	0	18	0
1000 flints,	0	18	0
4 doz. jews-harps,	0	14	0
1 doz. boxes,	0	1	0
1cwt. 2qrs. 0lb. bar lead,	3	0	0
2 qrs. shot,	1	0	0
2 half barrels gun-powder,	13	0	0
Pennsylvania money.	£.220	15	0

The above quantity of goods were accordingly given the Indians, as agreed on by both parties; after which, our commissioners ordered me to go to Mr. Worrall, and desire him to send some punch for the sachems, which was accordingly done; and after they had severally drank health to the commissioners, and the compliment returned by the latter, the Indians retired to their wigwams, and the honourable commissioners went to their lodgings about 12 o'clock. [...]

Friday, June the 29th, 1744, A. M.

Our commissioners and the Six Nations had a private conference in the court-house chamber, when they jointly proceeded to settle the bounds and quantity of land the latter were to release to Lord Baltimore, in Maryland; but the Indians, not very well apprehending our commissioners, in their demand respecting the bounds of the lands to be released, occasioned a great delay in the finishing of that business; however, it was wholly settled in the afternoon, upon Mr. Weiser's conference with the Governor of Pennsylvania, his Majesty's commissioners of Virginia, and those of Maryland, and also with the Indians in council, where he debated the matter more fully; and explained our commissioners' demands in so clear a manner, that they came to such an amicable determination, as proved agreeable to each party. We again presented the sachems, here, with bumbo punch, with which they drank prosperity and success to their Father, the great King over the waters, and to the healths of our commissioners. [...]

Saturday, 30th June, 1744, A.M.
[...] At ten, his Majesty's commissioners had a conference with the Indians in the court-house chamber, to which no other persons than themselves were admitted.

One o'clock, P. M. The twenty-four chiefs of the Six Nations, by invitation of yesterday from the honourable commissioners of Maryland, dined with them in the court-house; when were present, at other tables, his Honour the Governor of Pennsylvania, the honourable commissioners of Virginia, and a great many gentlemen of the three colonies. There were a large number of the inhabitants of Lancaster likewise present to see the Indians dine.

We had five tables, great variety of dishes, and served up in very good order. The sachems sat at two separate tables; at the head of one, the famous orator, Cannasateego, sat, and the others were placed according to their rank. As the Indians are not accustomed to eat in the same manner as the English, or other polite nations do, we, who were secretaries on this affair, with Mr. Thomas Cookson, prothonatary of Lancaster county, William Logan, Esq. son of Mr. President Logan, and Mr. Nathaniel Rigbie, of Baltimore county, in Maryland, carved the meat for them, served them with cider and wine, mixed with water, and regulated the economy of the two tables. The chiefs seemed prodigiously pleased with their feast, for they fed lustily, drank heartily, and were very greasy before they finished their dinner, for, by the bye, they made no use of their forks. The interpreter, Mr. Weiser, stood betwixt the table, where the governor sat, and that, at which the sachems were placed, who, by order of his Honour, was desired to inform the Indians he drank their healths, which he did; whereupon they gave the usual cry of approbation, and returned the compliment, by drinking health to his Honour and the several commissioners.

After dinner, the interpreter informed the Governor and commissioners, "That as the Lord Proprietary and Governor of Maryland was not known to the Indians by any particular name, they had agreed, in council, to take the first opportunity of a large company to present him with one: And, as this with them was a matter of great consequence, and attended with abundance of form, the several nations had drawn lots for the performance of the ceremony; and the lot falling on the Căhūgă nation, they had chosen Gāchrādōdŏn, one of their chiefs, to be their speaker, and he desired leave to begin;" which being given, he, on an elevated part of the court-house, with all the dignity of a warrior, the gesture of an orator, and in a very graceful posture, spoke as follows:

"As the Governor of Maryland has invited us here, to treat about our lands, and brighten the chain of friendship, the united Six Nations think themselves so much obliged to him, that we have come to a resolution, in council, to give the great man, who is proprietor of Maryland, a particular name, by which we may hereafter correspond with him: And as it hath fallen to the Cahugaes' lot in council to consider of a proper name for that chief man, we have agreed to give him the name of Tŏcărў-hō-gōn, denoting Precedency, Excellency, or living in the middle, or honourable place, betwixt Asserigoa, and our brother Onas, by whom our treaties may be the better carried on."

And then, addressing himself to his Honour the Governor of Pennsylvania, the honourable the commissioners of Virginia and Maryland, and to the gentlemen then present, he added:

"As there is a company of great men now assembled, we take this opportunity to publish this matter, that it may be known Tocary-ho-gon is our friend, and that we are ready to honour him, and that by such name he may be always called and known among us; and, we hope, he will ever act towards us, according to the excellence of the name we have now given him, and enjoy a long and happy life."

When the speech was ended, all the other chiefs expressed their assent, and great satisfaction at what was said to our commissioners, insomuch that they sent forth five several cries of approbation.

Gachradodon having finished his complimentary oration, Mr. Commissioner Jenings, in the name of the other commissioners, and on behalf of Lord Baltimore, spoke in reply to the sachem: "That his Lordship was much obliged to the six nations for distinguishing him by the name of Tocaryhogon, esteeming it a mark of kindness and honour: That his Lordship would entertain the most unfeigned friendship for them; and that the government of Maryland would ever be ready and desirous to render them its best offices, conducive to their tranquillity and undisturbed safety;" which Mr. Weiser, by command, interpreted to the Indians; and at the same time was ordered to acquaint them, that the governor and the commissioners were then preparing to drink his Majesty's health; all which was done, and the chiefs expressed a sincere joy by their cry of approbation, and drank the same in bumpers of Madeira wine. The governor, commissioners, and indeed all the persons present, except the Indians, gave three several huzzas, after the English manner, on drinking the King's health; which a good deal surprised them, they having never before heard the like noise.

Upon ending the ceremony of drinking healths, the governor and commissioners retired some little time; but within an hour, the commissioners of Virginia and Maryland entered the court-house, and afterwards went up into the chamber, as likewise the several chiefs, Mr. Weiser, and a great many of the young gentlemen. Here, by order of our commissioners, I produced the engrossed release for the lands, with the seals fixed. We were obliged to put about the glass pretty briskly; and then Mr. Weiser interpreted the contents of it to the sachems, who, conferring amongst themselves about the execution of it, the major part of them seemed very inclinable to sign and deliver it; but upon Shukelemy, an Oneydoe chief's remonstrance, some of the others, with himself, refused, for that day, executing it; which refusal of Shukelemy, we imputed, and that not without reason, to some sinister and underhand means, made use of by the Pennsylvanians, to induce the sachems not to give up their right to the lands by deed, without having a larger consideration given them, by the province of Maryland, than what was specified in the release. Shukelemy, who before, we had esteemed one of our fastest friends, put us under a deep surprise and confusion, by his unfair behaviour; yet we, in some measure, extricated ourselves out of them, by the honest Cannasateego's, and the other sachems, to the number of sixteen, delivering the deed after the forms customary with the English, to which there were a great many gentlemen signed their names as witnesses. Mr. Weiser assured the commissioners, that he, with Cannasateego and some other chiefs, would so effectually represent the unfair dealing of Shukelemy, and his partisans in council, that he did not doubt to induce him and them totally to finish this business on Monday next, maugre all the insinuations and misrepresentations agitated by the enemies of Maryland; and indeed Mr. Interpreter proved successful, as is evident in the transactions of Monday, and may be seen in the printed treaty.

Monday, July the 2d, 1744, A. M.

The honourable commissioners of Maryland, with Mr. Weiser, met at the house of George Sanderson, in this town, when the several chiefs, who had not signed the deed of release, and renunciation of their claim to lands in Maryland, did now cheerfully, and without any hesitation, execute the same, in the presence of the commissioners, and Mr. Weiser; which latter they caused to sign and deliver it on behalf of a nation not present, both with his Indian name of Tarachiawagon, and that of Weiser. Thus we happily effected the purchase of the lands in Maryland, by the dexterous management of the interpreter, notwithstanding the storm on Saturday, that threatened to blast our measures; and hereby gained not only some hundred thousand acres of land to Lord Baltimore, who had no good right to them before this release, but an undisturbed and quiet enjoyment of them to the several possessors, who, in fact, had bought of that Lord's agent.

The names of the chiefs, who signed and delivered the deed, were,

Cannasateego, Tacanoontia, Johnuhat, Caxhayion, Toruchdadon, Netokanyhak, and Rotierawuchto, sachems of the Onondago nation.

Saguchsonyunt, Gachradodon, Hutasalyakon, Rowanhohiso, Osochquah, and Seyenties, sachems of the Cahugäes.

Swadamy, alias Shukelemy, Onichnaxqua, Onochkallydawy, alias Watsatuha, Tohashwanrarorows, Arughhocththaw, and Tiorhaasery, sachems of the Oneydöes.

Sidowax, Attiusgu, Tuwaiadachquha, sachems of the Tuscaroroes.

Tanasanegos, and Tanachiuntus, chiefs of the Senikers, or Senecäes.

The deed was delivered by Mr. Commissioner Jenings, on his return to Annapolis, to his clerk, Mr. Richard Burdus, who recorded it among the land records, in the provincial court office of Maryland, in libro. E. I. fo. 8, 9, 10, 11. [...]

Tuesday, 3d July, 1744.

At 11 o'clock, this morning, the Governor, and all the honourable commissioners, had a meeting with the Six Nations in the court-house, when his Honour made a speech to them, as did the commissioners of Virginia and Maryland; and each party presented strings and belts of wampum; on receipt of which, the Indians gave the usual cry of approbation, and in a stronger and more cheerful tone than heretofore. They were served with plenty of rum at the conclusion of the speeches, and drank it with a good *goút*. [...]

Thursday, 5th July, 1744.

This morning, Mr. Peters, secretary to the Governor, Mr. Black, secretary to the honourable commissioners of Virginia, and myself, examined the whole treaty, and finished all matters any way relating to it. At 12, Colonels Colvill and King, with the Virginia commissioners, settled our accounts with Mr. Worrall. Here we dined, and immediately afterwards mounted our horses, and went from this filthy town to our kind, facetious landlord's, Mr. Hughes, at Nottingham township, by the Gap-Road, so called from a space or gap being open in the ridge of blue mountains, which extend a great way to the south-westward of Virginia, and north-eastward of Pennsylvania. [...]

Further Reading

Jennings, Francis, ed. *The History and Cuz of Iroquois Diplomacy: An Interdisciplinary Guide to the Treaties of the Six Nations and Their League.* Syracuse, NY: Syracuse University Press, 1985.

Merrell, James H. *The Indians' New World: Catawbas and Their Neighbors from European Contact through the Era of Removal.* Chapel Hill: University of North Carolina Press for the Institute of Early American History and Culture, 1989.

Merrell, James H. *Into the American Woods: Negotiators on the Pennsylvania Frontier.* New York: W. W. Norton, 1999.

Richter, Daniel K. *The Ordeal of the Longhouse: The Peoples of the Iroquois League in the Era of European Colonization.* Chapel Hill: University of North Carolina Press for the Institute of Early American History and Culture, 1992.

White, Richard. *The Middle Ground: Indians, Empires, and Republics in the Great Lakes Region, 1650–1815.* New York: Cambridge University Press, 1991.

4

Cherokee Removal

Introduction

In the early nineteenth century, the Cherokee Nation and other Indians living east of the Mississippi faced a great crisis. Powerful forces in the United States government wanted them to remove to the West. Deeply attached to their land in the Southeast, the Cherokees fought removal by raising supporters among Christian missionaries and American politicians, sending delegations to Washington, D.C., with petitions and appeals, circulating their anti-removal newspaper *The Cherokee Phoenix* widely throughout the United States, and ultimately bringing their cause before the United States Supreme Court. The resulting court cases, *Cherokee Nation v. Georgia* (1831) and *Worcester v. Georgia* (1832), eventually became the foundation for much of US Indian law. Although technically a victory for the Cherokees, *Worcester v. Georgia* did not save them from removal because President Andrew Jackson refused to enforce the Court's decision. Literally at gunpoint, the Cherokees removed to Indian Territory, now Oklahoma, in the winter of 1838–9. Four thousand Cherokees, one fifth of their total population, died as a consequence of this forced migration known as the Trail of Tears.

The devastating effects of Cherokee removal stand in sharp contrast to the benevolence allegedly intended by the policy. Andrew Jackson, Lewis Cass, and other removal advocates contended that removal would protect Indians from the violent intrusions of white settlers. By moving west, Indians would have sufficient land to carry on a hunting economy and could become "civilized" at their own pace. If Indians remained in the East, so the argument went, they would become demoralized, degenerate, impoverished, and dependent. Cherokee leaders such as John Ross, Major Ridge, his son John Ridge, and Elias Boudinot countered this rhetoric by pointing to how "civilized" the Cherokees had become. Indeed, there had emerged in the Cherokee Nation in the previous decades an elite social class, many of whom were more educated and wealthier in their plantations, ferry operations, and black slaves than most of their white neighbors in Georgia and Tennessee. With Sequoyah's invention of the Cherokee syllabary, a syllable-based system for writing the Cherokee language, the Cherokees could also claim a high rate of literacy.

In his article "Evidence of Surplus Production in the Cherokee Nation Prior to Removal," geographer David M. Wishart focuses on one issue within the larger debate about removal. Using economic data from the 1835 census of the Cherokee Nation, Wishart tests the pro-removal argument that the Cherokees were unable to make productive, agricultural use of their eastern lands. His findings would not have pleased Andrew Jackson or Lewis Cass but would have found favor with the Cherokee leadership. Wishart's analysis does seem to confirm their impression of the Cherokee economy as described in The Cherokee Phoenix, excerpts from which are also included in this chapter. In addition, Wishart's evidence raises questions about how Cherokee society changed in this time period. Several historians working on the pre-removal period concluded that, as the Cherokees adopted Euroamerican economic practices, Cherokee society became deeply stratified between an elite minority of "mixed bloods" (people of mixed Cherokee and white descent) who controlled the Cherokee government, and a poor, subsistence-oriented "full-blood" majority. Although this particular debate falls outside the bounds of Wishart's study, his statistical analysis of the Cherokee Nation in 1835 does provide information on social characteristics, such as literacy and white intermarriage, in addition to economics.

Evidence of Surplus Production in the Cherokee Nation Prior to Removal

David M. Wishart

The question of the continued economic viability of the Eastern Chero-kees in the southeastern United States was an important issue in the heated political debate during the 1830s over their removal to Oklahoma. For example, President Andrew Jackson, probably the most famous proponent of removal, bemoaned the lack of economic progress among the southeastern Indians. Jackson argued in his first annual message to Congress that the Indians had no right to "tracts of country on which they have neither dwelt nor made improvements, merely because they have seen them from the mountain or passed them in the chase," and felt that their inability to adopt white agricultural methods quickly would doom them to "weakness and decay" with "the fate of the Mohegan, the Narragansett, and the Delaware . . . fast overtaking the Choctaw, the Cherokee, and the Creek." Jackson elaborated on these views in a talk given to a Cherokee delegation visiting Washington in 1835 to protest the provisions of an early draft of the Treaty of New Echota, which ultimately set the terms for Cherokee removal. Jackson maintained that

> The game has disappeared among you, and you must depend upon agri-culture, and the mechanic arts for support. And, yet, a large portion of your people have acquired little or no property which can be useful to them. How, under these circumstances, can you live in the country you now occupy? (Remini 1984, p. 298)

Jackson promoted the view that removal to the trans-Mississippi west was a humanitarian policy essential for Cherokee survival. His remarks reflected a tone set by Lewis Cass, the Secretary of War during Jackson's second administration, who authored an anonymous piece titled "Removal of the Indians" for the 1830 volume of *The North American Review*. Cass, at that time the governor of Michigan, wrote at length about economic progress among the Cherokees. He admitted "that individuals among the Cherokees have acquired property, and with it

Wishart, David M. "Evidence of Surplus Production in the Cherokee Nation Prior to Removal." *The Journal of Economic History*, 55, No. 1 (March 1995): 120–38. (Cambridge: Cambridge University Press.)

more enlarged views and juster notions of the value of our institutions, and the unprofitableness of their own." But, he argued,

> the great body of the people are in a state of helpless and hopeless poverty. With the same improvidence and habitual indolence which mark the northern Indians, they have less game for subsistence, and less peltry for sale. We doubt whether there is, upon the face of the globe, a more wretched race than the Cherokees as well as the other southern tribes, present. (1830, p. 71)

In stark contrast, opponents of removal pointed to the significant progress that had been made by the Cherokees in adopting white agricultural practices. For example, the Reverend Samuel Worcester, a missionary who had lived with the Cherokees since 1826, asserted in a letter to removal advocate Reverend E. S. Ely that "the mass of the cherokee people have built them houses and cultivated lands with their own hands. ...There may be a few families among the mountains, who depend mostly on the chase for support, but I know not of one." Worcester proclaimed the success of the Cherokees' adaptation to agriculture in another letter to William Shorey Coodey, a member of a Cherokee delegation to Washington in 1830: "the land is cultivated with very different degrees of industry; but I believe that few fail of an adequate supply of food. The ground is uniformly cultivated by means of the plough, and not, as formerly, by the hoe only."

Disagreement about Cherokee economic progress prior to their removal west continues among contemporary scholars. The Jacksonian case that the Cherokees, along with the rest of the American Indians, were doomed to technologically inevitable destruction because of the high per capita land requirement associated with a hunter-gatherer existence has recently been advanced by Stanley Lebergott (1984, p. 16), who calculated that requirement for the pre-1825 Cherokees at 1,900 acres. Arguing along similar lines, prominent modern historians of Jacksonian Indian policy such as Robert V. Remini and Francis Paul Prucha characterized Jackson's policies as motivated by humanitarian concerns. According to Remini (1984, p. 314), Jackson left the White House "believing that he had saved the Indians from inevitable doom. And, indeed, he had." Prucha maintained that

> Jackson was genuinely concerned for the well-being of the Indians and for their civilization. Although his critics would scoff at the idea of placing him on the roll of the humanitarians, his assertions – both public and private – add up to a consistent belief that the Indians were capable of accepting white civilization, the hope that they would eventually do so, and repeated

efforts to take measures that make the change possible and even speed it along. (1969, pp. 533–4)

Theda Perdue (1979) and Don L. Shadburn (1990) presented a contrasting view, describing in great detail the use of African slaves in Cherokee agriculture and the growth of a planter class among the Cherokees. The adoption of white agricultural techniques suggests both a degree of assimilation into white culture and a significant reduction in the per capita land requirement for the Cherokees. R. Douglas Hurt, in his 1987 volume on American Indian agriculture, also described qualitative aspects of Eastern Cherokee agriculture that leave the reader with the impression that average Cherokee households and members of other southeastern tribes were proficient farmers. However, little in the way of statistical evidence is mustered to support this view.

The dearth of Cherokee economic data in the published literature is surprising, given the detailed statistics that were collected by the federal government in the process of removal. The Census of the Eastern Cherokees, 1835 is the most comprehensive statistical record available covering property holdings and economic activity by household for an Indian population in the antebellum period. In fact, the 1835 census includes agricultural statistics for Cherokee farmers of a kind that were not collected systematically for white farmers until the 1840 Schedules of Mines, Agriculture, Commerce, and Manufacturing, and then only for county-wide aggregates. The 1835 census allows us to address an important question relevant to the removal debate: What proportion of Cherokee households were producing food surpluses in 1835?

William G. McLoughlin carefully examined the 1835 census in a 1977 article (with Walter H. Conser, Jr.) and in his 1986 book, *Cherokee Renascence in the New Republic*. McLoughlin and Conser's detailed examination and interpretation of the census data focused on the way racial characteristics of households and communities were related to the distribution of skills and assets inside the nation. Their analysis portrayed a "bourgeois socioeconomic structure" with "not only an expanding Cherokee bourgeoisie but also a growing planter or upper-class gentry who lived very much on the same scale and with the same values and style of life as the surrounding white planter class" (p. 697). McLoughlin's 1986 work emphasized a high degree of stratification in the Cherokee social structure, with a small elite of planters, a somewhat larger group of yeoman farmers, and a large class of impoverished subsistence farmers. McLoughlin and Conser's work was based on a typed version of the 1835 census that was prepared "under the direction of Acting Secretary of Interior J. D. C. Atkins in 1897." The typescript covers 2,637 of the 2,669 households included in the original manuscript.

McLoughlin and Conser posed an important question when they considered the relative sizes of social classes in the Eastern Cherokee population, but they did not reach firm conclusions on this issue in respect to the Cherokees prior to removal. If, however, a bourgeois Cherokee household is defined simply as one that produced surpluses, thus creating a source for investment, it is possible, based on data from the original manuscript of the 1835 census, to calculate a lower bound for the percentage of households that achieved surplus production and to estimate the magnitude of household surplus or deficit production. A lower bound for aggregate surplus production for the Eastern Cherokees can also be estimated. By comparing household production with subsistence requirements, more definitive statements can be made about the number and percentage of households that could have achieved something like bourgeois status in the Eastern Cherokee population.

The purpose of this article is to shed more statistical light on the impressionistic views of Cherokee economic development presented during the removal debate of the 1830s and in the current literature. I examine economic data in the 1835 census for evidence of surplus production by Eastern Cherokee households. First, I describe the stated purpose of the census and the categories of information it recorded. I then present a comparative analysis of summary statistics for the sections of Tennessee, Alabama, North Carolina, and Georgia that comprised the Eastern Cherokee Nation as well as statistics on literacy and skill levels among the Cherokees for each state. In the following section I use the census results to evaluate the extent of surplus Cherokee agricultural production and to calculate a lower-bound estimate for the percentage of households that attained at least subsistence levels of food production. I also estimate aggregate surplus production. I conclude with observations that relate my analysis to the debate over Cherokee economic progress and the removal program.

The Census of the Eastern Cherokees, 1835

Major Benjamin F. Currey was the acting Indian agent at the Cherokee Agency East and the Superintendent of Cherokee Removal in charge of conducting the 1835 census. He stated (albeit unclearly) that the purpose of the census was "to be fully possessed of a knowledge of [the Eastern Cherokees'] number, the number of each man's houses, the number of his farms, with the quantity of land under cultivation, the proportions of tillable land, the mineral resources and water privileges of the country, etc., [that] the commissioners would be able to fix a true estimate upon the value of the country in case the whole title does not

Table 1 Summary statistics (households)

Variable	Tennessee Mean	N	Alabama Mean	N	North Carolina Mean	N	Georgia Mean	N	Totals Mean	N
Males -18 yrs.	2.12	314	2.15	172	2.01	472	2.19	1,033	2.13	1,991
Males +18 yrs.	1.61	356	1.59	220	1.50	600	1.72	1,259	1.64	2,435
Females -16 yrs.	2.18	305	1.91	172	1.91	435	2.11	1,024	2.06	1,936
Females +16 yrs.	1.60	389	1.63	228	1.56	617	1.80	1,309	1.70	2,543
Cherokees	5.96	424	5.80	245	5.61	650	6.63	1,350	6.20	2,669
Male slaves	5.76	42	4.15	34	1.20	10	4.79	76	4.69	162
Female slaves	4.33	55	4.27	37	1.92	12	4.55	89	4.27	193
Total slaves	8.42	57	7.48	40	2.33	15	8.01	96	7.61	208
Whites married	1.01	77	1.00	27	1.00	10	1.00	67	1.01	181
Cultivated acres	27.05	399	36.17	198	10.96	628	15.19	1,271	17.69	2,496
Houses	4.44	408	2.78	214	1.53	635	3.71	1,289	3.20	2,546
Bushels of wheat cultivated	35.43	28	95.00	2	0.00	0	43.55	29	41.44	59
Bushels of wheat sold	18.78	9	0.00	0	0.00	0	20.76	17	20.08	26
Bushels of corn cultivated	380.54	366	477.92	189	126.45	622	222.80	1,201	242.17	2,378
Bushels of corn sold	129.61	209	454.52	31	93.38	63	103.08	513	122.47	816
Corn income ($)	57.75	209	234.90	31	46.62	63	63.18	440	67.41	743
Bushels of corn purchased	59.31	150	34.18	34	108.00	2	19.42	119	41.27	305
Grain expenditure	21.89	150	16.62	34	54.00	2	10.11	119	16.9	305
Readers in English	2.34	169	2.07	92	1.97	31	2.12	179	2.18	471
Readers in Cherokee	1.97	242	2.28	139	1.77	313	1.92	715	1.93	1,409

Notes: N, and therefore the mean, for each variable refers only to those households for which non-zero values were reported for that variable. A handful of observations on some variables in the census were recorded with half units; these were rounded up to the nearest integer in the data-entry process.

Source: Census Roll, 1835 of the Cherokee Indians East of the Mississippi and Index to the Roll, Records of the Bureau of Indian Affairs, Record Group 75.

approve of the gross sum fixed upon already." Major Currey submitted the completed census to the Commissioner of Indian Affairs on 27 February 1836.

The 1835 census records household-by-household data on 13 demographic categories, 9 agricultural categories, and 9 categories of physical capital and skills. Demographic information includes the number of Cherokees per household grouped by sex and by age (above and below age 18 for males, above and below 16 for females). Cherokees are also categorized by racial mix with columns for half-breeds, quadroons, full bloods, mixed Catawbas, mixed Spaniards, and mixed Africans. The number of African slaves held by households is recorded by sex. The census shows no evidence of the use of Indian slaves by the Cherokees. Whites connected by marriage are also listed.

Agricultural data include the number of farms, the total number of acres cultivated, bushels of corn raised and sold, bushels of wheat raised and sold, gross income from corn sales, bushels of corn purchased, and cash outlays for corn purchases. A serious drawback of the census as a source of agricultural data is that crops other than wheat and corn and the amount of livestock held per household are omitted. It is also not clear what defines a farm for those households with more than one farm listed.

Physical capital recorded (but, unfortunately, not valued) in the census includes the number of houses, mills, and ferryboats per household. Skills possessed by household members are listed in six categories: farmers over age 18, mechanics over age 18, weavers, spinners (listed as "spinsters" in the manuscript), and readers in English and readers in Cherokee per household.

Summary statistics from the census of the Eastern Cherokees, 1835

The statistics presented in table 1 calculated from the population of Eastern Cherokee households reflect the situation experienced by the average Cherokee household in each state just prior to removal. Note that the number of observations for each variable changes because statistics were calculated only for those households with non-zero values reported for specific variables. Production measures are listed per household rather than per farm because it is not clear how a farm is defined in the manuscript and the focus of this study is household production.

Household sizes were roughly similar in all the states, ranging from six to seven Cherokee members throughout the Eastern Cherokee

Table 2   Cherokee literacy by state

State	Percent of households		Percent of population	
	Cherokee	English	Cherokee	English
Tennessee	57.1	39.9	18.9	15.6
Alabama	56.7	37.6	22.3	13.4
North Carolina	48.1	4.7	15.2	1.7
Georgia	53.0	13.2	15.3	4.2
Overall	52.8	17.6	16.4	6.2

Notes: These figures are computed from table 1. The first two columns give the percentage of households with at least one literate member. The second pair of columns gives the literacy rate as a percentage of the total Cherokee population.

Source: See table 1.

Nation. The average number of acres cultivated per household varied from 11 in North Carolina to 36 in Alabama. Bushels of corn output per household averaged 126 in North Carolina, 223 in Georgia, 381 in Tennessee, and 478 in Alabama. Average corn sales per household making a sale were $46 in North Carolina, $58 in Tennessee, $63 in Georgia, and $235 in Alabama. The percent of households that sold corn was 10 in North Carolina, 13 in Alabama, 38 in Georgia, and 50 in Tennessee. Rates of slaveownership were highest in Alabama and Tennessee, with some 16 percent of households owning an average of seven to eight slaves in Alabama and 12.5 percent of Tennessee households owning an average of eight to nine slaves.

For the Eastern Cherokee Nation as a whole, only 173 of 2,669 households, or 6.5 percent, had no acreage in cultivation. The average cultivated acreage was slightly less than 18 acres for all households engaged in farming. Some 89 percent of households produced a corn crop; the average annual harvest per household was 240 bushels. Almost 31 percent of households sold some corn; the average amount sold was 122 bushels. Approximately 8 percent of Cherokee households owned slaves with an average of seven to eight slaves per household.

Literacy rates for the Cherokee language varied little among states. However, a big difference in English literacy shows up when Tennessee and Alabama are compared to North Carolina and Georgia. (See table 2.) The proportion of households with at least one member literate in English was 39.9 percent in Tennessee and 37.6 in Alabama, as contrasted with 4.7 percent in North Carolina and 13.2 percent in Georgia. On the other hand, over half of the households in every state except North Carolina (where the figure was 48 percent) had at least one member who was literate in Cherokee.

Table 3 Cherokee physical and human capital statistics by state

	Tennessee	Alabama	North Carolina	Georgia
Houses	1,803	596	978	4,801
Farms	412	262	714	1,667
Grain mills	8	2	6	9
Ferryboats	45	9	0	13
Farmers over 18	581	327	822	1,933
Mechanics over 18	209	9	13	100
Weavers	547	159	325	1,410
Spinners	863	274	721	2,202

Source: See table 1.

Data for physical and human capital among the Eastern Cherokees are presented in table 3. The number of houses far exceeds the number of households for all four states, and the number of farms is greater than the number of households for every state but Tennessee. Apparently, households frequently made investments in land clearing in different locations, perhaps to better ensure a successful crop or to take advantage of differences in soil and growing conditions. Weavers and spinners were found in most households. Tennessee and Georgia are notable for the large numbers of ferryboats owned by the Cherokees and the number of mechanics counted in the census.

Estimating the Extent of Surplus Agricultural Production for the Eastern Cherokee

Data from the 1835 census can be used to test the competing views regarding the ability of Cherokee households to produce their own subsistence. The data are well suited to the calculation of a lower bound for the percentage of households that achieved at least subsistence levels of output because Cherokee agriculture is known to have been fairly diversified. It is widely accepted that many other crops besides corn and wheat, in addition to substantial herds of livestock, were raised by the Cherokees.

McLoughlin and Conser, for example, cited an 1828 census taken by the editors of the Cherokee newspaper, *The Phoenix*, that listes 22,405 "black" cattle, 7,628 horses, 38,517 swine, and 2,912 sheep (p. 681). Citing contemporary accounts of Cherokee agriculture, Perdue noted that the Cherokee cultivated "corn, gourds, melons, cucumbers, squash, cymlins [cymlings], beans, and a 'red pease'" (perhaps kidney beans) during the colonial period (p. 15). Hurt maintained that pumpkins, sunflowers, cabbage, potatoes, peaches, leeks, and garlic were grown in the mid-eighteenth century, in addition to the crops noted above (p. 32) McLoughlin also cited Cherokee accounts of their agricultural practice in 1826 that refer to production of wheat, rye, oats, sweet potatoes, apples, butter, and cheese, as well as to widespread cotton cultivation, mostly for domestic use (p. 301). A mixture of corn meal and boiled beans baked as a bread was a traditional staple of the Cherokees. This undoubtedly nutritious but bland fare was supplemented with hunting and fishing activities in the mountainous regions of North Carolina. Douglas Wilms refers to peach orchards in Georgia during the 1830s that were so extensive that the surplus peaches not dried for winter consumption were fed to hogs. Wilms also notes that Georgia Cherokees were involved in the hog trade, providing both hogs for market and corn for feed to hogs that were driven through Georgia for sale on plantations (1973, pp. 113, 139).

Given this evidence of diversification in food production, a plausible lower-bound percentage of self-sufficient households could be estimated by comparing the size of households' corn crops with an appropriate threshold level of corn output for self-sufficiency. If the corn crop alone was large enough to provide for a household's subsistence (including slaves and intermarried whites), then almost certainly, given diversification in production, the household produced some surplus food. Thus, the percentage of households producing above the threshold would be a lower bound for the percentage achieving at least self-sufficiency. Following David Weiman's work (1987, pp. 627–47) on production by up-country farmers in the counties of Dekalb and Floyd (which were part of the Cherokee Nation) in Georgia in 1859, I chose 20 bushels of corn per consumer equivalent as an appropriate threshold for calculating a lower bound for self-sufficiency for Cherokee farmers. Using methods similar to Weiman's, I calculate consumer equivalents per household by summing the adult populations of both sexes, the slave population, whites married to Cherokees, 0.5 times the females under 16, and 0.5 times the males under 18. The amount of corn potentially available for human consumption can be computed by taking 0.95 times the corn output per household to allow 5 percent of the corn produced for seed. These calculations can be made from the figures presented in table 1.

Lower-bound estimates for the percentage of households that achieved self-sufficiency in corn production and the magnitude of surplus corn production are presented by state and for the Cherokee Nation as a whole in table 4. These results show that in Tennessee and Alabama, 75 percent, at a minimum, of the households that produced corn produced surpluses. When non-corn-producing households are included, the percentages producing above the threshold fall to 63.7 percent for Tennessee and 59.1 percent for Alabama. Somewhat lower percentages of households exceed the lower-bound threshold in North Carolina and Georgia. At least 48.4 percent of North Carolina households and 52.1 percent of Georgia households that produced corn produced surpluses. When non-corn-producing households are included for these states, the percentages fall to 46.1 percent for North Carolina and 46.4 percent for Georgia. Overall, 56.5 percent of households that produced corn in the Cherokee Nation produced above the lower-bound threshold, and just over half of all households exceeded the threshold.

The magnitude of surplus corn production is recorded by state and for the Cherokee Nation as a whole in the last column of table 4. These are minimum estimates because they are based on the lower-bound threshold for self-sufficiency of 20 bushels per consumer equivalent. The

Table 4 Percentages of households achieving self-sufficiency in corn production and the magnitude of surplus corn production

State	All households	Corn-producing households	Total surplus corn (bushels)
Tennessee	63.9 (270)	74.0	86,224
Alabama	59.1 (145)	76.7	59,367
North Carolina	46.1 (300)	48.4	18,916
Georgia	46.4 (626)	52.1	106,419
Cherokee Nation	50.1 (1,341)	56.5	270,758

Notes: These figures are computed from tables 1 and 5. The figures in parentheses are the numbers of households producing surpluses.

Source: See table 1.

aggregate corn requirement for subsistence is 20 bushels per consumer equivalent times the number of consumer equivalents, and surplus corn is equal to the difference between this figure and 95 percent of total corn output. The surplus varies from a high of 106,419 bushels in Georgia to a low of 18,916 bushels in North Carolina. The aggregate surplus is 270,758 bushels. The surplus could have been used for livestock production, for redistribution to households that were unable to produce adequate amounts of food, for sale in the market to earn a cash income, or for insurance against future crop failures.

A more detailed picture of the distribution of Cherokee corn output per consumer equivalent is presented by state and for the Cherokee Nation as a whole in table 5. These data are striking in that a substantial percentage of Cherokee households fall below the threshold for self-sufficiency of 20 bushels per consumer equivalent. However, for several reasons, the Jacksonian conclusion regarding the high level of misery in these households may not be warranted.

First, the 20 bushels per consumer equivalent is a very stringent lower-bound threshold as is revealed by an examination of Weiman's (1987) study of up-country Georgia farmers. Floyd County, Georgia, one of the counties Weiman included in his 1859 sample, was also part of the Eastern Cherokee Nation prior to removal. It seems reasonable that agricultural production of many Cherokee farmers in 1835 would have been similar to that of white farmers in Floyd County in 1859 because

Table 5 The distribution of Cherokee corn output per consumer equivalent by state in 1835 (number and percentage of households)

Bushels of corn available for consumption per consumer equivalent	Tennessee		Alabama		North Carolina		Georgia		Cherokee Nation	
	N	%	N	%	N	%	N	%	N	%
0–0.99	110	26.0	73	29.8	158	24.3	493	36.5	834	31.2
1–9.9	52	12.3	17	6.9	130	20.0	344	25.5	543	20.3
10–19.9	43	10.2	27	11.0	192	29.5	231	17.1	493	18.5
20–29.9	36	8.5	28	11.4	110	16.9	158	11.7	332	12.4
30–49.9	71	16.8	45	18.4	118	18.2	208	15.4	442	16.6
50–69.9	49	11.6	17	6.9	29	4.5	87	6.4	182	6.8
70–99.9	46	10.9	19	7.7	23	3.5	84	6.2	172	6.4
100–149.9	27	6.4	18	7.3	13	2.0	54	4.0	112	4.2
>150	41	9.7	18	7.3	7	1.1	35	2.6	101	3.8

Notes: Consumer equivalents per household were calculated by summing the adult populations of both sexes, the slave population, the whites by marriage, 0.5 times the females under 16, and 0.5 times the males under 18. Corn available for human consumption was computed by taking 0.95 times corn output for the household, thus allowing 5 percent for seed. These methods follow those used by Weiman (1987). The category 1–9.9 excludes those households that were recorded as having raised no corn.

Source: See table 1.

most of the Cherokees in the Southeast in 1835 were upcountry farmers. Weiman uses 20 corn-equivalent bushels per consumer equivalent and 36 corn-equivalent bushels per consumer equivalent as the lowest and highest thresholds for self-sufficiency in his analysis. The more detailed statistics listed in the 1860 Census of Agriculture allowed him to convert non-corn food crops to corn-equivalent bushels in his calculations of the percentage of farms that were self-sufficient in foodstuffs. For example, tenant farmers in Floyd County, the least diversified farmers in Weiman's sample, produced non-corn food crops that accounted for 1.32 times as many corn-equivalent bushels than corn itself. If one assumes that, on average, Cherokee farmers were as diversified as white tenants in Floyd County in 1859, then a Cherokee household just achieving the threshold of 20 bushels of corn per consumer equivalent would also produce 1.32 times 20, or some 26.4 corn-equivalent bushels of non-corn food crops for a total of 46.4 corn-equivalent bushels per consumer equivalent. Thus, assuming diversification in Eastern Cherokee agriculture that is on par with white tenants in the same region some 15 years later, the threshold of 20 corn-equivalent bushels per consumer equivalent greatly exceeds

Weiman's highest threshold of 36 corn-equivalent bushels per consumer equivalent.

Because white tenant farmers would have been under pressure to specialize in crops for sale in the market in order to generate cash income to pay rent, it seems reasonable that Cherokee farmers, who were under no similar pressure, would have been inclined to push diversification further in order to insure against specific crop failures. But even if we assume that the Cherokees achieved only the limited levels of diversification of white tenants, 10 bushels per consumer equivalent of corn production would have been accompanied by 13.2 bushels per consumer equivalent of non-corn food crops, putting all of the 493 households in the category of 10 to 19.9 bushels per consumer equivalent in table 5 over the threshold of 20 bushels per consumer equivalent. If these households are counted as self-sufficient, the percent of all households achieving self-sufficiency becomes 68.7 and the percent of self-sufficient corn-producing households becomes 77.2. Indeed, these percentages can be taken as conservative upper-bound estimates for the share of Cherokee households that achieved at least self-sufficient levels of production.

Clearly, the analysis presented here hinges on the assumption of extensive diversification in Cherokee agricultural practice. Unfortunately, direct statistical evidence on levels of diversification appears to be nonexistent. However, it is possible to strengthen the anecdotal case for extensive diversification with statistical analysis of the data on corn production, wheat production, and cultivated acres listed in the 1835 census. The fact that corn yields per acre (total bushels of corn produced divided by total cultivated acres) computed from data in table 1 are low suggests diversification. These yields range from a high of 13.8 bushels per cultivated acre for Georgia to a low of 11.4 bushels per cultivated acre for North Carolina and an average for the entire population of 13 bushels per cultivated acre. The national average yield for corn in 1840 was 25 bushels per acre. Wilms cites corn yields for the year 1914 of 30 to 40 bushels per acre with little or no fertilizer in the northwestern portion of what had been Cherokee Georgia (1973, p. 61). Even if the Cherokees were only half as efficient as white farmers in Floyd County in 1914, the calculated yields should have been in the range of 20 bushels per acre.

In fact, the data presented in table 6 show that Cherokee corn yields measured per capita rather than per acre were in the same range as those for southern up-country whites in the antebellum period. The Cherokee corn output per capita figure of 31 bushels in 1835 even exceeds the figures reported by Lewis Gray for white Virginia farmers in 1850. A complete comparison of Cherokee and white farming practice in the region under study is beyond the scope of this article. However, a spot

Table 6 Per capita corn output in selected regions of the Southeast in 1850, 1840, and for the Cherokees in 1835 (bushels per capita)

Region or group	Output
Valley of Virginia	21.37
Valley of East Tennessee	49.41
Middle Tennessee	65.26
Kentucky Blue Grass region	82.66
Virginia mountains	26.97
Kentucky mountains	39.07
Cumberland plateau	42.16
Northwest Georgia	41.89
Floyd County Georgia in 1840	55.06
Dekalb County Georgia in 1840	27.99
Tennessee Cherokees in 1835	45.15
Alabama Cherokees in 1835	51.70
North Carolina Cherokees in 1835	21.31
Georgia Cherokees in 1835	27.34
Floyd County Cherokees in 1835	30.85
Eastern Cherokees in 1835	31.44

Notes: Cherokee output per capita is computed from data in table 1 by dividing total corn output by the total population including slaves and whites by marriage. White output per capita for Dekalb County and Floyd County, Georgia, in 1840 is computed by dividing total corn output in these counties by total population. Other figures for 1850 are listed in Gray (1958).

Sources: See table 1; Gray (1958), vol. 2, p. 876; Schedules of Mines, Agriculture, Commerce, and Manufacturing, 1840, Records for Dekalb County and Floyd County, Georgia; Dekalb County and Floyd County, Georgia, Manuscript Census, 1840.

comparison of Floyd County Cherokee farmers with white farmers in Floyd and Dekalb Counties in 1840 shows that Floyd County whites produced significantly more than the Cherokees per capita, who in turn produced roughly the same amount as Dekalb County whites per capita. Dekalb County is an interesting county to compare with Floyd County in 1835 and 1840 because Weiman found that farmers in Floyd County were producing greater surpluses and were better integrated into markets for their surplus produce than farmers in Dekalb County on the eve of the Civil War. Weiman attributes this differential performance to differences in natural endowments and internal infrastructure development between the two counties (p. 627). It appears, however, based on per capita corn production statistics from 1840, that Floyd County farmers were well ahead of Dekalb County farmers just two years after the Cherokee removal in 1838. These data suggest that white Floyd County farmers may have experienced systematic gains from taking over Cherokee investments in farm capital compared to the situation faced by nearby farmers in Dekalb County, who may have incurred more significant farm-making costs. A comparative study of the Cherokee data from 1835 with county-wide data from 1840 for white farm production on former Cherokee land and white production on adjacent non-Cherokee land could shed greater light on the extent of gains for white farmers who moved onto Cherokee land relative to white farmers who did not.

The case for diversification can be further strengthened by estimating corn yields and the number of acres in crops other than corn, using OLS regression techniques. The expression

$$Y = Q/A$$

where Y is the yield per acre, Q is the output, and A is the acreage, can be rearranged to give

$$A = Q/Y.$$

For all crops $i = 1, \ldots, n$ one may write

$$\sum_{i=1}^{n} A_i = \sum_{i=1}^{n} Q_i/Y_i$$

Assuming that cultivated acres listed in the census includes all crops harvested, one can estimate the equation

$$A = a + b_1 Q_1 + b_2 Q_2 + e_i$$

where a is a constant representing the acres devoted to crops other than corn, and wheat and b_1 and b_2 are the crop-yield reciprocals for corn and wheat, respectively. Thus, a second estimate for crop yields can be computed from the crop-yield reciprocals. If these estimated yields are higher than those computed directly from the census, then acres were likely devoted to crops other than corn. Moreover, a significant positive constant term represents an estimate of the number of acres that were devoted to non-corn food crops.

Because of the small number of wheat-producing households in Alabama and North Carolina, regression equations that include wheat production could not be estimated for these states. Therefore, the

Table 7 Regression estimates of corn and wheat yields and acreages in other food crops

| State | N | With corn output as the dependent variable | | Yield |
		Constant	Coefficient	
Tennessee	361	6.22**	0.0566**	17.67
		(5.45)	(34.04)	
Alabama	189	5.27*	0.0665**	15
		(2.02)	(24.33)	
North Carolina	622	4.20**	0.0539**	18.55
		(14.62)	(41.80)	
Georgia	1,200	3.29**	0.0558**	17.92
		(6.92)	(61.36)	
Cherokee Nation	2,372	3.72**	0.0591**	16.92
		(10.19)	(87.89)	

| State | N | With wheat and corn output as independent variables | | | | |
		Constant	Wheat Coefficient	Corn Coefficient	Wheat Yield	Corn Yield
Tennessee	27	18.18	0.2160	0.0470**	4.63	21.28
		(1.93)	1.40	(7.99)		
Georgia	29	13.33	−0.0825	0.0571**	—	17.51
		(0.956)	(−0.317)	(8.24)		
Cherokee Nation	58	11.53	0.17	0.0537**	5.88	18.62
		(1.33)	(1.22)	(11.19)		

* = Significant at the 5 percent level.
** = Significant at the 1 percent level.

Note: The figures in parentheses are *t*-statistics.

Source: See table 1.

dependent variable, cultivated acres, was regressed as a function of corn output alone for all four states and for the Eastern Cherokee population. Cultivated acres was then regressed as a function of wheat output and corn output for Tennessee, Georgia, and the Eastern Cherokee population.

The estimated constants, coefficients, *t*-statistics, and yields are reported in table 7. For the equations with corn as the only independent variable, all constants and coefficients are significant at the 1 percent level, except for the constant term in the equation for Alabama households, which is significant at the 5 percent level. These results point to somewhat higher yields for corn than are generated by using the quotient

Table 8   Distribution of skills held by households with two or fewer cultivated acres

Skill	Tennessee	Alabama	North Carolina	Georgia
	(N = 50)	(N = 52)	(N = 61)	(N = 243)
Mill owner	1 (1)	1 (1)	0	0
Ferryboats	10 (3)	4 (3)	0	0
Mechanics	14 (9)	1 (1)	0	21 (20)
Weavers	38 (32)	27 (27)	10 (9)	170 (137)
Spinners	65 (43)	45 (41)	65 (45)	290 (184)
Farmers	45 (36)	42 (37)	60 (50)	253 (180)
No skills	(3)	(3)	(1)	(26)

Notes: The *N* listed below the states refers to the number of households with two or fewer cultivated acres. The first number listed in each column is the number of people with the skill (except for the mills and ferryboats lines where the number is the actual number of mills and boats). The figures in parentheses are the numbers of households with such capital or skill.

Source: See table 1.

of total bushels of corn raised and the total cultivated acreage found in the census. They suggest yields that run from a low of 15 bushels per acre for Alabama to a high of 18.55 bushels per acre for North Carolina. The estimated corn yield in the Cherokee Nation is 16.92 bushels per acre. These higher yields are consistent with a level of diversification in which less than the total cultivated acreage would be devoted to corn production. Furthermore, the significant positive constant terms suggest that some acreage was devoted to other crops. As a percentage of the average culti-vated acreage per household calculated from the census, the proportion of land devoted to crops other than corn suggested by the regression results ranges from 38.3 percent for North Carolina to 14.6 percent for Alabama.

The equations including wheat production as an independent variable show constants that are larger but insignificant at the 5 percent level. Wheat coefficients are also insignificant. However, corn coefficients are significant and the computed yields are approximately 17 to 20 bushels per acre. Again, these are higher yields than those computed directly from the census, indicating that crops other than corn were raised on the cultivated acreage listed in the census.

A second reason to discount the Jacksonian contention that the Chero-kees were unable to procure a living from the resources available to them in the Southeast is that many Cherokee households depended on other human and physical capital to make a living. Evidence to support this assertion is presented in table 8, which shows that, among the 406 house-holds listed with two or fewer acres in cultivation, 98.8 percent had at least one member with some skill or owned physical capital of some type.

Third, the demographic characteristics of the 173 households with no acres in cultivation suggest that a significant number were comprised of aged Cherokees. Approximately 21 percent of these households con-sisted of a single adult male, a single adult female, or an adult couple with no children. Five of these households had members who were all males below age 18 or females below age 16, forming another smaller class of dependents. The largest group of households with no acres in cultivation consisted of adults living with children. These zero-acre households with adults and children were 4.7 percent of total house-holds in Tennessee, 12.6 percent in Alabama, 2.6 percent in North Carolina, and 4 percent in Georgia. Alabama's concentration of larger Cherokee farms could have afforded employment opportunities to those with no acreage of their own. Many of these families may have hired out their labor to nearby farms.

Finally, it is possible that household production is the wrong unit of measure by which to judge Cherokee economic performance relative to subsistence, especially for the North Carolina households. Anthropo-logical evidence for the North Carolina Cherokees suggests that town-centered, communal, aboriginal forms of production were operative well into the second half of the nineteenth century. These towns and their production systems were called the *gadugi* and operated under the direction of a benevolent community chief. Production was split between private plots and, in some cases, community fields with com-munal labor employed throughout. Sharing of the output was ritualized in the *gadugi*. It would have been possible for a household to produce less than a subsistence amount of food on its private plot, yet earn a livelihood in the context of the *gadugi*. Clearly, a communal system of labor organization could cause the *gadugi* to be noticeably less inclined toward surplus production than private farmsteads. Once subsistence was produced by the *gadugi*, labor likely ceased.

Taken together, the evidence presented in the foregoing discussion points to a large majority of Cherokee households that were either farm producers at levels well in excess of subsistence or were procuring a living some other way with other types of human or physical capital. Many of the households with no visible means of support were likely comprised of aged and orphaned Cherokees. The extent of surplus production across Cherokee households is surprising given the widely accepted view of extreme Cherokee social stratification. As presented by McLoughlin, this view polarizes the Cherokees into "a small group of well-to-do, influential merchant-traders, large planters, slave-owning farmers, and entrepreneurs, . . . a somewhat larger group of farmers and herdsmen who mixed small-scale farming with another enterprise . . . and by far the largest class, . . . the small farmers who barely made enough to live on. . . ." (1986, p. 327). Mary Young supports the same position in a recent article, stating that ". . . most Cherokees were self-sufficient hillbilly farmers. . . ." (1990, p. 46). To be sure, the results presented here indicate that perhaps there were many farmers who resembled hillbillies and produced at or below the margin of subsistence. However, at a minimum, my calculations also point to a clear majority of households producing surpluses in Tennessee and Alabama, and just under 50 percent doing so in North Carolina and Georgia. Contrary to McLoughlin's and Young's conclusions, the largest class of Cherokees consisted of households producing more than enough to live on.

Conclusions

With at least half of Cherokee households producing substantial surpluses, advocates for the Cherokee removal were on shaky ground when they used economic arguments to justify imposing the costs of forced migration on a developing economy as a humanitarian policy. However, it still remains possible that Jackson and his followers were motivated by feelings of benevolence to support the policy of Indian removal. The evidence presented here shows clearly that there were many poor Cherokee households in the Southeast prior to removal. Perhaps the obvious presence of these indigent Cherokees caused Jackson and his supporters to overlook the larger number of Cherokee households that were producing substantial surpluses. There is no doubt that supporters of removal claimed that they had carefully weighed the evidence for Cherokee progress against the evidence that suggested increasing misery. For example, Cass asserted:

> We are as unwilling to underrate, as we should be to overrate, the progress made by these Indians in civilization and improvement. . . . We hope that our opinion upon this subject may be erroneous. But we have melancholy forebodings. That a few principal men, who can secure favorable cotton lands, and cultivate them with slaves, will be comfortable and satisfied, we may well believe. . . . But to form just conceptions of the spirit and objects of these efforts, we must look at their practical operation on the community. It is here, if the facts which have been stated to us are correct, and of which we have no doubt, that they will be found wanting. (1830, pp. 71–2)

Did supporters of the Cherokee removal deliberately understate the extent of economic progress in the Eastern Cherokee Nation? Certainly, the political end of instituting a general policy of Indian removal was well

served by understating the size of the surplus-producing class of Cherokees. Moreover, the practical effect of removal was the transfer of rents in
the form of improved acreage capable of surplus production to white
farmers. A thorough analysis of the political economy of the Cherokee
removal might find that the policy was a politically pragmatic transfer of
wealth from Cherokee households to white farmers, even if the supporters of removal believed at the time that it was also a humanitarian
policy toward an indigenous population.

References

Cass, Lewis, "Removal of the Indians," *The North American Review*, 30 (Jan.
    1830), pp. 62–120.
Gray, Lewis C., *History of Agriculture in the Southern United States to 1860*, 2 vols.
    (Gloucester, MA, 1958).
Hurt, R. Douglas, *Indian Agriculture in America: Prehistory to the Present* (Lawr-
    ence, KS, 1987).
Lebergott, Stanley, *The Americans: An Economic Record* (New York, 1984).
McLoughlin, William G., *Cherokee Renascence in the New Republic* (Princeton,
    1986).
McLoughlin, William G., and Walter H. Conser, Jr., "The Cherokees in Transi-
    tion: A Statistical Analysis of the Federal Cherokee Census of 1835," *The
    Journal of American History*, 64 (Dec. 1977), pp. 678–703.
Perdue, Theda, *Slavery and the Evolution of Cherokee Society: 1540–1866* (Knox-
    ville, TN, 1979).
Prucha, Francis Paul, "Andrew Jackson's Indian Policy: A Reassessment," *The
    Journal of American History*, 66 (Dec. 1969), pp. 527–39.
Remini, Robert V., *Andrew Jackson and the Course of American Democracy, 1833–
    1845*, 2 vols. (New York, 1984).
Shadburn, Donald L., *Cherokee Planters in Georgia: 1832–1838* (Roswell, GA,
    1990).
Weiman, David F., "Farmers and the Market in Antebellum America: A View
    from the Georgia Upcountry," *Journal of Economic History*, 47 (Sept. 1987),
    pp. 627–47.
Wilms, Douglas C., "Cherokee Indian Land Use in Georgia, 1800–1838"
    (Ph.D. diss., University of Georgia, Athens, 1973).
Young, Mary, "The Exercise of Sovereignty in Cherokee Georgia," *Journal of the
    Early Republic*, 10 (Spring 1990), pp. 43–63.

Documents

After Cherokee lands were sold to the United States as part of the removal
process, individual Cherokees were then to be compensated for their houses,
outbuildings, and fields. To determine the value of each family's "improve-

ments," US agents conducted a census as called for in the Treaty of New Echota (1835). Since removal pressures had already thrown the Cherokee economy into disarray, the 1835 census cannot completely capture Cherokee society free from US intervention. Chief John Ross, for example, is listed on the 1835 census as living in Red Clay, Tennessee. His home was actually in Georgia, but the state of Georgia had dispossessed him and other prominent Cherokees of their lands as a way to pressure the federal government to proceed with Cherokee removal. Still, as David Wishart points out, this census is an unusually detailed document for its time and a valuable resource for historical study.

Wishart analyzed the entire sample of data from the 1835 census with the help of a computer, which is the ideal approach. However, the raw data are also worth studying with an eye to picking out patterns: Were there any characteristics shared by the majority of Cherokees? Were there significant differences within Cherokee society? Listed below are data on sixty households from throughout the Cherokee Nation. To conserve space, this version reprints about a third of the queries appearing on the original census form. The original form asked close to forty questions, many of which remained blank for most households. Few Cherokee families owned mills, grew wheat, or identified as "Mixed Catawbys," "Mixed Spaniards," or "Mixed negroes." Of these sixty households, only two men, Jonathan Mulkey and John Ross, owned ferry boats. In contrast, nearly every household had "spinsters" and almost as many "weavers," women who were spinning and weaving cloth, probably from cotton the Cherokees grew themselves.

In the abridged version below, the first three columns list the number of Cherokee men over age 18 and Cherokee women over age 16 followed by the total number of Cherokees, including children, living in each household. Thus, Quatie Hare of Red Clay, Tennessee headed a household of seven Cherokees: two men over 18, four women over 16, and to bring the total up to seven, one child. Quatie, by the way, is a woman's name. The column labeled "Whites" refers to "Whites connected by marriage." In terms of agricultural statistics, the census asked mainly about corn production – how much was raised, sold, or bought. Although Cherokee agriculture was diversified, corn was an important staple, which the censusmakers intended to use to measure productivity and land value. The census also asked how many in each household could read English and how many could read Cherokee. Finally, the original census form asked how many in the household were "Half-breeds," "Quadroons" (which appears to have meant one-fourth Cherokee), or "Full blooded." As a racial category, quadroon never caught on; so few checked the "quadroon" category, there was little point including it here. We know that Chief John Ross was genealogically one-eighth Cherokee and that the single "Full blooded" person in his household was probably his wife. And yet, his children were not listed as "quadroons." According to the

Census Roll, 1835, of the Cherokee Indians East of the Mississippi, Microcopy No. T-496

Household Head	Cherokees			Slaves	Whites	Acres Cultivated	Bushels of corn			Readers		Blood	
	M18+	F16+	Total				Raised	Sold	Bought	Eng.	Cher.	Half	Full
(p. 5) Red Clay, TN													
Quatie Hare	2	4	7			55	400	150	4	3	3	4	2
James Chisolm		2	3		1	2	700	400	60	1		3	1
Five Killer	1		6		1	10				1			
Feather	2	1	8			10	200		35		3		8
David Timpson	1	1	7			9	200	60		4		7	
Sam Smith	3	3	14			24	175			4	7	14	
Saml. Ballard		1	5		1	70	600			1			
Ruthy Taylor		2	8			8	50		15	1		8	5
Susy Otterlifter		3	3	3		8	60		5	2	1	3	
William Conner	1		8		1	20			40	3			
David Downing			2		1	1			10			2	
Jonathan Mulkey	1	1	3	3	1	20			15	2			
John Ross	2	1	7	19		60			100	5	1	6	1
Cotaquesky	1	1	10				150						1
Black Fox	2	1	3			2							3
(p. 16) Wills Valley, AL													
Pipe	1	1	4			10	200				2		4
Young Duck	4	4	14			5	60				4		14
Cumberland	2	2	6			8	80			1	3		6
Alley Lasley	1	2	7			20	300			4	2	5	2
Wm. Lasley	3	2	9	2		117	3,000	500		3		7	2
Crawler	1	1	4			3	50			3	2		4
David Gage	1	3	4		1	152	3,000			1			3
Nelson K. Harlin	1	1	2	1		12	100			2	2	2	
Ooh tah he tah	4	6	27								1		27
John O. Nicholson	1	1	2	1		15	200			2			
(p. 16) Turkey Town, AL													
Path Killer	1	2	5			1	10				3		5
Senoway	1	1	3								1		1
Writer	1	1	8			10	150						8
Johnson	1	1	4			5	100						4

(Contd)

Seeds	4	1	7			5	75					7
(p. 33) Haywood County, NC												
The Shy Fellow	1	1	3			2	20					3
Nanney Reed		3	11						1	8	10	1
Ootiee	2	2	7			8	150					7
Widow Bags	2	2	8			4	50			4		8
Slim Jakee	1	1	6			4	30			1		6
Cholah	1	1	5			2	20					5
Chickasatter	1	1	7			3	60					7
Coluti	1	3	8			2	20			1		8
Ground Squirrel		1	3			6	100			1		3
Ned	1	2	5			4	30					5
Heawlugah	2	1	7			3	30			1		7
The old man	1	2	3			2 1/2	25			3		3
Alekah	1	1	4			8	25			2		4
Allbones	1	2	5			6	30			1		5
Saka		3	3			1/4	5					3
(p. 45) Ahmacolola River, GA												
Scouteha	3	3	11			25	300	14				11
Paunch Lifter	1	2	6			25	500			1		6
Snip	1	1	2			18	200	20				2
Beaver Toter	1	1	6			10	100					6
Black Bird	2	3	10			12	200	8		1		10
Cloud	2	2	8			8	80			3		8
Nancy		2	6			3	40				2	4
(p. 45) Etowah, GA												
James Landrum	5	3	15	8	1	218	750			2	12	
Charles Landrum	1	1	3	1		20	300			1	1	
Sam Thommas		1	3		1	10	230	50		1		
Charles Bag	1	1	3									
Jesse Cochran	1	1	4			25	80	30		1	2	2
Cheuy	1	1	4			4	50	6				5
John Proctor Sr.	2	2	7			40	500	250		1		7
John Proctor Jr.	1	1	4			30	375	160		1		4

Excerpts from *Census Roll, 1835, of Cherokee Indians East of the Mississippi.* **National Archives Microfilm Collection T496.**

census, his household consisted of one "Full blooded" person and six "Half-breeds." "Mixed blood" and "full blood" became commonly used terms in Cherokee society in the nineteenth century. Although seemingly biological or racial categories, "mixed" and "full" more often encapsulated a person's lifestyle, clothing, social values, and associations.

★   ★   ★

As the official newspaper of the Cherokee Nation, *The Cherokee Phoenix* represented the Nation's formal position on removal and opposed it. When Elias Boudinot, editor of the newspaper, determined in the early 1830s that the Cherokees' only viable choice was to accept removal and negotiate for the most favorable terms, Chief John Ross insisted that Boudinot give up his position as public spokesman of the Nation's sentiments. The following documents come from 1828 and 1830 issues of the *Phoenix*, when Boudinot was still in charge of the newspaper and still anti-removal. The first document is a summary of a census the Cherokee Nation conducted in 1824 to measure their economic progress. The eight districts of the Cherokee Nation, by which the 1824 census is organized, equate to state boundaries roughly as follows: Aquohee (North Carolina); Ahmohee (Tennessee); Chattooga (Alabama); and Chickamauga, Taquohee, Coosawattee, Etowah/High Tower, and Hickory Log (Georgia). Then, there are two Boudinot editorials, both of which take US removal advocates to task for misrepresenting Cherokee economic conditions.

Three Excerpts *from* The Cherokee Phoenix

Statistical Tables of the Several Districts Composing the Cherokee Nation (Wednesday June 18, 1828)

In 1824 a resolution was passed by the Legislature of the Cherokee Nation, appointing and authorising eight persons to take the census of the Nation, and to prepare correct statistical tables of each District. The general result has been laid before the public. Our object in inserting the following tables which we copy from a pamphlet is to show that, if possessions can be considered as indicating the progress of civilization, some of the Districts are considerably farther advanced in improvement than others.

Three excerpts from *The Cherokee Phoenix*: "Statistical Tables of the several Districts composing the Cherokee Nation," June 18, 1828; "Indian Emigration," May 14, 1828; untitled, April 21, 1830.

COOSEWAYTEE DISTRICT.

POPULATION.

Males under 18 years of age	529	
Males from 18 to 59 years of age	515	
Males over 59 years of age	67	
Total number of males	—	1,111
Females under 15 years of age	476	
Females from 15 to 40 years	174	
Females over 40 years of age	539	
Total number of females	—	1,205
Total of males and females		2,316
Male slaves 168 ⎱ Total		
Female slaves 127 ⎰		295
Whole Population		2,611

In this District, there are twenty-seven white men married to Cherokee women, and twenty Cherokees married to white women.

There are in this District, 2,944 black cattle, 1,207 horses, 4,965 swine, 369 sheep, ninety one goats, 113 looms, 397 spinning wheels, thirty-three wagons, 461 ploughs, five saw-mills, five grist mills, ten blacksmith shops, two Missionary Schools in operation, in which are twenty one scholars of both sexes.

TAHQUOA DISTRICT

Males under 18 years of age	357	
Males from 18 to 59 years of age	301	
Males over 59 years of age	35	
Total number of males	—	693
Females under 15 years of age	301	
Females from 15 to 40 years	328	
Females over 40 years of age	37	
Total number of females	—	666
Total of males and females		1,359
Male negroes 7 ⎱ Total		
Females negroes 17 ⎰		24
Whole population		1,383

There are in this District, eight white men married to Cherokee women, and one Cherokee man married to a white woman.

There are in this District, 211 spinning wheels, one grist mill, one blacksmith shop, 308 ploughs, fifty-three looms, 323 sheep, 2,419 swine, 1,506 black cattle, 554 horses.

CHICKAMAUGA DISTRICT.

Males under 18 years of age	484	
Males from 18 to 59 years of age	396	
Males over 59 years of age	43	
Total number of males	—	923
Females under 15 years of age	298	
Females from 15 to 40 years	374	
Females over 40 years of age	131	
Total number of females	—	803
Total of males and females		1,726
Male negroes 90 ⎱ Total		187
Female negroes 97 ⎰		
Whole population		1,913

There are in this District, fifteen white men married to Cherokee women, and four Cherokee men married to white women.

There are in this District four Schools and seventy-two scholars of both sexes, a grist mill, two saw-mills, one cotton gin, 121 looms, 368 spinning wheels – eighteen wagons, 354 ploughs, 1,175 horses, 2,505 black cattle, 8,900 swine, 111 goats, eleven blacksmith shops, five ferries, four stores, and 397 sheep.

HICKORY LOG DISTRICT.

Males under 18 years of age	397	
Males from 18 to 59 years of age	300	
Males over 59 years of age	42	
Total number of males	—	739
Females under 15 years of age	345	
Females from 15 to 40 years	336	
Females over 40 years of age	113	
Total number of females	—	794
Total of males and females		1,533
Male slaves ⎱ Total		
Female slaves ⎰		
Whole population		1,533

There are in this District, twenty Cherokees married to white women, and forty white men married to Cherokee women.

There are in this District, five blacksmith shops, thirty-two wagons, one cotton gin, one saw-mill, two stores, 187 head of sheep, twenty-four goats, 3,178 swine, 1,733 black cattle, 520 horses, 232 spinning wheels, 76 looms, and farming utensils in proportion, of all descriptions.

AQUOHEE DISTRICT.

Males under 18 years of age	561	
Males from 18 to 59 years of age	607	
Males over 59 years of age	77	
Total number of males	—	1,245
Females under 15 years of age	699	
Females from 15 to 40 years	522	
Females over 40 years of age	98	
Total number of females	—	1,319
Total of males and females		2,564
Male negroes	10 ⎫ Total	
Female negroes	9 ⎭	19
Whole population		2,583

There are in this District, four white men married to Cherokee women.

There are in this District, one Missionary School of fifty scholars, 1,191 horses, 1,799 black cattle, 5,544 swine, 765 sheep, thirty-seven goats, one saw-mill, one grist mill, 446 ploughs, 145 looms, 346 spinning wheels, five blacksmith shops, seven wagons.

AHMOHEE DISTRICT.

Males under 18 years of age	386	
Males from 18 to 59 years of age	300	
Males over 59 years of age	31	
Total number of males	—	717
Females under 15 years of age	338	
Females from 15 to 40 years	299	
Females over 40 years of age	58	
Total number of females	—	695
Total of males and females		1,412
Male slaves	73 ⎫ Total	
Female slaves	69 ⎭	142
Total population		1,554

There are in this District, eleven Cherokees married to white women, and twenty-eight white men married to Cherokee women.

There are in this District, five Schools and twenty-seven scholars of both sexes, seven blacksmith shops, one turnpike, five ferries, six public roads, one threshing machine, one store, ninety-three goats, 243 sheep, 6,080 swine, 1,730 cattle, 845 horses, 372 ploughs, seventy looms, 327 spinning wheels, twenty-nine wagons, three saw-mills, six grist mills, two cotton gins.

CHATTOOGA DISTRICT.

Males under 18 years of age	420	
Males from 18 to 59 years of age	400	
Males over 59 years of age	30	
Total number of males	—	850
Females under 15 years of age	339	
Females from 15 to 40 years	365	
Females over 40 years of age	95	
Total number of females	—	799
Total of males and females		1,649
Male negroes 122 ⎫ Total		292
Female negroes 170 ⎭		
Total population		1,941

There are in this District, eighteen white men married to Cherokee women, and three Cherokee men married to white women.

There are in this District, 6 schools in which are ninety-two scholars of both sexes; and 1,318 horses, 7,018 cattle, 4,654 swine, 335 sheep, fifteen goats, 124 looms, 307 wheels, 446 ploughs, eleven blacksmith shops, five grist mills, two cotton gins, one sawmill, and two stores.

HIGH TOWER DISTRICT.

Males under 18 years of age	347	
Males from 18 to 59 years of age	325	
Males over 59 years of age	26	
Total number of males	—	698
Females under 15 years of age	300	
Females from 15 to 40 years	306	
Females over 40 years of age	71	
Total number of females	—	677
Total of males and females		1,375
Male negroes 43 ⎫ Total		79
Female negroes 36 ⎭		
Total population		1,454

In this District, there are four white men married to Cherokee women, and two Cherokee men married to white women.

There is in this District one School, in which are twenty scholars of both sexes; and 818 horses, 3,170 cattle, 3,777 swine, 298 sheep, 67 goats, 67 looms, 65 ploughs, five blacksmith shops, two mills, 240 wheels, and eleven wagons.

Indian Emigration

(Wednesday May 14, 1828)

Col. Thomas L. McKenney, late special Agent to the Southern Indians, in a letter to the Secretary of war, dated Choctaw Country, Oct. 10th, 1828, makes an estimate of the probable expense of removing the Chickasaw Indians. The utmost extent of cost is estimated at 494,750 dollars, including the cost of a visit to examine the country, the cost of their houses, mills, work shops, orchards, fences, and their stock of all kinds, all which are to be replaced by the United States. According to the foundation which Col. McKenney has laid down, we make the following estimate of the probable cost of the removal of the Cherokees (if that were to be the case).

The population of the Cherokee Nation, we will put down at 13,000, (which is below the actual number). We will suppose (following Col. McKenney's suppositions) the families to average five souls, which will give 2,600 houses. These houses, we do not suppose can be built for less than an average cost of 200 dollars, which in our opinion is quite moderate. Most of these houses it is true, are poor, and may be built for a small amount, yet there are many which will require the double and trible of what we put down as an average cost. – Few of the best houses cannot be built for less sums than two, three, and four thousand dollars, including barns, cribs, &c. – This part of the expense will then be $520,000.

The number of mills, grist, and saw, is fifty, which may be replaced for the sum of $25,000, supposing each mill to cost $500.

Their shops are sixty two in number, and these estimated at $50 each will cost $5,000.

Their orchards perhaps may be replaced for $3,000.

The fences of the Chickasaws are estimated by Col. McKenney at $50,000. $200,000 will then be but a moderate estimate for this item of the expense attending the removal of the Cherokees.

There are in this Nation 7,683 horses, these at $40 per head, will cost $307,320.

22,531 black cattle at $10 per head will cost $225,310.

46,700 hogs owned by the Cherokees, at $3 per head, will cost $140,100.

The probable cost of a visit to examine the country, may be the same as estimated by Col. McKenney, $10,000, and of their removal to it, $350,000. This is by no means an extravagant estimate, for Col. McKenney puts down the cost of the removal of the Chickasaws, who are but four thousand in number, at $100,000.

The total amount of cost, then, for the foregoing items, will be $1,783,730. And supposing we add a fourth for the expense of the

Government, the Schools, the military, and other items not enumerated, the whole amount of expense in removing the Cherokees beyond the limits of any State or Territory will be $2,229,662.

If this project is intended, as we are told by its advocates, for the good and civilization of the Cherokees and other Indians, cannot this sum be put to a better use? – Supposing with this money, the United States begin to establish Schools in every part of this Nation? With this money let there be a college founded, where every advantage of instruction may be enjoyed. Let books, tracts, &c. be published in Cherokee and English, and distributed throughout the Nation and every possible effort be made to civilize us, let us at the same time be protected in our rights. What would be the consequence? If we fail to improve under such efforts, we will then agree to remove.

(April 21, 1830)

The Committee on Indian Affairs in the House of Representatives, in page 21 of their report say:

"That the greatest portion, even of the poorest class of the Southern Indians, may, for some years yet, find the means of sustaining life, is probable; but, when the game is all gone, as it soon must be, and their physical as well as moral energies shall have undergone the farther decline, which the entire failure of the resources of the chase has never failed to mark in their downward career, the hideous features in their prospects will become more manifest."

Whoever really believes that the Cherokees subsist on game, is most wretchedly deceived, and is grossly ignorant of existing facts. *The Cherokees do not live upon the chase*, but upon the fruits of the earth produced by their labour. We should like to see any person point to a single family in this nation who obtain their clothing and provisions by hunting. *We* know of no one. We do not wish to be understood as saying that they do not hunt – they do hunt some, probably, about as much as white people do in new countries, but they no more depend upon this occupation for living than new settlers do. Game has been nearly extinct for the last thirty years, and even previous to that, when the Cherokees depended upon the chase for subsistence, they were obliged to obtain their full supply of meat and skins out of what is now the limits of this nation. Cut off the last vestige of game in these woods, and you cannot starve the Cherokees – they have plenty of corn, and domestic animals, and they raise their own cotton, and manufacture their own clothing.

The committee do not mean to exaggerate, either in the statement of facts, as they are believed to exist, or in the deductions which they make from them, as to the future prospects of the Indians.

The Committee have, nevertheless, greatly exaggerated – all their statements, of what they call *facts*, are nothing but unfounded assertions.

"The intelligent observer of their character will confirm all that is predicted of their future condition, when he learns that the maxim, so well established in other places, 'that an Indian cannot work,' has lost none of its universality in the practice of the Indians of the South; that there, too, the same improvidence and thirst for spirituous liquors attend them, that have been the foes of their happiness elsewhere; that the condition of the common Indian is perceptibly declining, both in the means of subsistence, and the habits necessary to procure them; and that, upon the whole, the mass of the population of the Southern Indian tribes are a less respectable order of human beings now, than they were ten years ago."

The maxim of our enemies, "that an Indian cannot work," the committee suppose "well established," and it would most certainly be well established if they could but prove their naked assertions. We know of many Indians who not only *work*, but work *hard*. Who labors for the Cherokee and builds his house, clears his farm, makes his fences, attends to his hogs, cattle and horses; who raises his corn, his cotton and manufactures his clothing? Can the committee tell? Yes, they have an answer at hand. He has no house, no farm, no hogs, cattle, no corn to save him from starvation, and clothing to cover him from nakedness. We know not what to say to such assertions. The above maxim has been received by many as truth, but not by the intelligent observers of their character, but by their enemies and such as have not had the means of knowing facts. But suppose it was once well founded and correctly applied, it has long since lost its universality. We invite any person who may be hesitating on this point to come and see and judge for himself – we are not afraid that the truth, the whole truth, should be known – we desire it – we invite "the most rigid scrutiny."

"That an Indian has an inherent thirst for spirituous liquor," is another maxim which the committee think is well applied to the Cherokees. On the charge of intemperance, we are very far from pleading *not guilty* – we have ourselves raised our voice against this crying sin. But if the charge is, that the Cherokees have greater thirst for spirits than whitemen, we unhesitatingly deny it. It is not so – we speak from personal observation. Facts form the only proper criterion in this case, and what is the actual state of things? We know, most certainly know that among the whites of the surrounding counties intemperance and brutal intoxication (at which humanity may well shudder,) may be witnessed in every neighborhood. Go to their elections and courts and number those who are under the influence of inebriating drink, and then come into the nation, and visit the Indian elections, courts and the General Council and make a disinterested comparison, and we pledge ourselves that there is less intemperance exhibited here on these occasions than among the whites. It is an incontrovertible fact, for the truth of which we appeal to all honest eye-witnesses, that on these public occasions, particularly at the General Council, which continues four weeks, a drunken Indian is seldom to be seen. We are sorry that intemperance does exist, but is it not universal? There has been of late considerable reformation among the Cherokees, in common with other parts of the country.

Against the statement of the committee that "the condition of the common Indian is perceptibly declining," we must give our unbiassed testimony, and appeal to facts repeatedly made public – *the common Indian among the Cherokees is not declining, but rising.*

"The Cherokees are generally understood to have made further advances in civilization than the neighboring tribes, and a description of their real situation may make it of less importance to notice, in detail, the condition of the others. Upon this point, the committee feel sensibly the want of that statistical and accurate information, without which, they are aware that they cannot expect their representations to be received with entire confidence. To supply this deficiency, however, they have sought information from every proper source within their reach, and do not fear that the general correctness of their statements will be confirmed by the most rigid scrutiny."

Here then is the great mystery – *the committee feel sensibly the want of* STATISTICAL *and* ACCURATE *information!* This accounts for their misrepresentations. – But was it impossible to obtain correct statistical information? They thought so we presume, for they sought it "from every *proper source.*" If they had only applied for testimonies which disinterested persons would not consider *improper*, the information would most easily have been obtained. *We* could have furnished them with a true copy of a statistical table taken in 1824, & by inquiring at the Agency, we doubt not they could have found another taken in 1810. By comparing these they would have formed a true foundation for facts and accurate deductions. But no, such a course would not possibly answer – they must seek information from somewhere else, not from documents, and resident whitemen, but from the enemies of the Indians, who are looking with eager expectation to their removal, that they may take possession of the spoil, obtained by means the most unmanly and iniquitous.

Further Reading

McLoughlin, William G. *Cherokee Renascence in the New Republic.* Princeton: Princeton University Press, 1986.

Perdue, Theda, ed. *Cherokee Editor: The Writings of Elias Boudinot.* Knoxville: University of Tennessee Press, 1983.

Perdue, Theda. *Slavery and the Evolution of Cherokee Society, 1540–1866.* Knoxville: University of Tennessee Press, 1979.

Thornton, Russell. *The Cherokees: A Population History.* Lincoln: University of Nebraska Press, 1990.

Wallace, Anthony F. C. *The Long, Bitter Trail: Andrew Jackson and the Indians.* New York: Hill and Wang, 1993.

Wilkins, Thurman. *Cherokee Tragedy: The Ridge Family and the Decimation of a People.* 2nd edn. Norman: University of Oklahoma Press, 1986.

5

Sacred Places

Introduction

The Battle of Little Big Horn was a fight for the Black Hills, *Paha Sapa* to the Lakotas (Sioux). The mountainous western part of South Dakota, *Paha Sapa* was the heart of the Lakota nation in the nineteenth century. A century or two before, the Lakotas had lived further to the east, in what is now the eastern Dakotas and Minnesota, but then, for a variety of reasons, they had migrated onto the northern plains. Most important, Europeans brought horses to the Americas. Adopting the horse made the Lakotas more mobile. They traversed greater distances and became more dependent on buffalo as the mainstay of their economy. Other factors are a matter of scholarly debate. Some historians argue that, despite the impact of European diseases, the Lakotas flourished in the eighteenth and nineteenth centuries, and as a consequence their expanding population impinged on lands inhabited by the Crows, Pawnees, and other Indians to the Lakotas' west and south. Another common explanation for the westward migration is that European settlement created a domino effect across the continent. As Europeans occupied the eastern seaboard, Indians were both drawn west to keep up with the fur trade and pushed west by the loss of land. Warfare between Indian nations escalated as the Ojibwes moved onto Dakota territory; the Dakotas then pushed their relatives the Lakotas farther west onto Crow territory.

In any case, by the mid-nineteenth century, the United States began to express interest in the northern plains, particularly as a wagon and railroad thoroughfare for American settlers heading to the west coast. In the 1868

Treaty of Fort Laramie, the Lakotas and US treaty commissioners formally demarcated the boundaries of the Great Sioux Nation, at the center of which stood the Black Hills. Within a few years, however, a gold discovery brought hordes of prospectors to the area, accompanied by American soldiers purportedly instructed to maintain order. When Lakota appeals to the United States to honor the treaty went ignored and when the Lakotas refused to sell *Paha Sapa*, war broke out. The Battle of Little Big Horn, though a victory for the Lakotas and their allies the Cheyennes and Arapahoes, brought the US army out in full force. With the help of a harsh winter and dwindling buffalo herds, the United States defeated the Lakotas. In the Fort Robinson Agreement (1877), the United States took possession of the Black Hills. In a 1979 ruling, however, the United States acknowledged that the Fort Robinson Agreement violated the Treaty of Fort Laramie, and the Lakotas were awarded $17½ million, plus interest, as compensation for the Black Hills. The eight Sioux Tribes encompassed by the ruling refused to accept monetary payment, declaring that "The Black Hills are not for sale." The money, now over $500 million, sits in a US bank account held in trust for the tribes, should they ever vote to accept it.

The Black Hills judgment arrived at the figure of $17½ million by calculating the economic value of the land acre-by-acre but did not grapple with how to put a value on the Black Hills as a sacred place. Linea Sundstrom's "The Sacred Black Hills: An Ethnohistorical Review" argues that there is considerable evidence in nineteenth-century records to show that the Lakotas and other Indians on the northern plains thought of the Black Hills in this way. The region served as a rendezvous for the Sun Dance, a site for young men to retreat to for powerful visions, and a repository of important historical, or mythological, landmarks: Harney Peak (Owl Maker Hill), Bear Butte, the Racetrack, Wind Cave, and others. That the Lakotas migrated to the area a few centuries ago has diminished, in some eyes, their claims to the area as sacred; however, this view presumes that Lakota culture cannot change without becoming less Lakota. As Sundstrom suggests, Lakota history, religion, and relationships to land – their sacred geography – would be better conceptualized as constantly adapting through a mix of the old and the new.

The Sacred Black Hills: An Ethnohistorical Review
Linea Sundstrom

The Black Hills area is widely recognized as sacred in the context of traditional Lakota and Cheyenne belief systems. Questions arise, however, regarding the authenticity and historical depth of these beliefs. Some researchers assert that the concept of the sacred Black Hills is little more than a twentieth century scheme to promote tourism or part of a legal strategy to gain the return of Black Hills lands to Lakota and Cheyenne tribal governments. While many Lakotas and Cheyennes today express a strong spiritual link to the Black Hills, some historians have questioned whether today's beliefs about the Black Hills have historic precedents. Watson Parker questions whether the Lakotas could have developed a sacred geography in the relatively short time they occupied the Black Hills. Donald Worster concedes that the Black Hills are now widely regarded as sacred to the Lakota people, but asserts that the area was not viewed as holy ground prior to the 1970s.[1]

The position that the Black Hills held little significance to Indians is most frequently based on two sources: Richard I. Dodge's *The Black Hills*, written in 1875, and Edwin Denig's *Five Indian Tribes of the Upper Missouri*, written in 1854. Both assert that the Lakotas then living in the area made little use of the Black Hills, venturing in only to gather tipi poles. Dodge and Denig state that the Lakotas avoided the Black Hills because game was scarce, pasturage was insufficient for horses, and there were "superstitions" about evil spirits inhabiting the mountains. This information has been cited with little regard to the historical context in which it was compiled.

Denig reported that "much superstition is attached to the Black Hills by the Indian," incorrectly attributing this "superstition" to volcanic action causing smoke and loud noises in the interior mountains. While later writers mentioned loud, booming noises in the Black Hills, there is no evidence for any recent volcanic activity in the area, and the phenomenon remains unconfirmed and unexplained. Denig's informants told him the noises were the groans of a Great White Giant condemned to lie under the mountains as punishment for intruding into the Lakotas' hunting ground

Sundstrom, Linea. "The Sacred Black Hills: An Ethnohistorical Review." *Great Plains Quarterly* 17 (Summer/Fall 1997): 185–212. Illustration: From Amos Bad Heart Bull and Helen H. Blish, *A Pictographic History of the Oglala Sioux*. Lincoln: University of Nebraska Press, 1967, p. 289.

and as a lesson to all whites to stay out of the area, a story clearly meant to scare whites away from the Black Hills. Denig himself had no personal interest in the opening of the Black Hills to white settlement, but seems merely to have been repeating what his informants told him.

The same cannot be said of Dodge. The thesis of his later book, *Our Wild Indians*, was that Native Americans entirely lacked morality and were something less than human, and the theme of *The Black Hills* was the need to get the area into the hands of whites who could extract wealth from the natural resources wasted under Indian occupation. He foresaw stock ranches, cities, and tourist hotels springing up in the country as soon as the "miserable nomads" could "be got rid of."

In this context, Dodge quotes a Lakota named Robe Raiser, whom he had met with two mixed-blood men, all prospecting for gold on Rapid Creek. According to Robe Raiser, Indians of his band entered the Black Hills only occasionally to hunt or cut tipi poles and usually avoided the area because it was the abode of spirits, had little game and many flies, was too rainy, was bad for horses, and had frequent violent thunderstorms. Dodge implies that other Indians confirmed Robe Raiser's information, but nowhere in his diary or book does he specifically mention speaking with any other Indian. Robe Raiser's comments, like those of Denig's informants, imply that the interior Black Hills were avoided at least in part because they were considered holy ground, "the abode of spirits."

Overall, both *The Black Hills* and *Our Wild Indians* are rife with error and should not be cited uncritically. For example, Dodge's statement that the interior Black Hills contained no evidence of Indian habitation is now entirely refuted by more than 3,000 archaeological sites recorded for this area. Even Dodge's own diary and the report of the 1874 Black Hills Expedition specifically mention discovery of old Indian campsites in the Black Hills.

Dodge's Black Hills diary is a study in self-contradiction. One passage describes "a great Indian trail as large as a wagon road." Another mentions seeing the remains of Indian camps "all along the day's route." Later, however, these observations are replaced with assertions that the area was never used except for gathering lodge poles. The changes coincide with Dodge's recognition of the great potential of the Black Hills to white entrepreneurs, but whether they were truly coincidental is impossible to know. In alternately describing the Black Hills as void of evidence of Indian habitation and full of such evidence, Dodge seems to have made a distinction between the interior uplift and peripheral zones. In fact there is much less evidence for sacred places in the interior than in the outer edges of the Black Hills.

Neither Dodge nor Denig contradicts the assertion that the Black Hills were sacred to the Lakota people. The "superstition" they noted is simply a biased description of the Indians' religious beliefs about the area. In Dodge's Black Hills diary, he reports finding the site of a Medicine Lodge (Sun Dance) encampment on Castle Creek, well inside the western Black Hills. If the Indians did not use the area for camps, it was not because the mountains lacked religious significance. Neither writer addressed the possibility that the Black Hills were sacred to earlier groups inhabiting the area.

From a more objective perspective, Donald Worster writes that the Lakotas did not mention anything about the sacredness of the Black Hills until the dawning of a religious revitalization movement in the 1970s.[2] Worster implies that current views of the sacredness of the Black Hills are the product of this revitalization movement, which followed decades of frustration in attempting to regain an economic foothold after the extinction of the bison herds that had been their mainstay and the forced removal of the Lakotas to non-arable lands. Worster notes that Lakota testimony before various treaty and claims commissions stressed the economic, not spiritual, value of the Black Hills and asserts that no documentary evidence before the 1970s suggests that the Black Hills were the Lakotas' sacred place.

The question of the sacredness, or lack thereof, of the Black Hills to Native American groups demands a more exacting view. The question must be rephrased: what portions of the area, if any, were considered sacred, when, and by whom?

Published ethnographic and ethnohistoric accounts provide evidence of whether the Black Hills were considered sacred historically by various Native peoples or whether their "sacredness" is merely a product of a clever tourist promotion or legal strategy. Such information explores the historical depth of present-day traditions and beliefs and provides a framework for building more detailed understandings of the traditional or sacred landscape. Ethnographic and historic sources used here are generally limited to information collected at least fifty years ago, long before the 1970s and within the lifetimes of people who had enjoyed the freedom of movement, and concomitant geographic competence, of the pre-reservation era. In some instances, more recent information, such as James LaPointe's 1976 compilation of Lakota legends, is included when it is consistent with and supported by older references.[3]

Lakota Sacred Places

Historic and ethnographic sources indicate that both specific locations and specific kinds of places were sacred to the Lakotas. Specific locations in and near the Black Hills mentioned as sacred include Bear Lodge

Figure 1 *Amos Bad Heart Bull's map of the Black Hills.* Reproduced from *A Pictographic History of the Oglala Sioux*, by Amos Bad Heart Bull, text by Helen H. Blish, by permission of the University of Nebraska Press. Copyright © 1967 by the University of Nebraska Press. Copyright © renewed 1995 by the University of Nebraska Press.

Butte (Devils Tower), Bear Butte, the Racetrack or Red Valley, Buffalo Gap, Craven Canyon, Gillette Prairie, the Hot Springs-Minnekahta area, Inyan Kara Mountain, Harney Peak, Black Buttes, White Butte, and Rapid Creek Valley.

A historic Lakota map of the Black Hills shows most of these localities. Between 1890 and 1913, Amos Bad Heart Bull made an extensive series of drawings, interpreted and printed after his death, that record the history and traditions of the Oglala division of the Lakota alliance. His map of the Black Hills (figure 1) shows eight features of known religious significance. A yellow band surrounding the Black Hills is labeled *Ki Inyanka Ocanku* (The Racetrack). This refers to a circular depression surrounding the interior uplift, still known as the Racetrack or Red Valley. Other features shown and labeled on the map are: *Mato Tipi Paha* (Bear Lodge Butte or Devils Tower); *Hinyankagapa* (Inyan Kara Mountain); *Baha Sapa* (Black Buttes); *Re Sla* (Gillette Prairie); *Mato Baha* (Bear Butte); *Mini Kata* (Hot Springs); *Pte Tali Yapa* (Buffalo Gap); and *Miniluzan* (Rapid Creek). Each of these features is discussed separately below.

Was Bad Heart Bull participating in a latter-day conspiracy to designate the Black Hills sacred land so that the Lakotas could demand their return? Such a conclusion ignores the historical context of the creation of the map. Bad Heart Bull made the map, and the rest of his pictographic history, simply to record the story of his people as tribal historians remembered it. He never attempted to publish or publicize his work, and few people outside his family knew of it until it was "discovered" in 1926, thirteen years after his death. His family, extremely reluctant to share the manuscript with outsiders, eventually agreed to let Helen Blish record and study the drawings and their notations. When Bad Heart Bull's sister died in 1947, the manuscript was interred with her. Bad Heart Bull was hardly attempting to mislead whites about the religious significance of the Black Hills. Neither he nor Blish's Oglala informants identified the map specifically as a chart of sacred locales, although other information confirms the sacred nature of the features shown on the map. Besides being literally buried, the map was figuratively buried among the 408 drawings comprising the entire manuscript.

Inyan Kara Mountain. Bad Heart Bull's written notation on the map identifies one peak as *Hinyankagapa*, which Blish translates as Ghost Butte. Similarly, Cheyenne informants told John Bourke in 1877, "Inyan Kara Peak they [the Lakotas] call *ihancaja-paja*, that is to say the hill where the ghosts live." These terms are variants of *Iⁿyaⁿ Kaga Pa* (or in corrupted form, Inyan Kara Butte). Although they are consistent in drawing a connection between Inyan Kara Mountain and ghosts, the translations do not make sense. The Lakota word for ghost is *wanagi* (the soul when separated from the body) or *wica nagi* (a person's ghost) or *wamaka nagi* (animal's ghost) or simply *nagi* (spirit). *Iⁿyaⁿ* means stone; *Kaga* refers to the action of creating or imitating; and *Pa* means peak, butte, or hill. The location of this butte on Bad Heart Bull's map, on the western edge of the Black Hills, west of Gillette Prairie and south of Black Buttes, confirms that Inyan Kara is represented.

The term *I^{n}ya^n Kaga* can be translated several ways. *I^{n}ya^n* refers both to rock and to a superior being from whose blood the earth and sky were created. The spirit *I^{n}ya^n* literally bleeds dry and hardens into stone in creating the earth. In this sense *I^{n}ya^n* is one of sixteen "aspects" of *Waka^{n}Ta^{n}ka* (Great Sacredness or Great Mystery). *I^{n}ya^n* is one of four beings that existed prior to creation and is the creator of sky and earth. *Kaga* means to make, create, or imitate. This same term is used for one who makes, creates, or imitates. *Kaga* also refers to the performance of a ceremony in which a spirit is evoked or imitated. The name of this mountain thus has meaning on several levels. Translated as Stone Maker, the name may refer to the creation of the earth through *I^{n}ya^n*'s self-sacrifice – i.e., Stone creates [the world]. This would identify *Inyan Kara* as the place where creation began or ended or where creation is manifest in the visible features of the mountain.

On another level, the name refers to the geologic origin of the mountain. *Inyan Kara* is an igneous intrusive thrust up through the main ranges of the northern Black Hills. The semi-volcanic origin of the feature and resulting odd shape of the mountain is expressed as stone creating [itself]. An early translation of the place name is "the peak makes the mountain." This seems to express the same idea; however, the term follows English, rather than Lakota, syntax, and thus is probably not correct. Lakota syntax indicates the phrase is "the stone makes" or "the stone is made"; the term *pa* simply means the name refers to a peak. A reporter accompanying the 1874 Black Hills Expedition translated the name as "The Mask." The Lakota word for mask is *iteha*; thus, the idea of imitating or evoking an image, rather than a mask in the literal sense, is suggested here.

In the final sense of the term, *I^{n}ya^n Kaga* would refer to the performance of a ceremony in which *I^{n}ya^n* is invoked. According to a recent study of Lakota ethnoastronomy, Lakotas preparing for the Sun Dance first traveled to Inyan Kara to gather stones to be used in the purification (sweat bath) preceding the Sun Dance. I have not found any historical references to this practice.

The name *I^{n}ya^n Kaga* thus can refer to the act of creation, to the creation of the particular feature, and perhaps to a ceremony through which this act was commemorated and renewed, or to those conducting such a ceremony. The name may also refer to any combination of these.

Harney Peak. There has been some confusion as to the identity of the mountain that Bad Heart Bull labeled *Hinyankagapa.* A footnote to the text says that one informant spelled the name *Hinhan Kaga*. This indicates an entirely different name for the mountain, rather than just an alternative spelling. The word *Hi^{n}ha^n* means owl; the entire phrase might be translated Owl Maker Hill. This is one of the Lakota names for Harney Peak.

In one story in the Lakota Fallen Star myth cycle, the term Owl Maker (Owl Imitator) is used to refer to the evil spirit Double-Face. The people rescue a child taken by Double-Face in the guise of an owl-like monster. This event is said to have taken place at Owl Maker Butte. Although the specific location is not given, Owl Maker Butte would translate to *Hi^{n}ha^n Kaga Pa*, the term supplied by Blish's informants for Harney Peak. Blish's informants apparently thought that the map showed Harney Peak, rather than Inyan Kara. The location of the feature on Bad Heart Bull's map is correct for Inyan Kara, but not plausibly for Harney Peak, which is east, not west, of Gillette Prairie *(Re Sla* on Bad Heart Bull's map).

On the Bad Heart Bull map, Inyan Kara is pictured with horns and a human face. In Cheyenne tradition, this indicates a spirit being. Horned humans were also sometimes drawn by the Lakotas to depict spirit beings. The tradition of a ghost or evil spirit inhabiting either Harney Peak or Inyan Kara, or both, apparently originated with the Cheyennes. Blish's informants told her that Ghost Butte was the Cheyenne name for the mountain in question. This term could either be a poor translation for "spirit being" or a correct translation for ghost. In the Cheyenne language, the same word, *mis tai*, is used for ghost and owl. In Cheyenne tradition ghosts are said to fly around at night like owls, preying on young children, and are said to make a sound like an owl hooting. Such ghosts occupy high peaks. The Lakotas, by contrast, use separate terms and concepts for ghosts and owls but sometimes call the old woman who guards the Ghost Road (Milky Way) *Hi^{n}ha^n Kaga* or Owl Maker. It seems plausible that the Lakota name for Harney Peak, Owl Maker [or Owl Imitator] Butte, is a translation of the Cheyenne word Ghost [or Owl] Hill. A Cheyenne story tells of a girl who is captured by a huge Ghost Owl and eventually escapes to a "high mountain" with the aid of some hawk people. This may refer to Harney Peak, but unlike the Lakota version of the story, no specific place-name is given. It does, however, suggest that the mountain may have been incorporated into the mythology of both groups.

Another source provides a sacred term for Harney Peak. Nicholas Black Elk made several references to Harney Peak in telling his life story to John Neihardt in 1931, always referring to it as "the center." In Lakota theology the center of the universe could be (and was) anywhere. One established a center by making an altar or praying with the sacred pipe to the seven directions – south, west, north, east, up, down, and center. In Black Elk's account, Harney Peak was the center both because it marked the center of the Lakotas' territory at that time and because it was the center from which he had received instruction and knowledge of the four directions of the universe. The term translated as "the center of the earth" was part of a sacred language, distinct from everyday speech and used in religious discourse. Thus, the term refers as much to the religious significance of Harney Peak to Black Elk as to its physical location. It is clear, however, that Black Elk referred specifically to the Black Hills as the center or heart of the earth and to Harney Peak as the center of that center.

Bear Lodge Butte (Devils Tower). Bad Heart Bull shows a feature in the Black Hills that unmistakably represents Devils Tower, despite a somewhat distorted geographic placement. I have used the name for this feature, the Bear Lodge, that was used in common by Lakotas, Cheyennes, Arikaras, Arapahos, and Crows. This name is indicated pictographically on the Bad Heart Bull map by showing a bear's face at the base of the butte and is preserved in the adjacent portion of the Black Hills, known as the Bear Lodge Range. The name refers to an old myth, widely told on the northern Plains, about the formation of both Bear Lodge Butte and the Black Hills. As a girl and seven brother helpers attempt to escape from a monstrous bear, the Black Hills rise up as a barrier between them and their pursuer. The Bear's Lodge is formed when the girl and her seven helpers pray to the rock to rise up and save them from the bear. From the top of the towering rock, the people rise up to the sky to dwell there as the stars of the Big Dipper or Pleiades. (See discussion of Kiowa and Kiowa-Apache traditional beliefs, below.)

Few historic Lakota versions of this story were recorded. One version, collected both historically and recently, refers to two boys, who are set upon by a great bear and run to the rock for refuge. The butte is formed as the rock rises up carrying the boys to safety. In another version, collected in 1933, the youngest of seven brothers goes to rescue his sister-in-law from the leader of a den of monster bears. All eight escape by praying to a rock that rises to become Bear Lodge Butte. Unlike the Kiowa, Cheyenne, Arikara, and Arapaho versions of the story, the older Lakota texts do not associate the feature with the Big Dipper or the Pleiades. The Lakotas did make a connection between Bear Lodge Butte and stars – one of their principal constellations was known as *Mato Tipila* or the Bear Lodge. In this case, it represents the butte itself, not the people who escaped from the great bear.

In addition to its mythological significance, some Lakotas believed Bear Lodge Butte to be an earth center (see discussion of Harney Peak) and the place from which the Great Spirit scattered game animals to provide food for them. Some Lakotas today associate Bear Lodge Butte with their Sacred Calf Pipe, but I could find no written historical precedent for this belief.

Sundance Mountain. Sundance Mountain is not shown as a separate feature on Bad Heart Bull's map but is known from other sources to have been a Lakota sacred site. According to Nicholas Black Elk, the Belle Fourche River was referred to as the Sun Dance River "in olden times" because it flowed near the old Sun Dance grounds and was only later referred to as the northern branch of the Good [Belle] River. A stream running through the Red Valley between Bear Lodge Butte and the Black Hills proper is still known as Sundance Creek. The importance of the traditional Sun Dance ground is also reflected in the name Sundance, Wyoming, and nearby Sundance Mountain. An account of the area around Sundance Mountain, written in 1886, refers to it as "a summer rendezvous of the Sioux who came [t]here to hunt, gather berries, and hold their sun dance."

One reach of Sundance Creek, known as Medicine Flat Creek, runs through the Red Valley just east of Sundance Mountain, between the Bear Lodge range and the Black Hills proper. This name is a translation of *Wapiya Oblaye I^{n}ya^n*, or "plain of the rocks that heal [or make fortunate]," and refers to porous rocks believed to have healing properties. This connection between porous rock and healing is confirmed by the English and Lakota names of another sacred site, *I^{n}ya^n Oka Toka*, or Medicine Rock State Park in southeastern Montana. The Lakota name refers to porous rock while the English name indicates the site was recognized as a place of healing.

Black Buttes. Bad Heart Bull's map includes the Black Buttes, just northeast of Inyan Kara in the Bear Lodge range, but no interpretation of this feature appears in the accompanying text. It is difficult to track down any specific ethnographic or ethnohistoric references to this feature, because its Lakota name, *Paha Sapa*, is one of the terms applied to the Black Hills as a whole. An older term, *He Sapa*, also means Black Mountains and refers less ambiguously to the Black Hills. Nevertheless, their presence on Bad Heart Bull's map suggests that Black Buttes bore a traditional significance.

Bear Butte. On the eastern edge of the Black Hills, Bad Heart Bull drew a butte in the form of a bear's head. Bear Butte *(Mato Paha)* is an important Lakota holy site, an area used for ceremonies and individual prayers, including the *Ha^{n}blecheya* (Crying for a Vision), prayers for fertility, and prayers of remembrance. During such prayers it was traditional to place stones or other objects in the forks of trees on the butte in remembrance of the ancestors, whose spirits were believed to congregate at the sacred mountain. Because of its importance as a holy site for various groups, Bear Butte was traditionally considered neutral ground. The various divisions of the Lakota nation held a council there in 1857 to discuss the incursion of whites into the Black Hills country. Bear Butte appears to have been included in a set of seven ceremonial sites (Star People Villages) that corresponded to constellations. Some Lakotas today associate the Sacred Calf Pipe, their holiest object, with Bear Butte, but this belief may lack historical precedent.

Rapid Creek Valley. The inclusion of Rapid Creek *(Mnilusahan)* on Bad Heart Bull's map suggests that it, too, had special significance for the Lakotas. According to James LaPointe, Rapid Creek was a favorite winter camping ground because it did not freeze in winter and game and shelter were abundant in the creek valley. LaPointe ties a Fallen Star myth to this area, suggesting that it may have had religious significance. In the 1940s, Nicholas Black Elk also related a Fallen Star story linked to Rapid Valley.

Black Elk's narrative about Fallen Star also refers to a place called *He Ska* or White Buttes, located north of the Black Hills. This probably was either the White Butte near the town of the same name in Perkins County, South Dakota, or the White Butte in nearby Slope County, North Dakota, both outside the Black Hills proper. The latter site is revered by the Hidatsas as one of the buttes associated with Earth-naming rites.

Hot Springs. Bad Heart Bull indicated the location of an area of hot springs in the southern Black Hills portion of his map. The identification of Hot Springs *(Mnikahta)* as a sacred locale is supported by a more recent statement by Stella Swift Bird:

> Hot Springs was called holy water or holy place. When people got sick they went there to drink the holy water. They drank four times and each time it had a different taste. They drank four mouthfuls and prayed.[4]

James LaPointe also collected recent Lakota beliefs concerning the warm springs of the southern Black Hills. According to his informants, the term *Mni awoblu makoce* (land of bubbling waters) was applied to this region of the Black Hills. The area was highly regarded both for its abundant plant and animal resources and healing waters and for its religious significance.

> The Lakotas say these lands belonged to the "underground people," highly intelligent beings with supernatural powers, who inhabited subterranean

lands. . . . Legends say these people bred game animals for human consumption and kept perpetual fires ablaze to heat the waters that flow up to the surface, thus keeping the flowers in bloom and the medicinal shrubs growing the year round."[5]

These beliefs tied the warm springs area to the underground nation and the perpetuation of the buffalo herds, but I have found no written confirmation that these beliefs date before 1970.

The Racetrack. A ring of low relief surrounding the interior Black Hills is shown on Bad Heart Bull's map as *Ki Inyanka Ocanku,* the Racetrack. This valley is still known by that name, taken from an origin story known as the Great Race. The four-leggeds and two-leggeds race entirely around the Black Hills to determine which will eat the other. The earth and rocks there turn red from the blood flowing from the exhausted racers' mouths and feet. The two-leggeds win, establishing that people will thereafter eat bison instead of being eaten by them. This event established order in the universe. It accounts for the beginning of the Sun Dance and the use of the bow and arrow. All the Lakota versions of the story of the Great Race refer specifically to the Black Hills and to the Racetrack.

Eagle Shield further explained the significance of the Racetrack in terms of the Lakota Crow-Owners Warrior Society. Interestingly, he treated the animals' use of the Racetrack as an ongoing event, not as something from the remote past.

> The reason why the Black Hills were so long unknown to the white man was that Wakantanka [Great Spirit or Great Mystery] created them as a meeting place for the animals. The Indians had always known this and regarded the law of Wakantanka concerning it. By this law they were forbidden to kill any of the animals during their great gatherings. In the Black Hills there is a ridge of land around which is a smooth, grassy place called the "race-course." This is where the animals have the races, during their gatherings. Even small animals like the turtle are there. The crow is always first to arrive, and the other birds come before the animals, while insects and creatures like the frog travel slowly and arrive last. Sometimes it takes 10 years for all the animals to arrive, as they come from long distances and camp whenever winter overtakes them.[6]

Although the Racetrack is less well known than many of the other purported sacred sites in the Black Hills, it certainly is of primary importance, historically, as the place where order was established and the Sun Dance was begun.

Buffalo Gap. Bad Heart Bull identified a gate-like figure at the southeastern edge of the Black Hills as *Pte Tali Yapa,* the Buffalo Gap or

Buffalo Gate. As the name indicates, Buffalo Gap was the place where the great bison herds entered the Black Hills in the fall and came out again in the spring. It was also considered a gateway into the interior Black Hills for Lakota people as they sought winter quarters in the shelter of the mountains. A more recently collected story concerns the formation of the Buffalo Gap through the action of countless herds of bison passing through the area after emerging from Wind Cave.

Upland Prairies. Bad Heart Bull's map includes a feature labeled *Re Sla*, referring to an upland prairie or "bald," more commonly written *Pe Sla*. I could find no other historic references to this place, with one possible exception. In Black Elk's version of the Fallen Star myth cycle, the hero is traveling in the Black Hills country when he comes to a flat place, the home of Thunder-beings. Since the central Black Hills – unlike the lowland prairies – were often associated with the Thunders, this hints that Gillette Prairie was the place Fallen Star visited. Nothing in the story permits a definite identification, however.

Some Lakotas today associate the three upland prairies – Reynolds Prairie, Gillette Prairie, and Danby Park – with a spring ritual known as "welcoming back all life in peace." The largest of these, Gillette Prairie, was known as *Pe Sla* (Bald Place).

Other locations. Several other locations considered sacred by some Lakotas today are not included in Bad Heart Bull's map. Wind Cave is sacred to Lakotas today who recognize it as the place from which *Tokahe* (First Man) emerged from the underworld to bring wisdom and power to the Lakota people through his teachings. *Washu^n Niya*, the breathing hole, is the Lakota name for this feature. In other contexts, the cave is also seen as a doorway to the underworld. Some view the cave as the place from which the buffalo and other animals periodically emerge from the underworld to replenish the herds. A story published in 1951 relates that the cave was the home of a sacred white buffalo bull, while a later tradition tells of a Lakota man named *Taopi Gli*, who eloped with a maiden from the underworld nation and thereby ensured the prosperity of his people.

A creation story collected around the turn of the century explains that *Tokahe* appeared as the first messenger from the world of the sacred beings and taught the people how to be human. He gave them the concept of religion and taught them about the world of the sacred mysteries, how to heal sickness, and how to seek visions. He brought the Buffalo Ceremony celebrated at a girl's coming of age. Although this version does not link *Tokahe* to Wind Cave, he is said to have emerged from the underworld and eventually to have returned there. It is clear from LaPointe and Powers that these events are associated with Wind Cave in the minds of traditional Lakotas today, but the age of this tradition is not known.[7]

> When mankind first came upon the world, they did not know how to live so as to please the Gods. Therefore the Gods sent *Toka*, one of the *Pte* (Holy Buffalo) people who dwell in the regions under the world, to reach them. They did as *Toka* bade them and thus established their customs, their usages, and their ceremonies. *Toka* chose two of the people and gave into their charge the ceremonies that should be done according to the will of the Gods, and he taught them how to know and speak the wishes of the Gods. He told them the sacred mysteries so that they would have greater authority and powers than any which mankind could give them. *Toka* bade them teach this lore to those only who were worthy and acceptable to the Gods. He stayed with the people until they lived aright, and then he went from among them. Thus *Toka* established the order of holy men and they alone commune with the Gods and speak their will.[8]

Craven and Red Canyons, in the southern Black Hills, are recognized today as sacred locales, based on the presence of rock art there. Although the old name is no longer remembered, this is probably the place referred to by Nicholas Black Elk:

> There is a place in the Black Hills, also on the Little Big Horn, a bank of solid inscriptions that only a medicine man can read. It is a mystery [i.e., holy]. There is one in the Black Hills that only a medicine man can read (pictograph). We don't know who wrote it, but a medicine man can decode it and get the meaning. We would camp and when we came back there would be more writing.[9]

Another Lakota, John Around Him, provided a similar account at a later date:

> Up there in the Black Hills somewhere, I don't know where, a long time ago there was a piece of rock – a bank or something – the people went there every year. Every year there would be a different picture on the rock. Nobody knew who put the picture on the rock, but if there is going to be a war within the next year, there will be a picture of people laying there. That shows that there is going to be a war. If they go there and see pictures of buffalo and pictures of drying racks where they hang the meat to dry, if they see that, then they'll have a good year. Plenty to eat.[10]

A large panel of rock art in Craven Canyon may be of Lakota origin. It has many similarities to Lakota picture-writing, but cannot be directly "read" like other pictographic art. Another possibility is that the passage refers to the Pringle Pictograph site, 39CU70, an isolated rock art site containing many triangle designs and a few other painted designs. Its location, next to a spring and below a tall granite outcrop high in the Black Hills, suggests that it was used in a ritual context. A third rock art site, a panel of red drawings on the back of a small rock shelter in the bluffs overlooking the Cheyenne River, contains designs similar to those at Craven Canyon and the Pringle Pictograph. These three sites are stylistically similar to each other but are different from other Black Hills rock art.

Marie McLaughlin identifies a "mysterious butte" with a cave in it as a mystical or sacred site.[11] Based on the description of the cave and a Lakota drawing of its rock art that accompanies the story, I believe this legend refers to Medicine Creek Cave in the Bear Lodge range or to Ludlow Cave in the Cave Hills north of the Black Hills. The drawing reveals that the cave contained representations of bison, elk, deer, antelope, and mountain sheep heads, as well as a large number of hoofprints and a few anthropomorphic figures. These correspond fairly well to the rock art recorded from Medicine Creek Cave. On the other hand, the story refers to a drawing of a shield with an eagle or Thunderbird on it and many offerings, which fit better with Ludlow Cave in the northern Cave Hills. Unfortunately, most of the rock art once present in Ludlow Cave was destroyed before it could be recorded.

Two Lakota sources refer to Sylvan Lake as a holy place. These would seem to be anachronistic, because the lake did not exist until construction of a dam in 1892, but a more careful reading suggests that the place referred to is actually in the deep valley downstream of the lake. Here several natural pools are formed in the granite rocks over which the stream flows. One of the overlooking rocks resembles a human, identified in a story collected for the South Dakota Writers Project as a stately young woman, sent by the spirits to guard the pools from animals who might dirty the waters needed by the people in times of drought. According to an account given between 1928 and 1930 by Sitting Bull's nephews, One Bull and White Bull, the Hunkpapa Lakota leader received a vision near the present Sylvan Lake, in which he saw what looked like a man in the rocks above the pools and he heard singing. He climbed up to investigate and saw that it was an eagle. It flew away, but Sitting Bull remembered that it sang: "My father has given me this nation; in protecting them I have a hard time." This song meant that Sitting Bull was to devote his life to protecting his people.

The Black Hills area in visions. The Black Hills were important as a place where powerful visions were received. One of the great pieces of Lakota religious literature is the vision of the Oglala holy man, Black Elk, as related to John G. Neihardt in the 1930s. Neihardt presented Black Elk's vision in *Black Elk Speaks*. Later, in *The Sixth Grandfather*, Raymond J. DeMallie reproduced the actual transcripts of Black Elk's teachings as Neihardt collected them. Black Elk's teachings are too long and complex to relate here and are easily accessible elsewhere. Suffice it to say that the holy spirits transported Black Elk to Harney Peak, the center of the world, to receive their teachings. From this center Black Elk traveled in his vision to the north, south, east, and west edges of Lakota territory, always returning to Harney Peak.

Less well known is the vision of Brown Hat, also known as Battiste Good, a Lakota historian born about 1822. Brown Hat related his *Ha^nblecheya* as follows:

> In the year 1856, I went to the Black Hills and cried, and cried, and cried [i.e., prayed for a vision], and suddenly I saw a bird above me, which said: "Stop crying; I am a woman, but I will tell you something: My Great-Father, Father-God, who made this place, gave it to me for a home and told me to watch over it. He put a blue sky over my head and gave me a blue flag to have with this beautiful green country. My Great-Father grew, and his flesh was part earth and part stone and part metal and part wood and part water; he took from them all and placed them here for me, and told me to watch over them. I am the Eagle-Woman who tell you this.
>
> "The whites know that there are four black flags of God; that is, four divisions of the earth. He first made the earth soft by wetting it, then cut it into four parts, one of which, containing the Black Hills, he gave to the Dakotas, and, because I am a woman, I shall not consent to the pouring of blood on this chief house (or dwelling place) – that is, the Black Hills. The time will come that you will remember my words, for after many years you shall grow up one with the white people." She then circled round and round and gradually passed out of my sight. I also saw prints of a man's hands and horse's hoofs on the rocks [referring to rock art], and two thousand years, and one hundred millions of dollars. I came away crying, as I had gone. I have told this to many Dakotas, and all agree that it meant that we were to seek and keep peace with the whites.[12]

Recollections of Lakota people indicate that the Black Hills were frequently used for the individual vision quest. According to Frank Kicking Bear, his grandfather, Chagla, learned ritual and songs of the Sun Dance from a vision received in the Black Hills. Stella Swift Bird recalled six places where her grandfather, Fast Thunder, had fasted: one in the buttes above Beaver Creek in Nebraska, one at Scottsbluff, one in Montana, one in the Black Hills, one in North Dakota, and one on top of Bear Butte, "always on the highest butte he could find." The renowned Oglala holy man Chips prayed in the Black Hills in 1874. Peter Bordeaux related an account of huge eagles visiting a vision seeker in the Black Hills:

There were some white eagles, twice as large as the ordinary eagles, that increased and existed in the air and space above the vast country and nestled on the land of the Black Hills all the time prior to the year of 1875. A warrior observed the ceremony of the fast on the top of one of the Black Hills; on his third day, one of the said white eagles flew down and landed on the altar hill by the fasting warrior and talked to him in plain Sioux language. It said that the white men will invade your Black Hills in the very near future and will take over the resources under their possession and give you a bad time. Then the white eagles relinquished their roaming from the vast country of the Black Hills.[13]

A much earlier account of vision-seeking in the Black Hills was given by One Eye, the brother of Bull Bear. In 1846, he told Francis Parkman that he had fasted in a cave in the Black Hills as a boy, or approximately 1782.

While a vision might be sought at any secluded place, the repeated use of a particular place for vision seeking suggests a more specific religious significance for that place. Brown Hat's vision is perhaps the strongest ethnographic evidence that the Black Hills area as a whole was considered sacred ground. In this vision, the Eagle Woman told Brown Hat that the Great Father gave the Black Hills to the Lakotas as their dwelling place. Nicholas Black Elk also considered the Black Hills the "heart of the earth" and the promised land of the Lakotas, based on the story of the Great Race.

Cheyenne Sacred Places

Bear Butte, *Nowah'wus*, is the most sacred location in the traditional Cheyenne belief system. Known as Sacred Mountain Where People Are Taught, or Medicine Pipe Mountain, Bear Butte was central to many Cheyenne beliefs and ceremonies. "The old Proto-Tsistsistas and Tsistsistas [Cheyenne] concept of the spirit lodge derives from the configuration of the sacred mountain [Bear Butte] that itself is a spirit lodge and that is associated with *maheonoxsz*, the sacred caves, and *heszevoxsz*, the underground caverns where the animal spirits reside."[14] This belief is mirrored in the sweat lodge as a medium of renewal. Cheyenne sacred tradition involves a series of stories whereby the people are saved from crises by receiving sacred knowledge at Bear Butte. When the Cheyennes were starving, Sweet Medicine and Erect Horns brought them prosperity and cultural identity from the spirit beings residing within Bear Butte. Bear Butte as the source of the people's power and beliefs appears to be both old and fundamental to Cheyenne religion. The connection between Bear Butte and the Cheyenne people is very complex and intricate.

Today, Cheyenne pilgrims climbing Nowah'wus see the marks of the past all around them. Circles of rocks form the tipi rings of older camp sites. An eagle-catching pit is near. High on the butte itself, that great bird so close to Thunder still nests. Circling above the stone heights he watches the fasters down below. A spring marks the place from which the people gathered blue clay to make the sky color used in decorating the rawhide parfleches. And to the southwest lies the spot where the Buffalo People themselves first gave the Suhtaio the Sacred Medicine Lodge, the Sun Dance.

This is the heart of the Cheyenne sacred places and sacred ways. This is where the All Father and the Sacred Powers themselves gave Sweet Medicine the four Sacred Arrows.[15]

In his discussion of Lakota beliefs about the Black Hills, Donald Worster states that the Black Hills were not thought of as holy ground by earlier generations. "They [the Black Hills] were not exactly their equivalent of Mecca."[16] This statement certainly does not apply to the Cheyennes and Bear Butte. During Cheyenne ceremonies, villages, ceremonial structures, and supplicants were often oriented to Bear Butte. Like the Muslim praying toward Mecca, religious Cheyennes were constantly aware of their location in relation to the sacred mountain. John Bourke specifically stated in 1877 that "Bear Butte, at the northeast corner of the BlackHills, was once a sort of a Mecca for the Cheyennes" where they fasted, prayed, and honored the spirits of their dead. The location of various Cheyenne bands during their seasonal movements mirrored their arrangement around Bear Butte during gatherings for ceremonies.

The Racetrack, Buffalo Gap, Sundance Mountain, and Bear Lodge Butte (Devils Tower) are associated with Cheyenne traditions regarding the Great Race and the origins of the Sun Dance. The story of the Great Race plays an important role in Cheyenne cosmology, especially in establishing order among living things. As in the Lakota version of the tradition, the story is closely linked to the Racetrack. Two versions of the story place the beginning and ending point at Buffalo Gap. Other versions refer to the first Sun Dance near Bear Lodge Butte and Sundance Mountain.

The Cheyenne name for Bear Lodge Butte is *Nakoevë*, Bear Peak. It was revered in Cheyenne tradition as the place where the girl was saved from the giant spirit bear and is linked to the constellations Pleiades and the Big Dipper.

Like the Lakotas, the Cheyennes believed rock art sites were sources of power and information about the future. Beverly Badhorse notes that most incised rock art in the northern Plains was probably made by Lakotas and Cheyennes.[17] Recognizable Cheyenne motifs include

V-neck humans, lizards, turtles, circles with dots in the middle, and bisected circles, some of which refer to the Sun Dance. The Cheyennes say the V-neck human is a variant of the "man" symbol used in the Sun Dance and in other Cheyenne ceremonies. According to Badhorse, the lizard or horned toad is the most powerful religious symbol of the Cheyennes because it does its own Sun Dance. Lizard body-painting is common among modern sun dancers. At least one lizard and several V-necked humans are known from Black Hills rock art, and at least one Cheyenne shield motif is present.

Karl Schlesier argues that some or all of the stone alignments called medicine wheels are of Cheyenne origin. Whatever their exact origin, these features do tend to be associated with Algonkian speakers.[18] As the Cheyennes and their Arapaho allies were the only Algonkians in the Black Hills, it is reasonable to hypothesize that the single medicine wheel in the Black Hills was of Cheyenne origin. This circle of stones had five "arms" extending outward, each with a smaller circle of stones at its end and another about one-third of the way in from the end. The site lies on the eastern edge of the Black Hills, but most of the wheel has been destroyed by highway construction.

When a group of Cheyenne elders visited Bear Butte in 1940, they detoured on their way home to visit a hot spring in the southern Black Hills that was "famous in Cheyenne legend." They also visited a place called "hole in the wall" near the town of Mystic in the central Black Hills and the remains of a ceremonial antelope pit in the town of Belle Fourche.

Arapaho Sacred Places

Because the Arapahos were closely allied with the Cheyennes, we can assume that for the most part they shared the same sacred sites. An abbreviated version of an account of how the Arapahos acquired their seven sacred bundles, or "Medicine Bags" suggests that Bear Butte was a focal point of their religion, as it was for the Cheyennes:

> There was a vision in which a man found himself inside a cave. He saw the medicine arrows of the Cheyennes, but "they were too powerful." Instead, he took the seven medicine bags, which he gave to the seven most honored men in the tribe.[19]

The reference to the Cheyenne arrows strongly suggests that Bear Butte was the place visited in the vision. The Lakota holy man Fools Crow, who fasted at Bear Butte around 1914 and again in 1950, noted that Cheyennes and Arapahos alike made much use of the mountain.

The Arapahos have traditions about Bear Lodge Butte similar to those of the Cheyennes, Kiowas, and Lakotas. Their name for the feature translates to Bears' Lodge.

Kiowa and Kiowa-Apache Sacred Places

The identity of the Kiowa people was closely tied to the Black Hills. The Lakotas called the Kiowas the Island Hill people, referring to the island-like position of the Black Hills, surrounded by grasslands. According to the Lakota holy man Black Elk, "there was anothertribe that grew from this band, and they called them the Island Hill [*Witapaha*, Kiowas], by which I think they meant the Sioux called the Black Hills at that time the Island Hills." The Lakotas also used the term Island Hill people to refer to any ancient inhabitants of the Black Hills. This suggests that the Kiowas were in the Hills long enough to be considered the prehistoric inhabitants of the area.

Although much information has been lost, a few sources provide a glimpse of the sacred landscape of the Kiowas and their Kiowa-Apache allies in the Black Hills. Kiowa and Kiowa-Apache myths refer specifically to Bear Lodge Butte and Bear Butte Lake. It is reasonable to hypothesize that the entire northern border of the Black Hills from Bear Lodge Butte to Sundance Mountain to Bear Butte was sacred ground for the Kiowas, as it was for the Cheyennes and Lakotas who followed them.

According to James Mooney, the Kiowas had a myth accounting for the origin of the Black Hills, though he did not record the text or cite a source for it. The Kiowa name for the Black Hills, however, provides a link to Kiowa mythology. The Kiowas called the Black Hills *Sádalkañi K'op*, translated as stomach rind or manifold mountains.[20] The name refers to the rugged, broken nature of the Black Hills country. In one version of the story of Bear Lodge Butte, a girl and several warriors are pursued by a giant bear. They receive supernatural help from three spirit beings: a monstrous creature living under the waters of a river, a hill, and a rock. The rock becomes Bear Lodge Butte, lifting the people safely out of the reach of the bear. Before that, however, the hill offers to help, if the people will instruct it what to do.

> The little girl said, "I want you to turn into a buffalo's entrails. There is a certain part of the entrails that has some rugged gullies. You must become similar to buffalo entrails." And a miracle occurred. The land became hilly and full of canyons, and the men and girl ran ahead while the bear was slowed by these hills and gullies and canyons.[21]

The correspondence between the girl's description of the area as "entrails" and the Kiowa metaphor of stomach rind suggests that this part of the story refers to the creation of the Black Hills, the most prominent broken landscape near Bear Lodge Butte. Like the Lakotas, Cheyennes, and Crows the Kiowas associate Bear Lodge Butte with a constellation, either the Pleiades or the Big Dipper.

Another Kiowa version relates that the power of Bear Lodge Butte saved, not a girl or sisters, but the Kiowa culture-hero Sun-Boy or Half Boy. This supernatural boy had split himself in two; thus the two parts are often referred to as the Twin Gods, although each was half of the same person. In 1890 an old Kiowa woman related that about 1690, the Kiowas had settled in the Black Hills country near the Rock That Pushed Up the Boys, another name for Bear Lodge Butte. Because Sun-Boy brought the Kiowas their sacred spirit power, this story indicates that Bear Lodge Butte was an important religious place for the Kiowas.

According to Kiowa tradition, the Bear Kidney *taíme*, one of three great tribal religious objects, came from Bear Butte. This was a stone believed to house great supernatural powers.

A Kiowa-Apache tradition refers to a sacred lake in the northern Black Hills as a portal to the land of the dead. Here a Kiowa-Apache culture hero received one of the sacred bundles of his people. This apparently refers to Bear Butte Lake, the only natural lake in the Black Hills apart from a few small sinkholes. Its proximity to Bear Butte is reflected in its identification as the sacred lake of the Kiowas and Kiowa-Apaches. This echoes a Kiowa tradition of a sacred lake in the northern Black Hills.

Arikara Sacred Places

The Arikara story accounting for the origin of Bear Lodge Butte is similar to the Kiowas and also associates the feature with the Pleiades. In one version of the story, seven sisters were set upon by a bear while playing. They ran to a big rock which rose up, carrying them out of reach of the great bear. Their people could not get them down again, so they rose up into the sky to become the stars of the Pleiades.

The Arikaras told a series of stories about Bloody Hands, a poor orphan boy who lived with his grandmother at the edge of the village. Bloody Hands succeeded in various undertakings, despite his lack of wealth and physical beauty, because he possessed great powers. The story of Bloody Hands becoming an eagle is the last of the series, told in April, at the end of the storytelling season.

When Bloody Hands asked his grandmother's permission to join a war party, she refused, explaining that the other warriors would make fun of him because he was so ugly and pitiful. His feelings hurt, Bloody Hands turned into an eagle. Heedless of his grandmother's pleas that he return to his natural form, he flew off "where the highest of the Black Hills are." The grandmother followed him and attempted to bring him down by posing as bait – first a rabbit and then a deer. The eagle was not fooled and reached the Black Hills, where he lighted on top of a tall rock – Bear Lodge Butte. The grandmother begged him to come to the edge so that she could have one last look at him. When he did she turned into a bear that leaped up the sides of the rock, scratching it with her claws, but unable to reach him. When she grew tired, the eagle-grandson departed, where the grandmother could not follow. Thus they were separated.

> Now grandson, grandson, you have made it hard for me. It is impossible to go over there. It is only rocky land ... you have hurt my feelings here. And now we've separated. It is truly the way it is: we have separated. The eagle is going all around. He is going around in the Black Hills. But I'll go around pitifully over there.[22]

This story suggests that the Black Hills were beyond the usual territory of the Arikaras, a place where supernatural beings could live undisturbed by human interference. This echoes the Lakotas' view of the Black Hills as the abode of spirits.

Mandan Sacred Places

One version of the Mandan account of the Great Flood refers to Bear Butte. According to one source, Mandans made pilgrimages to Bear Butte annually to commemorate the flood and to pray that it not return. This account suggests a Mecca-like status for the mountain even before the Cheyennes made it the focus of their religion. Mandan oral tradition states that the group lived for a time in the Black Hills before establishing themselves on the Missouri River, a tradition supported by the presence of Initial Middle Missouri (proto-Mandan) archaeological sites in the eastern and northern periphery of the Black Hills.

Discussion

Groups occupying the Black Hills had traditional or sacred landscapes encompassing three kinds of properties: distinctive regions, such as the area around Sundance Mountain; specific points in the landscape, such as Inyan Kara or Bear Butte; and kinds of places, such as springs and caves. Table 1 summarizes references to the Black Hills in the mythology

Table 1   Stories referring to the Black Hills

Myth	Features named in myth	Group
The Monster Bear	Black Hills, Bear Lodge Butte	Kiowa, Lakota, Arapaho, Cheyenne, Arikara
Half-Boy Brings the Boy Medicine	Bear Butte Lake	Kiowa, Kiowa-Apache
Half-Boy Vanquishes the Monster Bear	Bear Lodge Butte	Kiowa
The Great Flood	Bear Butte	Mandan
Bloody Hands Becomes an Eagle	Bear Lodge Butte	Arikara
Erect Horns Gets the New Life Lodge Ceremony and Sacred Hat	Bear Butte	Cheyenne/Suhtai
Old Man and Old Woman Wolf	Bear Butte	Cheyenne
The Stone Buffalo Horn	Northern Black Hills	Cheyenne
Sweet Medicine Receives the Sacred Arrows	Bear Butte	Cheyenne
The Death of Sweet Medicine	Bear Butte	Cheyenne
The Great Race	The Racetrack, Sun Dance Mountain, Buffalo Gap, Inyan Kara	Lakota, Cheyenne
The Ghost Owl	Harney Peak	Cheyenne, Lakota
Emergence of the Holy Buffalo People	Wind Cave	Lakota
Taopi Gli Goes to the Underground World	Wind Cave	Lakota
The Great Flood and the Origin of the Lakotas	Harney Peak or Bear Lodge Butte	Lakota
Thunderbird stories	Harney Peak	Lakota
Uncigila's Seventh Spot	Black Hills (cave with rock art)	Lakota
Why the Crow is Black	Rapid Creek	Lakota
Fallen Star and the Chief's Arm	Bear Butte, White Butte	Lakota
The Seven Star Villages	Bear Lodge Butte, Bear Butte, Rapid Creek, possibly Gillette Prairie	Lakota

of various groups occupying the area. Groups new to the area often-adapted the sacred landscape of their predecessors to their own beliefs and traditions. As a group became separated from the Black Hills area in space and time, the number of remembered places became fewer and fewer. Thus, we have much information concerning Cheyenne and Lakota use of the Black Hills, less about Arapaho and Kiowa use, and little about Mandan and Arikara use.

The territories of ethnic groups often changed over time. In new territories, new ethnic markers were established. Often the sacred places of earlier – even evicted – groups were adopted because they were natural landmarks and powerful, impressive locations. In a sense, immigrating groups brought their sacred places with them. For instance, when the Suhtais lived in eastern South Dakota their sacred mountain was located in the Timber Mountains of southwestern Minnesota. When they moved to the Black Hills region around 1670, they adopted Bear Butte as their foremost sacred place and transferred to it the origin of the New Life Lodge ceremony that had belonged to the Minnesota mountain. Bear Butte was not a territorial marker but an important spiritual place for a number of ethnic groups in historic and prehistoric time.[23]

The very scarcity of prominent landmarks may help explain why they tended to be used in similar ways by different ethnic groups:

> Finally the Cheyennes reached the prairies where the rippling blanket of buffalo grass was cut by the swiftly flowing waters of the Yellowstone, the Tongue, and the Platte rivers. Ahead lay the apparently endless sweep of the plains country, its color changing with the shifting rays of the sun. Here, except for the pine hills and low-lying buttes, there were few places where a man could fast and pray. Thus the heights of the Sacred Mountain remained all the more deeply embedded in Cheyenne tribal memory.[24]

The Black Hills provides a prime example of this phenomenon. We can trace Lakota beliefs about Bear Lodge Butte and Bear Butte to the more elaborate Cheyenne traditions, which in turn appear to have derived in part from Arikara, Kiowa, or Crow traditions. The association of Devils Tower with bear taboos perhaps is a hold-over from when the Athabascan and Algonkian groups were living far to the north. That the Lakotas lacked this long-standing tradition of bear avoidance is evident in their rather abbreviated version of the myth. Nevertheless, they adopted both the place and much of the mythical context that had built up around it.

Religious traditions about the Black Hills clearly antedate the beginnings of tourism in the 1930s and the legal battles of the 1960s and 1970s, extending back at least several centuries. The Kiowas, Mandans, Arikaras, Cheyennes, and Lakotas all have traditional histories regarding extensive migration in precontact times. From the perspective of these traditional histories, the recognition of sacred places is sometimes a matter of having returned to a place remembered from the oldest times. It may also be viewed as a matter of perceiving an intrinsic sacredness of place that does not depend on beliefs specific to any one group for its definition.

New groups entering or reentering the area recognized the sacred sites of their predecessors and often adopted them as their own. Thus, the question of whether the Lakotas "had time" to develop religious traditions about the Black Hills reflects a naive view of culture change. Both the Lakotas and the Cheyennes placed old religious traditions into new (or renewed) geographic contexts as they entered (or reentered) the Black Hills area. Rather than having to invent such traditions, the Lakotas recognized and adopted the religious traditions of those who preceded them in the area. Myth structures permitted the reconciliation of old traditions to new places, as well as the adoption of new beliefs. Whether this was a process of borrowing new traditions or renewing old ones, the result was a complex sacred geography. For as far back as the historical and ethnographic record can take us, the Black Hills have been a physical manifestation of sacred relationships between earth, sky, and the underworld, between people and the spirit beings, and between the temporal and spiritual realms.

Whether the Black Hills, as a whole, were considered sacred is a more difficult question. At least thirteen places in the Black Hills are specifically referred to as sacred in historic and ethnographic documents. This does not count generic sacred places, such as rock art sites, caves, and high peaks associated with the Thunder-beings. Deciding whether thirteen sacred sites in a discrete area constitutes a holy land is a bit like asking how many angels can dance on the head of a pin. At least two Lakotas, Nicholas Black Elk and Battiste Good, specifically referred to the Black Hills as a promised land, but both were speaking after the loss of the area under the bitterest of circumstances. James H. McGregor, Indian agent at Pine Ridge in the 1930s, also described the Black Hills as the "special gift" of $Waka^n$ Ta^nka to the Lakota people, based on his conversations with Oglala elders. The Cheyennes believed that they were given all the territory around Bear Butte as their promised land. The beliefs of earlier groups in this regard are not recorded.

The northern Plains contains many places historically considered sacred by various Native American groups. Were the Black Hills more sacred than these other places? The answer certainly is yes as regards Bear Butte and Bear Lodge Butte (Devils Tower). The Racetrack and associated locales were also primary sacred sites for the Lakotas and Cheyennes, as was Bear Butte Lake for the Kiowa-Apaches. At the same time, those portions of the Black Hills richest in sacred sites were also richest in resources, especially after the introduction of the horse made the interior mountains less attractive to Native groups. In ceding the Black Hills in 1876, Lakota leaders made a last-ditch effort to reserve for themselves that portion of the Black Hills from the Racetrack outward.

Were these leaders acting to retain the lands containing their most important holy places, including Bear Butte, Bear Lodge Butte, Inyan Kara Mountain, Buffalo Gap, and the Racetrack? Or were they acting to retain the lands most accessible on horseback and most valuable to them economically? Since Lakotas viewed the abundance of resources in the Black Hills as an expression of the beneficence of $Waka^n$ Ta^nka, the two kinds of value were intertwined in their minds. Red Cloud clearly implied this by asking that the federal government provide for the Lakotas once the Black Hills were denied them: "God Almighty placed those hills there for my wealth, but now you want to take them and make me poor, so I ask so much [compensation] so that I won't be poor." It can be argued that hunting and other resource gathering in the Black Hills were as much religious as economic activities. In 1874 William E. Curtis wrote that "according to the evidence of Sitting Bull, the Indians had wont in former days to make their hunting [in the Black Hills] a mere accessory to – very possibly a part of – their worship." From the Lakota viewpoint, resource gathering did not preclude approaching the Black Hills in "a reverential mood."

In emphasizing the economic value of the Black Hills, the Lakota negotiators may simply have been trying to meet the whites on white terms. After all, a religious argument could hardly be persuasive to a people who considered Native religion ignorance at best and devil worship at worst. Such an argument was more likely to have had the opposite effect because the sooner the religion of the Lakotas could be broken down, the sooner they would become "good" (i.e., fully acculturated) Indians. Removing them from their purported holy land would only hasten the process. On the other hand, the whites were already grumbling about the cost of the annual treaty payments to the reservation Lakotas. Faced with this expense, perhaps the whites could be persuaded to reconsider their taking of the Black Hills.

The most revealing statements of white and Indian attitudes about the Black Hills in the 1870s come from newspaper accounts. Reporters accompanying the 1874 Black Hills expedition, with opportunity to discuss the Black Hills with Lakota, Santee, and Arikara scouts, were unanimous in describing the Black Hills as the holy land of the Lakotas and Cheyennes. N. H. Knappen of the *Bismarck Tribune* said the Indians regarded the Black Hills as the home of the Great Spirit. For the *New York World*, William E. Curtis described the Black Hills as the Indians' "earthly paradise" and "combined deer park and Mecca," and noted that the Black Hills were often the site of the annual Sun Dance, "most solemn of festivities." He concluded that, to the Indians, "the Black Hills are holy ground of the very holiest sort." With a perspicacity unusual for his day, Curtis hypothesized that Lakota religious leaders were increasingly stressing traditions about the sacredness of the area in order to preserve intact this last undisturbed remnant of their once vast territories. Samuel Barrows of the *New York Tribune* wrote that the Black Hills were the Indians' "fable-land," invested with legends and superstitions. Aris B. Donaldson of the *St. Paul Pioneer* also stressed that the Black Hills were sacred to the Indians.

It [the Black Hills] is the famed stronghold and favorite hunting ground of the red man. It is even dearer to him than the land of the "graves of his forefathers." He believes that the souls of the departed revisit these earthly abodes, and in spiritual forms pursue the spiritual game over the old, familiar hunting grounds. To the simple faith of the Indian, it is the most sacred spot on earth, to him the "holy of holies."

Nowhere in these newspaper accounts was the sacredness of the Black Hills questioned. It seems to have been the accepted knowledge of the day that the Black Hills were, indeed, the holy land of the Lakotas. At the same time, the reporters clearly show that they considered the issue of sacredness entirely irrelevant. Just as they were unanimous in recognizing the sacredness of the Black Hills, the reporters were unanimous in demanding that the area be quickly opened to white settlement. For example, after describing the Black Hills as the Lakotas' "holy of holies," Donaldson wondered how much longer the area would be left as only an occasional hunting ground for "the most obstinately depraved nomad" in the human race. In the 1870s, Indian beliefs about the Black Hills were either to be forbidden, reformed, or ignored. The real issue was how quickly the Indians could be either reformed or exterminated and the area opened to white use. The reporters, who reflected the prevailing attitudes of the day, had no motive for exaggerating the Indians' beliefs about the sacredness of the Black Hills.

When Lakotas asserted in the 1970s, with seeming suddenness, that the Black Hills were sacred ground, they were responding to the federal government's equally sudden policy that sacredness was relevant to their claims on the area. The rise of interest in Native American religious rights in the 1970s was to culminate in passage of the American Indian Religious Freedom Act in 1978. Public attitudes were changing rapidly. Instead of asking why the Lakotas were claiming sacred status for the Black Hills in the 1970s, we might more productively ask how the conventional wisdom of the 1870s – that the Black Hills were the Lakotas' holy land – came to be disputed in the 1970s. The answer seems to lie in the sudden relevance of sacredness to land claims disputes. The Black Hills have increasingly become a symbol of Native American resistance to acculturation, and because of this symbolic role, they are today sacred in ways that they historically were not. This does not, however, mean that the area had no religious significance in the past.

We may never know for certain the degree to which the Black Hills were considered sacred ground by their past inhabitants. At least portions of the area were sacred to many groups at many times. The presence of about a hundred rock art sites in the Black Hills, many illustrating recognizably religious themes and some dating back thousands of years, suggests that the area has had considerable religious significance for much, if not all, of its human history. The current religious revitalization movement among Lakota and Cheyenne people is as much a rediscovery as a reinvention of traditional beliefs, including beliefs about the Black Hills.

Notes

1 Watson Parker, "The Black Hills Controversy," paper presented at the annual meeting of the Dakota History Conference, April 1984, p. 4; Donald Worster, *Under Western Skies: Nature and History in the American West* (New York: Oxford University Press, 1992), p. 149.
2 Worster, *Under Western Skies*, p. 149.
3 James LaPointe, *Legends of the Lakota* (San Francisco: The Indian Historian Press, 1976).
4 Edward Kadlecek and Mabell Kadlecek, *To Kill an Eagle: Indian Views on the Last Days of Crazy Horse* (Boulder, CO: Johnson Books, 1981), p. 66.
5 LaPointe, *Legends of the Lakota*, pp. 45–6.
6 Frances Densmore, *Teton Sioux Music* (Bureau of American Ethnology Bulletin 61, 1918), p. 319.
7 LaPointe, *Legends of the Lakota*, pp. 79–85; Marla N. Powers, *Oglala Women: Myth, Ritual, and Reality* (Chicago: University of Chicago Press, 1986), p. 50.
8 James R. Walker, *Lakota Myth*, ed. Elaine A. Jahner (Lincoln: University of Nebraska Press, 1983), p. 206.
9 Raymond J. DeMallie, *The Sixth Grandfather: Black Elk's Teachings Given to John G. Neihardt* (Lincoln: University of Nebraska Press, 1984), p. 376.
10 Emily H. Lewis, *Wo'Wakita: Reservation Recollections* (Sioux Falls, SD: Center for Western Studies, Augustana College, 1980), p. 76.
11 Marie L. McLaughlin, *Myths and Legends of the Sioux* (1916; rpt Lincoln: University of Nebraska Press, 1990), pp. 104–7.
12 Garrick Mallery, *Picture-Writing of the American Indians* (Bureau of American Ethnology Annual Report 10, 1893), pp. 289–90.
13 Kadlecek and Kadlecek, *To Kill an Eagle*, p. 90.
14 Karl H. Schlesier, *The Wolves of Heaven: Cheyenne Shamanism, Ceremonies, and Prehistoric Origins* (Norman: University of Oklahoma Press, 1987), p. 63.
15 Peter J. Powell, *Sweet Medicine: The Continuing Role of the Sacred Arrows, the Sun Dance, and the Sacred Buffalo Hat in Northern Cheyenne History* (Norman: University of Oklahoma Press, 1987), p. 19.
16 Worster, *Under Western Skies*, p. 149.
17 Beverly Badhorse, "Petroglyphs: Possible Religious Significance of Some," *Wyoming Archaeologist* 23–24 (1979), 27–9.
18 Schlesier, *Wolves of Heaven*, pp. 83–7.
19 Virginia Cole Trenholm, *The Arapahoes, Our People* (Norman: University of Oklahoma Press. 1970), p. 80.
20 James Mooney, *Calendar History of the Kiowa Indians* (Bureau of American Ethnology Annual Report 17, 1898), pp. 156, 160.

21 Maurice Boyd, *Kiowa Voices: Myths, Legends, and Folktales*, vol. 2 (Fort Worth: Texas Christian University Press, 1983), p. 92.

22 Douglas R. Parks, *Traditional Narratives of the Arikara Indians*, vol. 4 (Lincoln: University of Nebraska Press, 1991), p. 513.

23 Karl H. Schlesier, Introduction to *Plains Indians, AD 500–1500: The Archaeological Past of Historic Groups*, ed. Karl Schlesier (Norman: University of Oklahoma Press, 1994), pp. xxiv–xxv.

24 Powell, *Sweet Medicine*, p. xxii.

Documents

Luther Standing Bear grew up in a time of great change for the Lakotas. Just a boy when his people defeated Custer's Seventh Cavalry at Little Big Horn, Standing Bear witnessed the near-extinction of the buffalo, the Lakotas' increased dependence on federal rations of beef and flour, their confinement to narrowly circumscribed reservations, and the institution of government boarding schools for Indian children. Standing Bear was in the entering class of students sent to the Carlisle boarding school in Pennsylvania when it opened in 1879 (see chapter 6). Later in life, he became a performer in Buffalo Bill's Wild West Show, a stuntman and film actor in Hollywood, and a writer of popular books and articles criticizing US Indian policies and describing the Lakota life he had known as a child. These two excerpts from his book *Land of the Spotted Eagle* (1933) explain the significance of the Black Hills to the Lakotas and the process and purpose of the vision quests undertaken by boys in their early teens, many of whom went to the Black Hills in search of visions and spirit helpers.

Land of the Spotted Eagle

Luther Standing Bear

[. . .] It is said that Nature makes the man to fit his surroundings. If that be the case, then a description of the land partly, at least, describes the

Standing Bear, Luther. *Land of the Spotted Eagle*. Lincoln: University of Nebraska Press, 1978 (originally published 1933): 42–5, 197–211. Reprinted by permission of the University of Nebraska Press. Copyright © 1933 by Luther Standing Bear. Renewal copyright 1960 by May Jones.

people. Our homeland was proportioned on a big scale. There seemed to be nothing small, nothing limited, in our domain. Our home, which covered part of North Dakota, all of South Dakota, and part of Nebraska and Wyoming, was one of great plains, large rivers and wooded mountains. So wide were the prairies that the sun seemed to rise out of one distant edge and in the evening to set in the opposite distant edge. The weather was extreme. The winter was cold with sleet and ice and the temperature often below zero. The winds were so strong they made us feel their strength. The summers were hot and violent with color. At times the skies were as blue as Lakota blue paint and as far as the eye could see the earth was a deep green, while the sun set in red as dazzling to the eye as the white of midday. The rain fell in streams and the storm warriors threw their lightning sticks to earth and shook our tipis with their thunder. We grew used to strength, height, distance, power.

Nature dealt vigorously with the Lakota and they with bodies almost bare became vigorous. What the body was fitted for the mind was fitted for also, and physical hardihood was matched with spiritual hardihood. There was little fear within. The mental reaction of the Lakota was one of unity with these tremendous forces, and rather than terror many times the attitude was a welcoming defiance. I have seen a brave, without uttering a word, strip himself to breechclout and walk out into a rain falling so heavily in sheets that a few paces from the door his form was lost to sight. He went out to be alone with Rain. That is true love of Nature.

Surroundings were filled with comforts for the body and beauty for expectant senses. Every morning the sun was received by each individual in a moment of silent reverence; and in the evening the sunset was watched, for it held the secret of the next day's weather. The springs and trees inspired songs and stories which we wrote in our minds and framed in our consciousness.

Of all our domain we loved, perhaps, the Black Hills the most. The Lakota had named these hills *He Sapa*, or Black Hills, on account of their color. The slopes and peaks were so heavily wooded with dark pines that from a distance the mountains actually looked black. In wooded recesses were numberless springs of pure water and numerous small lakes. There were wood and game in abundance and shelter from the storms of the plains. It was the favorite winter haunt of the buffalo and the Lakota as well. According to a tribal legend these hills were a reclining female figure from whose breasts flowed life-giving forces, and to them the Lakota went as a child to its mother's arms. The various entrances to the hills were very rough and rugged, but there was one very beautiful and easy pass through which both buffalo and Lakota entered the hills. This pass ran along a narrow stream bed which widened here and there but which in places narrowed so that the tall pines at the top of the cliffs arched their boughs, almost touching as they swayed in the wind. Every fall thousands of buffaloes and Lakotas went through this pass to spend the winter in the hills. *Pte ta tiyopa* it was called by the Lakotas, or "Gate of the buffalo." Today this beautiful pass is denuded of trees and to the white man it is merely "Buffalo Gap."

Two lovely legends of the Lakotas would be fine subjects for sculpturing – the Black Hills as the earth mother, and the story of the genesis of the tribe. Instead, the face of a white man is being outlined on the face of a stone cliff in the Black Hills. This beautiful region, of which the Lakota thought more than any other spot on earth, caused him the most pain and misery. These hills were to become prized by the white people for reasons far different from those of the Lakota. To the Lakota the magnificent forests and splendid herds were incomparable in value. To the white man everything was valueless except the gold in the hills. Toward the Indian the white people were absolutely devoid of sentiment, and when a people lack sentiment they are without compassion. So down went the Black Forest and to death went the last buffalo, noble animal and immemorial friend of the Lakota. As for the people who were as native to the soil as the forests and the buffalo – well, the gold-seekers did not understand them and never have. The white man will never know the horror and the utter bewilderment of the Lakota at the wanton destruction of the buffalo. What cruelty has not been glossed over with the white man's word – enterprise! If the Lakotas had been relinquishing any part of their territory voluntarily, the Black Hills would have been the last from the standpoint of traditional sentiment. So when by false treaties and trickery the Black Hills were forever lost, they were a broken people. The treaties, made supposedly to recompense them for the loss of this lovely region, were like all other treaties – worthless. But could the Lakota braves have foreseen the ignominy they were destined to endure, every man would have died fighting rather than give up his homeland to live in subjection and helplessness.

How long the Lakota people lived in these mid-west plains bordering the Black Hills before the coming of the white men is not known in tribal records. But our legends tell us that it was hundreds and perhaps thousands of years ago since the first man sprang from the soil in the midst of these great plains. The story says that one morning long ago a lone man awoke, face to the sun, emerging from the soil. Only his head was visible, the rest of his body not yet being fashioned. The man looked about, but saw no mountains, no rivers, no forests. There was nothing but soft and quaking mud, for the earth itself was still young. Up and up the man drew himself until he freed his body from the clinging soil. At last he stood upon the earth, but it was not solid, and his first few steps were slow and halting. But the sun shone and ever the man kept his face turned toward it. In time the rays of the sun hardened the face of the earth and strengthened the man and he bounded and leaped about, a free and joyous creature. From this man sprang the Lakota nation and, so far as we know, our people have been born and have died on this plain; and no people have shared it with us until the coming of the European. So this land of the great plains is claimed by the Lakotas as their very own. We are of the soil and the soil is of us. We love the birds and beasts that grew with us on this soil. They drank the same water we did and breathed the same air. We are all one in nature. Believing so, there was in our hearts a great peace and a welling kindness for all living, growing things. [. . .]

The Lakota loved the sun and earth, but he worshiped only Wakan Tanka, or Big Holy, who was the Maker of all things of earth, sky, and water. Wakan Tanka breathed life and motion into all things, both visible and invisible. He was over all, through all, and in all, and great as was the sun, and good as was the earth, the greatness and goodness of the Big Holy were not surpassed. The Lakota could look at nothing without at the same time looking at Wakan Tanka, and he could not, if he wished, evade His presence, for it pervaded all things and filled all space. All the mysteries of birth, life, and death; all the wonders of lightning, thunder, wind, and rain were but the evidence of His everlasting and encompassing power.

Wakan Tanka prepared the earth and put upon it both man and animal. He dispensed earthly blessings, and when life on earth was finished provided a home, *Wanagi yata*, the place where the souls gather. To this home all souls went after death, for there were no wicked to be excluded. *Wanagi yata* was a place of peace and plenty where all met in the peaceful pursuits of life – enmity, hate, and revenge having no place there. Not only did the soul of man repair to this place after leaving the earth, but the souls of all things. *Wanagi yata* was a place of green plains on which roamed the buffalo; where lakes gleamed in the sunshine, and myriads of birds hovered over fields of the sacred sunflower. [. . .]

For the most part the Lakota was a silent and solitary worshiper, though in many of the religious rituals prayer was offered in speech and song. Prayer, however, was not so much a matter of supplication as it was of thanksgiving, and favorite words for beginning a prayer were, *Tunka sila le iyahpe ya yo*, which translated says, "Father, receive my offering." [. . .]

Now the medicine-man derived his knowledge from the infinite source – Wakan Tanka. For him knowledge was not in books, nor in the heads of professors, but in the works of Wakan Tanka as manifested in the creatures and beings of nature. This association of knowledge with all the creatures of earth caused him to look to them for his knowledge, and assuming their spiritual fineness to be of the quality of his own, he sought with them a true rapport. If the man could prove to some bird or animal that he was a worthy friend, it would share with him precious secrets and there would be formed bonds of loyalty never to be broken; the man would protect the rights and life of the animal, and the animal would share with the man his power, skill, and wisdom. In this manner was the great brotherhood of mutual helpfulness formed, adding to the reverence for life orders other than man. The taking of animal life for food and clothing only became established, and frugality became regarded as a virtue. Animal life took its place in the scheme of things, and there was no slavery and no torture of four-footed and winged things. By acknowledging the virtues of other beings the Lakota came to possess them for himself, and for his wonder and reverence and for his unsurpassed humbleness and meekness Wakan Tanka revealed himself to the medicine-man.

In order to place himself in communication with the other earth entities the Lakota submitted to the purification ceremony, the fast and vigil in solitude, for only in so doing could he experience the vision or dream during which the dumb creatures could converse with him. But not every man who tried was fortunate enough to receive the vision. It was a test which required fortitude and strength, and though most young men tried, few were successful. Nevertheless, every boy longed for the vision, and even as children we tried to hear and see things that would add to our knowledge and power. We watched the medicine-men and repeated their acts in our play until the time came to try to be a dreamer. If the young man in solitude was unable to meet and talk with some spirit entity he could never share its powers, and even though he met every sacrifice the communion might not come about; and if it did not he would never be a medicine-man.

To go into the vision was, of course, to go into the presence of the Great Mystery, and this no Lakota man would attempt to do without first cleansing himself physically and spiritually. Accordingly he began the task of purification; he purged himself of material things, putting aside the thought of food, the chase, fine clothes, the ceremony, and dance. In the solitudes the dream-seeker felt that he would come into the precinct of spiritual power; would speak to beings with whom he could not speak in life's daily existence, and in recognition of his high resolve they might offer to him the gift of their powers and for this exalted contact he wished in every way to be worthy. Earnestly a young man endeavored to cast fear from his mind. The danger from prowling enemies was ever constant and he would be defenseless and, perhaps, weak in body from the fast; so, however devout in his purpose a youth might be, he did not always go through with his self-imposed task. Sometimes a young man stayed his allotted time only to be unrewarded for his vigil, while another's youthful fears brought him home without accomplishing his dream.

A young man having decided to begin purification, asked the assistance of the medicine-man, for only occasionally did a man get a dream without taking the purification ritual, and still less occasionally did a woman receive a dream and become a medicine-woman, for they never took the fast and the lonesome vigil. Upon request, the medicine-man arranged the sweat-lodge, carpeted it with wild-sage, and built an altar in front of its door. He, and perhaps some friends of the dream-seeker, went into the lodge and the purification ceremony began with the smoking of the pipe. All in the group took the sweat while the medicine-man sang, and when the ceremony was over each one rubbed his body with the leaves and branches of sage. This ceremony might be repeated for several days, or until the young man felt that he was thoroughly pure in body, and by that time the songs would have strengthened and fortified him in mind and spirit also.

The youth then started on his journey to the place of his vigil, wrapped only in his robe. The friends who accompanied him, usually two in number, carried for him the four staffs to mark the four corners of his resting place, and when they arrived there, they planted the staffs in the earth and tied to the top of each a flag of red or blue cloth or buckskin. Sometimes ten small sticks, each topped with a small bundle of tobacco, were placed at the foot of each large staff. A buffalo robe was spread in the center of the square marked by the four staffs and on the robe the young brave lay or sat, the pipe clasped in his hands. His friends then left and he was alone. Were he fortunate and received a dream, he was thereafter known as a dreamer or medicine-man.

The Lakotas had some wonderful medicine-men who not only cured the sick, but they looked into the future and prophesied events, located lost or hidden articles, assisted the hunters by coaxing the buffalo near, made themselves invisible when near the enemy, and performed wonderful and magic things. Last Horse was one of our famous medicine-men and was an exception in that he was a splendid warrior as well. When I was a boy I noticed that Last Horse at the ceremonies always came out and performed a dance around the fire by himself before the other dancers came in. When I became older I came to know that Last Horse was a Thunder Dreamer and that it was his place to bless the dog feast, always served for Thunder Dreamers, before the others partook of the food. The powers that helped Last Horse were the Thunder Warriors of the sky, and oftentimes he, and other Thunder Dreamers also, combed their hair in a peculiar way, as they imagined the warriors of the sky did. Their long hair was brought forward and tied in the middle of the forehead, and into the knot a feather, which pointed back, was fastened. This made them look fierce and warlike, as they supposed the thunderous sky warriors must look.

In 1878 I saw Last Horse perform one of his miracles. Some of my band, the Oglalas, went to visit the Brule band and by way of entertainment preparations were made for a dance and feast. The day was bright and beautiful, and everyone was dressed in feathers and painted buckskin. But a storm came up suddenly, threatening to disrupt the gathering, so of course there was much unhappiness as the wind began to blow harder and rain began to fall. Last Horse walked into his tipi and disrobed, coming out wearing only breechclout and moccasins. His hair streamed down his back and in his hand he carried his rattle. Walking slowly to the center of the village he raised his face to the sky and sang his Thunder songs, which commanded the clouds to part. Slowly but surely, under the magic of the song, the clouds parted and the sky was clear once more.

White Crow was a Stone Dreamer and the stones told him many wonderful things. One day when my father was away, my stepmother became ill and lay on her bed in great pain, unable to arise. I sent for White Crow, who brought with him no medicine-bag, rattle, nor the usual drum; neither did he sing or talk to mother, but merely sat and looked at her as she rolled in pain. After a while he took a small piece of root which he had with him and cut it into two smaller pieces, telling mother to chew one of the pieces and swallow it and also to chew the second piece and rub it on her chest where the pain was. This mother did as quickly as possible, for she was seriously ill. Her recovery was almost immediate, for it seemed no more than five minutes before she was up and preparing food for White Crow. I was so delighted and curious, that I offered White Crow my best horse if he would give me the name of the plant. He refused, and I then offered him fifty dollars for it, but I found that it was not purchasable at any price.

Chips was another Stone Dreamer and his fame was wide among his people, for he would go into the sweat-bath and there locate lost articles or horses and absent people. While taking the purification ceremony the *tunkes*, or hot stones, brought great inspiration to Chips, so when he went to the place of vigil they came to him in spirit and offered him service. So Chips always carried stones, some of them painted in colors, in his medicine-bag. When he was making medicine they would fly to him and they could be heard striking the tipi and after we moved into houses I have heard them dropping down the chimney and have seen them lying about on the floor where they had fallen.

There were many men, medicine-men and those who were not, who, in my early youth, did marvelous and unexplainable things. Sorrel Horse, the wonderful scout, had a medicine which, I believe, was the wolf, for he could travel with ease through snow so deep and weather so cold that it tried even the strongest of Lakota braves. It was a common saying in my time that Sorrel Horse "traveled like a wolf." I never will forget the sorrow of Sorrel Horse when his grandmother perished one winter in a deep snow-drift. She had attempted to go home alone one night from a dance and, being very old, had stumbled into the snow and had frozen to death. Sorrel Horse stripped and mounted his horse and rode through the high snow-drifts, singing his brave songs and lamenting for the lost one. When he came near my home he was blue with the bitter cold, but still singing, so I induced him to come in and consoled him until he was willing to clothe himself against the storm.

Crazy Horse also had a medicine, though he never claimed to be a medicine-man. The Lakotas believed that the hawk was his protecting power, for he escaped so many dangers, and the father of Crazy Horse always said that had his son had less faith in the white man and made his medicine before going to Fort Robinson on that fateful day his death would have been prevented. The white man laughs at the "magic" of the Indian, but that is because he does not understand the Indian's touch with nature.

The Thunder Dreamers were the *heyokas*, or clowns. They painted *zigzag* stripes on their bodies to simulate lightning, and arrows and war horses, and were, unlike most medicine-men, excellent warriors, many times using their powers to bring on a storm that would place their enemies at a disadvantage; also in olden days, before their powers were destroyed, they could stop the rain at the pleasure of their people; but in that day there was no dearth of rain as now, and the land of the Lakota was a paradise of green with an abundance of small streams, lakes, and springs which have since dried up and disappeared. Besides their serious business, which they carried on with the help of the sky powers, the Thunder Dreamers furnished fun and amusement at the various gatherings and festivities. They always made great sport around the kettle of hot dog soup which was served at the ceremonies by plunging their hands and arms into the boiling liquid and flinging it about, making the others run to safety. Many times I have seen a large kettle emptied of its contents in this manner, but so powerful was their medicine that they were never injured and any one but a Thunder Dreamer would have been severely burned. Much of the fun created by the fun-makers was by doing things opposite to the usual way; for instance, going into the tipi by crawling under instead of walking in by the door, or by coming out feet first. Now and then a Thunder Dreamer carried on his joking all the time, and one of these fellows was Break Shells. This dreamer did so many funny things that he made a sort of Bill Nye reputation for himself. Break Shells' sister once made for him a fine pair of moccasins with a great deal of quillwork on them; finishing them, she threw them to him across the tipi, saying, *"Ohan"*, or "wear them," as he full well knew; but since the word *ohan* means "to cook" as well as "to wear," Break Shells promptly threw one of the moccasins into the kettle of boiling soup. The sister was so disgusted that she walked out of the tipi without a word. It was customary with the Lakotas to remove one moccasin and with the bare foot hop across a stream that was too wide to jump across, but one day when Break Shells came to a stream he took off his moccasin, held up his bare foot, and hopped across with his shod foot. Everyone, of course, laughed. Another time Break Shells was driving some beef cattle from the plains to a corral near the village. One of the animals gave him a lot of trouble by running back toward the open country every time it got near the gate. Break Shells' father came out to watch, and seeing that his son's blanket was hanging and flying in the wind, yelled to him, "Drop the blanket and shoot!" Break Shells threw his blanket to the ground and as quickly as he could turn his horse, which was running, back to where the blanket lay on the ground, he shot it twice. With a gesture of hopelessness, the father turned and went back into his tipi.

That our medicine-men had great powers there was never any doubt among us, and it was only when their hearts became filled with unrest and defiance that their powers waned. They helped to make our lives joyful, to bring the rain so the grass would grow, to bring the buffalo near, and to get in closer touch with the forces of goodness. They were with us all through life, in sickness, and in death.

⋆   ⋆   ⋆

In the 1930s, about the same time as Luther Standing Bear wrote *Land of the Spotted Eagle*, another Lakota man was telling his life story to the Nebraska poet John Neihardt. Nicholas Black Elk had been graced with powerful visions as a young boy. By the time he met Neihardt, Black Elk had converted to Catholicism and risen to the respected position of catechist in the mission church at Pine Ridge Reservation. How and why Black Elk became Catholic is never explained in John Neihardt's *Black Elk Speaks* (1932), the epic saga of Plains Indian life based on Black Elk's reminiscences. As Black Elk said of his visions, he was not sure they were suited to twentieth-century Lakota life on a reservation, and among many accommodations he made, he chose not to heed his visions in their entirety. Still, Black Elk remembered and respected their power, for he described his visions in great detail to Neihardt. The excerpt here comes from Neihardt's notes, which Raymond DeMallie edited and published in *The Sixth Grandfather: Black Elk's Teachings Given to John G. Neihardt* (1984). The places mentioned in this account are landmarks in the Black Hills.

The Sixth Grandfather: Black Elk's Teachings Given to John G. Neihardt

Raymond J. DeMallie

Black Elk is Taken to the Center of the Earth and Receives the Daybreak Star Herb

[The] western black spirit said: "Behold this day, for this day is yours."
[*I will have the power to shed many happy days on people, they tell me.*]
"Take courage, for we shall take you to the center of the earth." They
[the spirits] said: "Behold the center of the earth for we are taking you
there." As I looked I could see great mountains with rocks and forests on
them. I could see all colors of light flashing out of the mountains toward
the four quarters. Then they took me on top of a high mountain where I
could see all over the earth. Then they told me to take courage for they
were taking me to the center of the earth. All the sixteen riders of the four
quarters were with me going to the center of the earth and also this man
by the name of One Side.

We were facing the east and I noticed something queer and found out
that it was two men coming from the east and they had wings. On each
one's breast was a bright star. The two men came and stood right in front
of us and the west black spirit said: "Behold them, for you shall depend
upon them." Then as we stood there the daybreak star stood between
the two men from the east. There was a little star beside the daybreak
star also. They had an herb in their hands and they gave it to me, saying:
"Behold this; with this on earth you shall undertake anything and
accomplish it." As they presented the herb to me they told me to drop
it on earth and when it hit the earth it took root and grew and flowered.
You could see a ray of light coming up from the flower, reaching the
heavens, and all the creatures of the universe saw this light. (Herbs used
by Black Elk are in four colors – yellow, blue, red, white flowers all on
one bush. The four-colored flowers represent the four quarters of the
earth. This herb is called daybreak star herb.)

[The] western black spirit said: "Behold all over the universe." As I
looked around I could see the country full of sickness and in need of

DeMallie, Raymond J., ed. *The Sixth Grandfather: Black Elk's Teachings Given to John G.
Neihardt*. Lincoln: University of Nebraska Press, 1984: 133–42. Reprinted by permission of
the University of Nebraska Press. Copyright © 1984 by the University of Nebraska
Press.

help. This was the future and I was going to cure these people. On the east and north people were rejoicing, and on the south and west they were sick and there was a cloud over them. They said: "Behold them who need help. You shall make them over in the future." After a while I noticed the cloud over the people was a white one and it was probably the white people coming.

The western black spirit sang:

> Here and there may you behold. (twice)
> All may you behold.
> Here and there may you behold. (twice)

They had taken me all over the world and showed me all the powers. They took me to the center of the earth and to the top of the peak they took me to review it all. This last song means that I have already seen it. I was to see the bad and the good. I was to see what is good for humans and what is not good for humans.

Black Elk Receives the Soldier Weed of Destruction

[The] black horse rider says: "Now your grandfathers, toward them may you walk" (meaning they are going back to the six grandfathers under the flaming rainbow). "You shall now walk toward your grandfathers, but before you there is a man with power. You shall see. Behold him!" I looked down upon the earth and saw a flame which looked to be a man and I couldn't make it out quite. I heard all around voices of moaning and woe. It was sad on earth. I felt uneasy and I trembled. We went to the north side of the flaming man. I saw that the flame really was a man now. They showed me the bad in the form of this man who was all in black and [had] lightning flashes going all over his body when he moved. He had horns. All around, the animals and everything were dying and they were all crying. (The black man represented war in general.)

They said: "Behold him. Some day you shall depend upon him. There will be dispute all over the universe." As they said this the man transformed into a gopher and it stood up on its hind legs and turned around. Then this gopher transformed into an herb. This was the most powerful herb of all that I had gotten. It could be used in war and could destroy a nation. (This was used in war and it was very destructive. If you touch this herb it will kill you at once. Nothing grows anywhere near it because it is killed immediately if it does.)

"Behold him. There will be dispute of nations and you will defend your people with this herb." (I was not old enough when I was supposed to use this herb or else I could have used it and killed many enemies. It was too terrible to use and I was glad that I did not get to use it. This herb is in the Black Hills. Every animal that nears it dies. Around where it grows there are many skeletons always. This medicine belongs only to me – no one else knows what this herb looks like. It looks like a little tree with crinkly leaves, reddish in color. I call this herb a soldier weed.)

Four riders came up – bay, gray, sorrel, white. The bay rider had a buffalo bonnet on and the latter [bonnet] was alive. You could see its eyes and nostrils flaming. The horns were long and curled and there were animals of all kinds standing on the horns. The gray rider had on a warbonnet which had many curved horns to the earth. There were only eagles on these horns. The white rider had on a spotted eagle for a bonnet and he had a lance also. The sorrel rider had a lance in his hand and it was a serpent. He had an eagle bonnet. These riders were on the left side of the soldier medicine. Then the four riders sang this song:

> My grandfathers, they have caused me to be sacred.
> They have caused me to be sacred.
> May you behold me.
> May you behold me.

As they finished the song, the four riders turned around and made a charge. There was so much smoke that I could not see the riders. I heard rapid gunfire and women and children wailing and the horses screaming in fear, dogs yelping. I heard them hollering for victory.

(I am glad that I did not perform this killing, for I would have not only killed the enemy but I would probably have killed the women and children of the enemy, but I am satisfied that I have not been well off. Perhaps I would have been a chief if I had obeyed this, but I am satisfied that I didn't become a chief.)

(Explanation of why they wore [the] helmets they did. The buffalo head meant great endurance. Some animals there had no power and had no right to be on the helmet. The eagle and the horse also had great endurance. These were to represent the people's endurance. The snake meant poison to the people. War itself is terrible.)

The smoke cleared away now and the warriors were in the fourth ascent. You could hear war all over the world. As they appear[ed], smoke covered up the herb and there was nothing but a skeleton as the smoke cleared away. This war was happening all over the world and the fourth ascent is yet to come. Then when the four riders reached the fourth ascent they turned into black-tailed deer. (Some black-tailed deer are sacred and if you try to kill them you cannot do it.) These deer had wounds on their sides which shone out like lightning. Here they showed me the power of the medicine and how to use it. Then the deer turned around and faced the herb from the east side. The black-horned man was standing there again and he changed himself into a gopher, then into an herb, and next into a skeleton.

(At the age of thirty-seven, Black Elk was to use this herb and it made him sad to think of what harm it would do to women and children. At this time he gave it up for the Catholic religion.)

(While performing his duties as a medicine man, Black Elk would hear women singing all over the room.)

[The] black spirit says: "Behold your herb; with it everything you face will be like it and the world will tremble" (meaning that whenever I have the herb I will be able to destroy). (Dispute of four ascents means war in the four quarters.) "There shall be a dispute of the winds, and then you shall depend upon the herb."

During this whole time I did not notice how I was dressed. But now I noticed that I was painted red and all my joints were black. There was a white stripe between the joints all over my body. And whenever I would breath, I would be breathing lightning. My bay horse had lightning stripes on it. The horse's mane was like clouds.

Black Elk Returns to the Six Grandfathers

They took me back to where the grandfathers were now: "Behold, you shall go back to where your grandfathers are." Then I saw the rainbow flaming and I saw the six grandfathers sitting there. (I [had] seemed to be traveling with them, but I found that I was traveling toward them instead.) Then I saw the first two men (turned to geese) that I had seen in the beginning of the vision. They were flying in four formations (circles) – one over the east, one over the west, one over the north, one over the south. The nation of geese sang this:

> In four circles they are flying
> In a sacred manner.
> May you behold them.

As they went around, the geese called thus: "B-p-p-p, b-p-p-p!" *[On earth Black Elk is to make the goose sound and he will get the goose power]*. The western spirit said: "Behold them, for they shall have a sacred voice for you." Here I was presented with the power of the goose voice.

They were taking me back now. Now I could see the house of the first grandfather. It was walled and roofed with cloud and above was lightning and underneath were the fowls of the air. Under the fowls are the beasts of the earth and men. The people on earth were rejoicing and the birds and animals and lightning and thunder were like laughter. They were saying: "Eagle Wing Stretches is coming home." Just before I entered the house, the black spirit said: "Behold your grandfathers; a great council they are having." The door was facing the side where the sun shines continually.

As I entered the door the grandfathers cheered for me and the lightning and the birds, beasts, and men cheered for me. I could hear many voices cheering. They were praising me. Some of them said: "He has triumphed!" As I entered, all the grandfather were sitting with their arms and palms out and said: "He has triumphed!" I could see nothing but millions of faces behind the grandfathers. The west spirit said (pointing to all the people trying to see me): "Behold your nation!"

(All the six men had wooden cups of water in front of them.) I took the cup of water from the west spirit and I could see a buffalo in the water. He presented it to me saying: "Behold the cup; in this cup your nation and you shall feed from it." (Meaning that this cup will be used for me and my nation – that they will all be relatives to each other, and the water is the power to give them strength and to purify them. This water will make the people happy.)

Again I looked toward the people and took good notice this time. I saw there were some animals [people?] in there of different tribes that I was to get along with on earth. I wasn't quite sure yet whether I saw a white man or not. (What I saw there actually happened, for now I have friends of all the different tribes, even of the whites. There will probably never be a time again when the Indians will fight each other; but the whites will fight each other and the Indians may have to fight in with the whites.) The people were happy, as I could see, after I took the cup.

The second (northern) grandfather spoke: "Grandson, all around the universe you have seen the powers and for what you have done your people rejoiced. You have given the men of earth the power they have given you, and with courage they are facing the wind" (meaning the wind of life). "Hundreds shall be sacred; hundreds shall be flames." He came forward and put butterflies' cocoons onto my arms – a red one on the right wrist and a brown one on the left wrist. (Brown is sacred and red is lightning power.) "All over the universe, all your grandfathers, the two-leggeds and on-earth walking, the day-fliers, they have had a council and appointed you and have given you their power. Now you shall go forth to the place from whence you came. Your people are in great difficulty. Behold them!"

As they [the grandfathers] said that I turned around and I could see that it was my own people. Everyone was happy and all the horses were happy except one who was sick. I took good notice and it was myself and I had been sick twelve days. This was probably the twelfth day when I was just going back to my body. I was shown the village and the second grandfather presented me with a cup of water, saying: "Behold this cup." In this cup I saw a man painted blue and he had a bow and arrow and he was in distress. He wanted to get out of the water and get away, but I was told to drink it down. They said: "Make haste and drink your cup of water." I took it and drank the man too. This blue spirit was a fish and I had drunk it down. From this I received strange power and whenever I was conjuring [*wapiya*] I could actually make this blue man come out and swim in the cup of water I used. (The fish represents the power of the water.)

The black spirit says: "Stand over to the third grandfather." (As each grandfather finished talking he would melt into the earth and come up again. Each time a grandfather spoke I was nearer to the earth.)

The third grandfather speaks: "Behold, there are two days relative-like they have given you." Pointing the cup of water to me he said: "Behold this; like unto this you shall live." There was a star in the third cup of water. He said again: "On earth the beings will be glad to see you. So take courage. Now you shall go forth back to your mother earth." Through this morning star in the cup of water I was to get all my wisdom to know everything.

The black spirit said to me again: "Stand over to the fourth grandfather." The fourth grandfather said (as he presented me with the cup I noticed the red road across the cup): "The road of the generations you shall walk. The ascents of your days shall be sacred. Take courage, your grandfathers shall watch over you in all the four quarters of the earth." The fourth grandfather sang this song:

> There is somebody lying on earth in a sacred manner.
>   I made him walk. (five times)
> There is somebody, on earth he lies.
> In a sacred manner I have caused him to walk.

(Black Elk uses this song in treating the sick.)

The black spirit says to me: "Stand over by the fifth grandfather." Then I noticed a cup which represented the Great Spirit. In this cup there was a spotted eagle outstretched. "Your grandfathers, whatever they have decided upon, you have finished. Take this." The eagle began to make beautiful sounds and I noticed his eyes were sparkling and he (the eagle) was dancing. "Every day this eagle shall be over you. He has eyes that will see everything (living eyes), and through them you shall also see. To your nation in a sacred manner you shall go."

[The] black spirit again asked me to stand over to the sixth grandfather. The sixth grandfather showed me a cup full of water and in it there were many small human beings. He said: "Behold them, with great difficulty they shall walk and you shall go among them. You shall make six centers of the nation's hoop." (Referring to the six cups of water, meaning that the six centers of the nation's hoop were the different bands or tribes: (1) Hunkpapas, (2) Minneconjous, (3) Brulés, (4) Oglalas, (5) Shihela [*Sahiyela*, Cheyennes] (6) Idazipcho (Black Kettle) [*Itazipco*, Without Bows].) "Behold them, this is your nation and you shall go back to them. There are six centers of your nation and there you shall go. Now in a sacred manner you shall walk. Your grandfathers shall make four goals" (four quarters).

Now the cloud house began to sway back and forth and everyone was moving around in it. The rainbow over the house was moving up and down. "Behold, the rainbow of your grandfathers shall be set where the sun shines continually." Then I could hear all living voices outside the rainbow tipi calling to me as I came out of the tipi: "Eagle Wing Stretches is coming out, so behold him!" Now I noticed that the sixth grandfather was myself, who represented the spirit of mankind.

"Your grandfathers have given you a good twelve days of happiness, and you shall have twelve sacred days. A day is appearing – behold its face as you come forth. It is so (hetchetu alo [*hecetu yelo*]). Your grandfathers shall go forth. You shall lead them. The living creatures of the earth's generations walk together as relatives."

When they showed me the star it was daybreak and then the sun came up and after it appeared they told me to go forth and I stood outside the rainbow tipi and this was the happiest moment of the vision. I looked to the four quarters of the earth and I saw all the riders. There were colors and lightning in the west and I saw black horses. In the north there were all kinds of birds flying and all different colors of horses. The same was true of the east. All sorts of horses started to mill around and in the south the buckskins were milling around. On earth the animals all rejoiced in happiness.

When I came out of the rainbow tipi the sixth grandfather was gone and I stood there in his place. The western grandfather led me out and the horses all neighed as I came out. As each grandfather came out of the rainbow tipi he was cheered for. They all took their places – north, south, and east. As the eastern man came out he took the rainbow with him and set it on the east side. The last grandfather was on earth and I did not know it and when I started to come back I was suddenly left alone. I heard a voice saying: "Look back and behold it." I looked back and the cloud house was gone. There was nothing there but a big mountain with a big gap in it. (Black Elk knows where this mountain is – Pike's Peak.)

The Spotted Eagle Guides Black Elk Home

I could see nothing but dust flying on the four quarters of the earth. I looked up and could see right above me a spotted eagle hovering over me and this was evidently who had told me to look back. I started back to the camp with the eagle guarding me. No one was with me then but the eagle, but I knew that I was coming back to the center of the nation's hoop by myself. I could see the people following me. Soon I saw my own tipi at home and I walked fast to get there. As I entered the tipi I saw a boy lying there dying and I stood there awhile and finally found out that it was myself.

The next thing I heard was somebody saying: "The boy is feeling better now, you had better give him some water." I looked up and saw it was my mother and father stooping over me. They were giving me some medicine but it was not that that cured me – it was my vision that cured me. The first thought that came to me was that I had been traveling and my father and mother didn't seem to know that I had been gone and they didn't look glad. I felt very sad over this.

Further Reading

DeMallie, Raymond J., ed. *The Sixth Grandfather: Black Elk's Teachings Given to John G. Neihardt.* Lincoln: University of Nebraska Press, 1984.

DeMallie, Raymond and Douglas R. Parks, eds. *Sioux Indian Religion: Tradition and Innovation.* Norman: University of Oklahoma Press, 1987.

Lazarus, Edward. *Black Hills, White Justice: The Sioux Nation Versus the United States, 1775 to the Present.* New York: HarperCollins, 1991.

Utley, Robert M. The *Lance and the Shield: The Life and Times of Sitting Bull.* New York: Henry Holt, 1993.

White, Richard. "The Winning of the West: The Expansion of the Western Sioux in the Eighteenth and Nineteenth Centuries." *Journal of American History* 65 (September 1978): 319–43.

6

Boarding Schools

Introduction

Chilocco was one of several dozen off-reservation boarding schools established by the federal government to educate, assimilate, and as anthropologist Tsianina Lomawaima says, "detribalize" American Indian children. The idea for government boarding schools originated with a former Army officer, Richard Henry Pratt, who became interested in Indian education while guarding a group of young warriors from western tribes imprisoned at Fort Marion, Florida. Pratt's Florida experience and a later, experimental Indian program at Hampton Institute, a post-Civil War school for black freedmen, led him to found the Carlisle Indian Industrial School in Pennsylvania in 1879. The Chilocco boarding school, built a few years later, followed the Carlisle model and subjected students to a regimented daily schedule of lessons, military-style drills, and work details. Intent on stripping Indian children of their cultural knowledge and loyalties, boarding school discipline also prohibited them from speaking their Native languages. By the late 1920s, assimilationist policies began to lose favor in Washington, D.C., and the momentum for off-reservation boarding schools waned. In the next few decades, most of the schools closed. Chilocco graduated its last class in 1980.

For *They Called It Prairie Light: The Story of Chilocco Indian School*, Tsianina Lomawaima interviewed over fifty former students, including her own father. This inside look at boarding schools from the students' perspective reveals a range of emotions. Using words like survival, resistance, and accommodation, Lomawaima shows how the assimilationist intent of Indian reformers met up against a powerful student culture. In the end, the student culture may have won. The book's last chapter, " 'Hm! White Boy! You Got No Business Here!' " describes how, ironically, boarding schools failed at their assimilationist mandate and resulted instead in a reaffirmation of tribal and Indian identities. Lomawaima presents her evidence in extended quotes drawn from the interviews. Each quote identifies a former student by name, the year he or she started school at Chilocco, the student's age or grade-level at the time, and the student's tribal background. Given Chilocco's eastern Oklahoma location, not surprisingly most of its students were Cherokee, Creek, Choctaw, or from other Oklahoma tribes. The chronological focus of Lomawaima's study is 1920 to 1940.

"Hm! White Boy! You Got No Business Here!"

K. Tsianina Lomawaima

The United States government established Indian boarding schools to detribalize and individualize Native Americans. They set out to mold a "successful" student – obedient, hardworking, Christian, punctual, clean, and neatly groomed – who would become a "successful" citizen with the same characteristics. Reality set in when school employees tried to regiment and homogenize a diverse, young, energetic student body through strict military discipline, all the while struggling to keep schools afloat that were chronically underfunded by Congress.

We need to understand the reality of school life in order to understand outcomes that policy did not foresee, for instance, that tribal and pan-Indian identity were reinforced, not diluted in Indian schools. [In *Ethnic Identity and the Boarding School Experience of West-Central Oklahoma American Indians* (1983), Sally] McBeth has made the point that boarding schools in Oklahoma unconsciously structured "interaction between tribes and promoted a pan-Indian sentiment. A variety of tribal groups came into prolonged contact in these educational facilities. Tribal identity retained its significance and at the same time an inter-tribal, 'Indian' identity emerged as an important cohesive concept" (1983, 141). Evi-

---

Lomawaima, K. Tsianina. Chapter 6: " 'Hm! White Boy! You Got No Business Here!' " *They Called It Prairie Light: The Story of Chilocco Indian School.* Lincoln: University of Nebraska Press, 1994: 129–67. Reprinted by permission of the University of Nebraska Press. Copyright © 1994 by the University of Nebraska Press.

dence from Chilocco complicates McBeth's point even as it supports
her.

The details of alumni memories indicate that student life was more
richly textured than a simple opposition to non-Indian authority and
consolidation of pan-Indian identity might indicate. Age, tribe, family
life, native language, and other salient factors operated meaningfully to
subdivide students while survival, shared experience, resistance to
authority, and enrollment in an "Indian" school knit them together. A
closely focused examination of Chilocco narratives reveals the arenas
and the ways tribal identity remained central or took on new significance
for students, as it reveals the circumstances that generated pan-Indian
sentiments.

We can't visit real daily life at Chilocco sixty years ago, but alumni
construct that reality for themselves and for others. They remember that
they controlled certain times and certain spaces of student life. Private
moments were the arena where gangs and cliques ruled, where tribe and/
or "Indian-ness" most often mattered. These relatively free spaces
existed in the interstices of regimentation and surveillance. Wherever
students escaped adult supervision, students set the rules for social
grouping and interaction.

Private Times, Private Places

Private moments fill treasured memories of boarding school. Students
controlled their spare time away from the watchful eye of the school
staff. Peer relationships were rich and complex and students organized
interaction within a miniature society of their own creation. Marian
describes student social control as she recalls her work detail in the
school kitchen.

> *Marian* 1934/18 Creek:
> I was assigned for my first detail in the kitchen. I weighed eighty-seven
> pounds and I was five-one. And upon my entering the kitchen, my detail
> was to cook the oatmeal. Every morning, for nine hundred students. The
> cook, realizing that I was quite short, built me a stool to stand on, so I could
> stir the large, wooden ladle in the oatmeal. And then immediately after
> emptying the pot, my job also was to wash the pot. One day, I climbed up
> on my stool, to wash my pot, and being very meticulous in my dress, and
> grooming, one of the older girls removed my stool while I had my stomach
> up on the rim of it [the pot], washing the bottom of it. And then she gently
> pushed me into the pot. I did not call out, I did not cry. I found my way out
> of the pot, and with a tea towel tied on my hair, I went to the cook, and
> asked her if I might go back to the dormitory. She resolutely got up, and

removed the tea towel from my hair, and asked me what happened. And I
told her that I slipped into the pot. From then on my days on this detail
were different. Because I had not elected to tell what really happened to me
I guess, I was accepted, among the larger and more controlling group in
the kitchen. Because in each society, there is a controlling group, and I
learned that, because even at home there was a pecking order among five
children.

Friendship and peer group control are certain, recurrent markers in the
landscape of Chilocco's social life. Because so many alumni foreground
these themes in their narratives, it is clear that student solidarity was the
most influential and enduring social relationship embedded in the structure of school society. Children at Chilocco turned to one another, not to
adults, to recreate and replace the close supportive ties of family and
community. Given the variety of student age, tribe, hometown, personality, and gender, peer group association was a complex whole with many
component parts, cliques, or gangs.

Male narratives are richer in private moment reminiscences than those
of female alumnae, perhaps because female students were more closely
chaperoned and not allowed free access to the outdoors and neighboring
communities. Women remember life in the dorms and a more restricted
range of spare-time opportunities. Men's stories are set in varied
environments of group activity or private thought. Men emphasize the
importance of gang membership, especially for the younger boys. The
relatively weaker adult surveillance of boys allowed, or possibly encouraged, the boys' reliance on physical violence and fighting to sort out their
differences.

The next few narrators map the restricted geography of the female
world at Chilocco. Surrounded by 8,000 acres, girls inhabited only their
dormitories and adjacent yards. Matrons chaperoned all outdoor activities and a good deal of what went on indoors.

Marian 1934/18 Creek:
Well, for fun, we were fixing up ourselves. [Laughter] We were doing our
hair, we had to pass the bobby pins around, and you did your hair. When
are you going to do your hair? I'm going to do my hair Thursday. O.K.
then, I'll do my hair Friday, and we'd use the same bobby pins. And we
sewed, we made our own little clothes, and we finally got to where we
could wear our own home clothes. And we played cards, and we danced
and we sang. And we could go for a walk, out on the oval, and we went to
the other dorms and visited girls and played cards with 'em. Sang, group
singing in the recreation room, and off and on we'd have formal teas, and
we'd invite our matron in. Just your little clique. And there wasn't much to
do, but that's what you did. If you ran out of that, then you got your books

out. They saw to it you had plenty of homework. ... And at nine o'clock, honey, you better be in that bed. Your light's out.

[...]

Juanita 1929/12 Cherokee:
One thing that I recall in Home 5, we had this nice kitchen. The other dormitories didn't have that, the old ones didn't have a kitchen. And the poultry yard, which was mammoth, had lots of chickens, lots of eggs, was right near Home 5. ... Somebody always had a boyfriend that could give you a chicken, kill you a chicken. And we would draw straws to see who was gonna go in Miss McCormick's office, get the key off the wall. ... But her room was so close by, to unlock the kitchen, to get in there, to cook the chicken in the middle of the night. [Laughter] ... Another thing we did, we put mattresses on the floor and we'd choke each other 'til we passed out, [Laughter] and they had the mattress there to fall over on. ... And piercing ears. ... That was another pastime, sort of, on Sunday afternoons, just bored stiff during quiet hour, piercing ears and ... that falling on the mattress, that was one of our pastimes. In the wintertime, playing freeze-out, opening all the windows in those barns, snow would blow in, you know! [Laughter] It was a challenge to think of something when you were so restricted. But we had a lot to keep us occupied, we had lots of sports, Chilocco was always first. We had arts and crafts and I can still see Edgar chasing butterflies, with a butterfly net. [Laughter] ... Oh, we did butterfly collections and beading, and tennis, we had a lot of tennis, we had racquets and tennis courts. They didn't get a swimming pool until later years. We did an awful lot of walking up to the state line and we had a radio and music in the ... music room.

[...]

Girls actively explored forbidden territory within the bounds of their restricted geography. "Wilderness" for the girls might mean the dorm kitchen or the fire escape.

Florence 1933/7th Choctaw:
You reminded me though, one time, the Home 4 had an old ... fire escape on the outside, it was always locked. [Laughter] It was also forbidden, you were not supposed to get into it ... but we found it unlocked, and we weren't up on the third floor, but we got down to the bottom of that thing and couldn't get out. But we [finally] managed to scramble back up and I remember thinking we're gonna be found here dead. [Laughter] You know wondering how many days and worrying about well how will they punish us? And then I thought well I'm gonna be dead and I won't have to worry anyway! [Laughter] It was really a frightening experience but we got back up I guess to the first floor ... and lived. Didn't get caught

even but it was just one of those crazy things that kids are going to do, I guess.

Women do not recount the same degree of overt resistance, of breaking major rules, as the men relate, but serious rule infractions such as drinking were a part of school society for girls as well as boys.

Florence 1933/7th Choctaw:
Has anyone told you, I was either in 7th or 8th grade . . . a group of the senior girls, by senior, I mean upperclassmen, got drunk on vanilla? [Laughter] . . . Oh, it was one of the funniest things, oh, it was probably pretty good vanilla, but it was a gay time for them, and I think they broke up a few things in the home ec department! [Laughter] I don't know what happened to 'em but it really made the grapevine!

Just as students found or created niches of responsibility and leadership within Chilocco's authoritarian framework, girls contrived physical spaces for free expression in their dorms and classrooms. Boys were not so hard pressed, as they had the run of the campus. Chilocco's acres were a refuge, a chance for privacy, a setting for gang membership, and a rich natural resource for hunting, trapping, and fishing. The wilderness of woods and prairies controlled by students contrasted sharply with the civilized campus controlled by staff. On evenings and weekends the boys slipped into a world of their own. It was easy.

Curtis 1927/9 Creek:
The old buildings all had big Virginia creepers, vines all over 'em, and the vines were as big as your arm. All you had to do was just slip out the window and climb down the vine, from the third floor, no problem, and go wherever you wanted to go, come back in, climb the vine, go right back into your room, your dorm. There was really no problem. You could go any time you wanted. They had bed checks every once in awhile, you just put a dummy in your bed and they never checked that.

Francis 1931/16 Cherokee:
We used to slip off to Ark City on Saturday nights, go listen to the big bands. I was in pretty good with the night watchman, I used to take turns for him, he was the one that checked the beds, so I could go to town and stay 'til one o'clock. All I had to do was tell him where I was going and when I'd be back.

Many boys were drawn to the open prairie, creek, and woods. The outdoor life figures significantly in their positive memories of the boarding school.

Albert 1926/13 Cherokee:
At Sunday noon was no duties, we were pretty much free, so we'd eat as
fast as we could on Sunday noon, get out and run down to the horse barn. I
think Mr. Halloway or Mr. Cobb had a hunting dog. He was a good
squirrel dog, and the first one that got down there and claimed that dog,
would get to hunt, hunt all up Chilocco Creek.

[...]

The great outdoors at Chilocco was a crucial environment, where
students developed and expressed mechanisms of social control. The
boys' gangs were strongest there, providing mutual support and physical
protection. Curtis and Edgar belonged to one of these smaller boys'
gangs, and they remember their gang's territory and home. [...]

Curtis 1927/9 Creek:
We even built little dugouts along some of the steep creek banks where the
water didn't come up anymore, dig out a place and put a roof over it and
sod it, and have a little place that we could go on our own. Even one year
we tore down one of the old buildings and it was nothing but junk lumber
that they were going to burn. We took that down in the woods and built a
little shack, put a tin roof on it, and a little loft in it. We filled that loft with
walnuts in the fall, put walnuts up in there to dry, had a little potbellied
wood burning stove in there, and go down there in the wintertime and
crack walnuts and sit in the warm shack. So there were a lot of little things
that other kids never had that grew up otherwise. Those things I remember
with great fondness. ... They'd have stomp dances out at night, in the
early years. They'd go out and build a fire, and parch corn, and then they'd
make little tom-toms out of tin cans with rubber stretched over the top,
and they'd have stomp dances around those fires at night, and it was a lot
of fun.

The Creeks, Cherokees, and other Southeastern tribes took part in the
stomp dances around the fires strung along Chilocco Creek in the
evenings. Stomp dances held the boys together in a shared cultural
context, and the very sociable pastime of parching corn united all tribes.
Parching corn symbolized group belonging and solidarity. The "parched
corn societies" were a focal point for boys' social relationships, and they
stand out in warm memories of boyhood camaraderie. [...]

Stomp dances and parched corn societies reinforced solidarity
among the boys and delineated their separation from the school's
control. The school administration never endorsed the dances but they
tolerated them. No accounts, oral or archival, document the school
administration taking aggressive steps to forbid or physically interfere
with stomp dancing. It is an anomaly of federal policy and practice at
that time.

Mason 1928/11 Cherokee:
Weekends and holidays were spent catching fur animals for hides to sell,
hides were hung and dried and sold in Arkansas City, money was divided
evenly with the group who had caught the hide. Fishing, stomp dancing
and parching corn at the trash dump were projects candidly looked down
on by faculty, but we did it.

Edgar 1929/10 Creek:
We also had, some of the Indians had their little stomp dances, Creeks
particularly, we Creeks would have their little fires and at night sometimes,
you'd see their fire burning and their stomp dances. 'Course this was
frowned on by the school authorities. As well as it was frowned on for
any of the students to speak their native tongue.

There are only two references to similar activities among the girls at
Chilocco.

Mary 1937/9th Cherokee:
[after discussing the boys' stomp dances along Chilocco Creek] The only
time [the girls] ever, we'd do it in our basement, in the dorm. Some of
those girls could do pretty good leading and singing, you know. Us green-
horns, we'd just get right in there and . . . I don't know if everybody did that
or not, but we did, in Home 3. I can't remember who it was that instigated
that.

Vivian 1929/14 Choctaw:
Some of the Poncas, I remember they would get in their rooms, and I
happened to be in this dormitory one time, [Laughter] and it had about
ten girls. Because I was late going back to school, I got put in the dormitory. I didn't have a room, and they [the other girls in the room] would
have their peyote meeting in the room. All I did was sit there on my bed.
[Laughter] I had never seen that, and so finally one of the girls came over
and told me to come over there and sit with 'em if I wanted to. So I went
over there, I set down, I didn't know what to *do*, I set down with 'em and
they passed that peyote button around, and I took a bite of it, but you
know what it tasted like? Uh, a green olive. And I said, "I don't like it."
And I took it out, you know, spit it out. They just laughed, didn't pay any
attention to me. [Laughter] And I don't know what they were doing, they
were, you know, in their own tongue, but they were all Poncas, Ponca
Indians. It sounded like they were praying, and then they'd sing and then
some more, like praying, and then they'd sing, somebody was beating on a
little gourdlike thing. It was quite an experience for me.

Participation in stomp dances or other covert religious activities was
an important way students could retain ties to their home cultures.
School authorities frowned on stomp dances but, for whatever reasons,

did not stop them. Authorities were quick to clamp down on other transgressions, and some student activities seem calculated precisely to flout authority. Students followed certain courses of action because of the reaction they provoked. Alcohol production and/or consumption was guaranteed to trigger a response. The concoction of home brew, a prime undercover pastime, demanded discretion, ingenuity, and perseverance. In the conflict between acquiescence and overt or covert resistance to authority, alcohol use emerged as a potent symbol of student collaboration and radical resistance. [. . .]

Curtis 1927/9 Creek:
We got fruit, peaches, and put those in a barrel one time, and water and sugar and malt or whatever, we put in that thing and let that ferment. That stuff stank to high heaven, [Laughter] you could smell it! I don't know how, why they never found any of those things, because all you had to do was get downwind of that, and you knew what was *there*. We took raisins and did the same thing, and grapes, we went over to the orchard and got big Concord grapes and we set those up in a barrel. [Laughter] We just put cheesecloth over the top of the barrel and *butterflies*! [Laughter] You could tell a half-mile away where it was because the butterflies were swarming in on these things. We had these barrels stashed all over the place! I don't think they ever knew about that, we were never questioned about it, anyway. . . . But that stuff was terrible, oh boy! But you got a buzz out of it. [Laughter]

[. . .] Alcohol abuse and alcoholism are pervasive tragedies among Indian families and communities. The focus on home brew, bootlegging, alcohol use, and drunkenness as important mechanisms of boarding school resistance raises difficult questions. Did the schools contribute substantially to alcoholism among Indian people? Was it a tragic consequence of students choosing a stimulus guaranteed to stir up school administrators that hurt students themselves most in the long run? Was there some element of self-destructive behavior at work for students who felt caught in a system they could not abide? Or, worse yet, could not leave? At least one tragedy at Chilocco speaks to these questions and to the further research they demand.

Curtis 1927/9 Creek:
TL: Was there any real bootlegging, with the older boys?
     They went to town, there was a lot of bootleggers in Arkansas City. Particularly in the summertime there were always some of the guys coming in from town just dead drunk with that stuff. One guy even died one night, from poisoned [liquor]. I think he did it deliberately though. He had graduated from high school and he was in his twenties, had no home. I can't remember where he came from or even what tribe he was. But he had

no home, no people at *all*, no relatives apparently, and they told him that he was gonna have to *leave*, because he had graduated. He didn't know where he was going or what he was gonna do; this was *home* to him. It was like kicking him out. And he came in that night, just dead drunk and died, and they think that he got, he poisoned that liquor and killed himself. I don't think they ever proved it, one way or the other, or whether he just got hold of some bad whiskey, but I've always felt like he killed himself drinking poisoned liquor.

For this student, Chilocco was the only home he knew, or could imagine. Other students shared their own little "homes" within Chilocco, whether a facsimile of home life in the practice cottages or real, warm shacks in the catalpa grove. The wilderness of the catalpa grove was more than a safe refuge for boys in search of privacy or camaraderie. It was a social arena in contradistinction to the controlled environment of the campus; what was most strongly sanctioned there was expressed most freely here. The tribal or Indian identity, for example, suppressed by the school seemed to flourish among the catalpas.

Boarding schools were designed to eradicate Indian ethnicity and tribal affiliation while rescuing the individual, hence Pratt's famous dictum "Kill the Indian, Save the man." At best, school staff ignored tribal identity; at worst, they punished students harshly for speaking native languages or practicing native religions. It was not so easy to ignore the basic fact that Chilocco students were Indians. It was an Indian school, after all. In private spaces and private moments, students sorted out for themselves who was who and what was what. Tribal identity dominated student interaction in particular places and situations, while it lay dormant or unexpressed elsewhere. Careful attention to how tribal identity was expressed at Chilocco produces a kind of peripheral vision. Focus on ethnicity, and you glimpse things previously hidden in the shadows: distinctions among students based on gender or hometown, for instance, and the different adaptations made by older and younger students.

Indians at Chilocco

Students responded individualistically to Chilocco's regimentation. What characteristics of individual personality or experience were linked to the decisions to accommodate or resist? How did tribe, family, gender, age, language, or degree of blood influence student response? Complex questions require complex answers. Evaluation of narrative reminiscence of intertribal relations yields clues. Native language proficiency, mixed blood versus full-blood, "eastern" versus "western" tribes were balanced in a complex equation of personal identity at Chilocco. These factors, in turn, balanced with other salient disparities among students. Young students/older students, children from broken homes/children from intact families: these distinctions made a difference for Chilocco students.

I asked Chilocco alumni, did students make friends or join gangs within their own tribe? What other factors – age, class, work details – if any, tended to define peer group association? Was there friction or hostility between tribes? Some alumni responded strongly and unequivocally, yes, tribes shaped peer association and there was friction, described in two instances as "intertribal warfare." Others responded just as strongly and unequivocally, absolutely not, there were no tribal divisions. In some cases, alumni did distinguish a salient dividing line between those of full Indian blood and those of mixed blood.

In making my own analysis of these disparate opinions, I have segregated the women's narratives from the men's because their discussion of private moments reveals important differences in their school experiences. The student interactions that took place in private times and places are the clearest indicators we have of student-organized peer groups and provide the clearest views of the criteria students used to sort each other into salient classes or categories. We know that girls at Chilocco were much more circumscribed than the boys; their experience of the school was different because of that. Differentiating the two genders makes it clear where men and women agree and where their accounts or perceptions diverge.

The Women Speak

Chilocco's alumnae express a wide diversity of opinion on the subject of tribal distinctiveness and/or divisiveness at the school. Clara, Maureen, Barbara, and Vivian all downplay student tensions along tribal lines. They recall group associations by age, or personality, or "status" on campus, specifically the popular athletes. Sarah agrees that Chilocco was "just one big family" but does comment on the clannishness of the Poncas.

> *Clara* 1923/10 Potawatomie:
> I really don't recall any kind of tension, or snobbery, along [tribal] lines, it seems like everyone got along together, it didn't make that much difference, were you a full-blood or mixed blood. Even those that only spoke English, and those that spoke their Indian languages seemed to get along.

> *Maureen* 1931/14 Choctaw:
> I never saw any animosity, I don't believe, between tribes. There was some infighting, a little bit. . . . But I thought as a whole, they got along pretty good.

Barbara 1928/12 Choctaw/Pawnee:
TL: Did (friendship) tend to follow tribal lines at all?
No, no. Not at all. It was just . . . I don't know what it would be, it would just be your personality, I guess, it must have been your personality. Because as I say, you were all in the same boat, you all wore these same clothes, and it would have to have been your personality or your background. I think it was more class, than it was whether you were full-blood or [not] . . . well, for instance, like the basketball stars and things like that, a lot of 'em would be full-blood and very dark but still they were up there.
TL: Big men on campus?
Yes, right.

Vivian 1929/14 Choctaw:
TL: People didn't stick together just with their own [tribe]?
Oh, I didn't think they did because I had a lot of Creek friends, see I'm Choctaw [Laughter] and I married, my husband was half Creek.

Sarah 1926/12 Shawnee:
TL: Did you have some friends that you would buddy around with?
Yes, we had what they called gangs, there'd be four or five, maybe six girls in a gang. [Laughter] . . . It was probably just around your age, or maybe your classmates, something like that.
TL: So . . . people just didn't mix with their own tribe?
Some did, like the Ponca girls, they were real close among themselves, but, you know, we were just one big family . . . and they'd always help each other, whatever ways they could.

Sarah's comment about the Ponca girls agrees with other narrators' perceptions about peer groups at Chilocco. Certain tribes tended to be singled out as "clannish," but it is difficult to say today whether they were actually more or less closed than other groups at Chilocco. It may be they have come to symbolize "tribalness" to contemporary alumni. Poncas did live close to the school, and Ponca runaways had only a few miles to go to reestablish contact with their families. Perhaps this proximity strengthened their awareness of their own tribal background and ameliorated the melting-pot effects of a multitribal student body drawn together by the difficulties of being far from home. There were never more than a handful of Ponca students at Chilocco, relative to the large student body, and Ponca-ness certainly did not define the limits of tribal clannishness. Typically, native language use is the factor identified today that bound together tribal members at Chilocco.

Ellen 1927/13 Creek:
They [the girls] just mixed quite a bit but those Creeks, lot of times they got together because they'd talk to each other, some of 'em could talk in Creek, you know.

Winona 1930/10th Cherokee:
There were some of the students up there that we hardly even knew, that
we just didn't even speak to them. Some of the tribes, you know, that were
clannish, and that would even speak their language when they were
together. Then there was students, see, that didn't want to participate in
a lot of the activities that the school had. They were, well, a lot of 'em were
full-blood Indians.

Winona's separation of full-bloods and mixed bloods recurs in many
narratives. Juanita and Irene both recall separation or at least distinctiveness along those lines but deny that the distinction led to any kind of
friction or hostility.

Juanita 1929/12 Cherokee:
TL: Did friendship follow tribal lines at all or did it cut across them?
   In my case, it cut across. Some of the full-bloods particularly that come
to my mind, the Creeks, they didn't even hang out with other
Creeks...they sort of hung together. And well I suppose there were a
few Cherokees that did that, that I can recall. The rest of us, it didn't
matter who was [what]. I loved the Comanches and the Cheyennes and
the Arapahoes, and one of my good friends was a Choctaw. One was a
Creek and one lived at the bottom of the Grand Canyon.

Irene 1929/15 Potawatomie:
TL: Did full-bloods tend to stay separate from mixed bloods?
   I think in a way it really was, but it never caused me to feel unwanted or
anything, I just stayed out of the way. [Laughter] It was always just someone else you could go be with.... [It's] hard to help that, maybe they all
came from some little community. But it never, I don't think it ever caused
problems.

The proportion of full-bloods declined at Chilocco throughout the
1920s and 1930s. Full-bloods constituted 54 percent of 954 students in
the 1924–25 school year; by 1940–41 that proportion had declined to 31
percent (of 811). In the peak enrollment years of the early 1930s, the
percentage of full-bloods hovered around 40 percent of over one thousand students. It seems unlikely that students knew each other's precise
degree of bloo,d as adumbrated in the schools' enrollment records,
which specified $^4/_4$, $^3/_4$, $^1/_2$, and $^1/_4$ Indian "blood."
   Students more likely made their judgments according to a complex
interplay of behavior, language proficiency, family background, and
looks, especially skin color. In this latter regard, they may have been
influenced by some tribes' hostility to people of African descent. School
authorities were certainly ever vigilant for offspring of African-American
parents trying, in federal eyes, to pass as Indians. Offspring of Indian and

black parents certainly existed at the time, but the government was not interested in making a place for them in federal schools. "Too dark" was the euphemism used in school records of suspect students. At the other end of the spectrum, employees favored lighter-skinned students. Some students recall a definite rift along the faultline of complexion as well as tribe and language.

Pauline 1929/16 Cherokee:
The first year I went, I didn't get to stay with my cousin. . . . [I was in] a dormitory, I would say fifteen to twenty beds in that dormitory. And they were all full-bloods, and they were all either Poncas or Creeks, and they all talked their [own] language, they didn't talk English. I tell you, I just felt so out of place. Here I was, I was blond-headed, light-complected, and they wouldn't have anything to do with me. They wouldn't talk to me, they wouldn't tell me anything, and if they did, I couldn't understand them. [Laughter] So I was away from home, and it was a long ways, and I didn't know a soul up there but my cousin. So I went to bawling, and went down to my matron on the floor and I told her, well I'm up there in that dormitory with all those full-bloods and they won't talk to me and they won't have anything to do with me. They won't help me and tell me anything, and I asked if I could move down there with my cousin. She said yes, and she let me come downstairs, and I was happy, even though there was six of us in that room, we were all jammed in one little old room. [Laughter]
TL: Was that usual, the full-bloods sticking together or people from one tribe sticking together?
Well, it was with those Poncas. Now there was other classmates that I had that weren't all full-bloods, there were a *lot* that weren't full-blood. And I would pick one out, I could see them, you know, around through the groups, especially in my class.

Pauline's unhappiness with her roommates led her to the matron, who intervened in her behalf and assigned her to a room with her cousin. Tillie recalls that matronly intervention often came at the point of room assignments themselves and may have played a role in shaping student peer groups along lines that seemed reasonable to the matrons.

Tillie 1939/13 Cherokee:
You were assigned your roommate for the year, every year it was assigned, you didn't have a choice. They knew you after awhile, they knew what girls would fit in with what other girls, and they would put you with someone compatible. Tribes sometimes determined that, the Poncas and Pawnees stuck pretty close together, for example. Others mixed pretty well. Some of the Creek girls might have been a little clannish, and the Kiowas, and Comanches.

What seemed reasonable to the matrons as criteria for discriminating among [or against] students?

Nora 1934/10th Cherokee:
Being lighter, the employees kind of favored me. I got ribbed a lot about it, but I was always too timid to really get into any trouble.

Women remembering tribal affiliation and peer group formation at Chilocco relate perceptions ranging from little or no tribalism to specification of groups closed by tribe, native language use, or degree of blood, or by some combination of these factors. Creeks and Poncas who spoke their own languages are mentioned several times as "clannish." Juanita comments that Creeks who were native language speakers differentiated themselves from Creeks who were not. With regard to native language proficiency, the sample of alumnae interviewed is quite imbalanced. Only two of the women entered Chilocco speaking their own language. Both are Creek, and neither commented on any tribalization among the girls. Almost all the alumnae represented here think of themselves as mixed blood, roughly half a dozen as full-blood: these categories reflect family background, behavioral characteristics, contemporary place of residence, and other factors in addition to superficial considerations of looks or skin color.

Women's narratives contain other clues to tribally influenced student associations in the comments that differentiated *eastern* from *western* tribes.

Norma 1925/12 Ponca:
Seems like the tribes would divide by eastern and western, you know. Like the western people pretty well stayed together and the eastern, from Creeks to Cherokees and them, they pretty well stuck [together]. They [the eastern tribes] even had different costumes than we did. They believed in the Stomp Dances, and the Corn Dance, these kind of things, and we didn't, we had another style. So there was a little separation there, but not very much. We were pretty much all together. I had a whole lot of Creek friends, and a lot of Cherokee friends, and I guess I'm the wrong person to talk to because I had no quarrel at all.

Eastern and *western* refer here to geographical and cultural differences. Eastern tribes had been removed from the South or East to eastern Oklahoma: such as, Creek, Cherokee, Choctaw, Chickasaw, Seminole, Euchee, Delaware, Shawnee. Western tribes by culture and geography included the Southern Cheyenne, Arapaho, Comanche, Kiowa, and Apache, who were located in western Oklahoma. Several tribes who were culturally closer to the western Oklahoma Plains tribes had been assigned lands close to Chilocco, and thus close to land areas settled by the so-called Five Civilized Tribes, or eastern tribes. The Poncas, Pawnees, Otoes, Kaws, and Tonkawas were geographically eastern but culturally western and students classed them among the western tribes.

The east/west dichotomy was probably exacerbated by school staff who discounted truly Indian heritage among the eastern groups, especially the Five Civilized Tribes. Real Indians in their judgment were western Indians. In the 1930s, as new administrators in Washington directed boarding-school personnel to value Indian cultures, Chilocco established an Indian Dramatics Club under the new arts and crafts teacher. The club's members were without exception western Indians: Kiowas, Comanches, Cheyennes, and so on, with a few Caddos just to confuse the issue. School records indicate the club gave performances, mostly off-campus, to represent the "Indian School" to the surrounding American public.

The arts and crafts teacher instructed students in "crafts representative of no certain tribe" since "many of the tribes represented at Chilocco have lost their tribal arts and crafts." The crafts of no certain tribe included spinning and weaving wool; beadwork; weaving rag rugs, yarn belts, and cornhusk place-mats; and cross stitch (an art, perhaps, of the least certain tribe). In 1935, the arts and crafts teacher expressed hopes of looking up Oklahoma Indian designs. She turned for help – not to the tribes – but to the Oklahoma Historical Society and the art department at the University of Oklahoma. Eastern Indians often agreed with this exotic perception of western Indians. Juanita (Cherokee) puts it eloquently:

> There's nothing in this world that will put me to sleep faster than a stomp dance...these Cherokees are so *colorless*, they have no feathers, no nothing...so now for our celebration every year we have the Plains Indians, now they can really get it on.

The Men Speak

Male narratives reveal the same broad range of opinions as the women's, from those who recall no tribal clannishness at all to those who describe intertribal "warfare." Men repeat the themes brought up by women, recalling close interrelations among the Five Civilized Tribes versus the western groups, and tribal clannishness linked with native language proficiency. [...]

Albert 1926/13 Cherokee:
I didn't notice it, really. Some of the Creeks, possibly, and some of the Choctaws that was from the [same] community at home may [have]. As

far as any kind of segregation, not segregation but cliques, I didn't notice any as far as tribes or even home towns or anything. Or even relatives, everybody seemed to be up there on their own. Now I mean you had your buddies but it was like, my close friends included a Kiowa, a Chicka-saw...a Creek, [and] a Choctaw boy.

[...] The men more often recall tribe as an operative factor in deter-mining student associations than the women do, and they stress more the associations resulting from hometown origin. *Hometown* in Okla-homa reflects tribal origin even today. When Indian Territory and Okla-homa Territory were consolidated into the state of Oklahoma, tribal governments were dissolved. Reservations as protected federal trust lands had already passed largely into (non-Indian) private ownership as a result of the Dawes Allotment Act. The eastern tribes, particularly the Five Civilized Tribes, no longer resided on reservations in the 1920s and 30s but lived in what are known today as "historic areas." Certain small towns in areas that had been historically designated as Creek or Cherokee or Choctaw lands maintained a population that was heavily of that tribal origin.

Ira 1936/? Cherokee:
Two things [mattered], tribe and hometown, for the large part. Some of the more outgoing boys, they made friends with people from all over the place.

Louis 1933/14 Cherokee:
I think the people who had a tendency to hang together, more or less as a group, because there were quite a few of them and that was the Kiowas and the Creeks. Now those two tribes did, and...used to slip around and try to talk their language. ...The Poncas were pretty clannish, but there wasn't too many of them up there, then. But the Five Tribes usually stayed pretty close to each other, I mean, you'll find that many of the Five Tribes intermarried into each other, quite a few of them did.
[...]

Hometown, tribe for some students but not all, native language, east-ern or western origin tended to bring the boys together in their small cliques or gangs. Although many of the boys came from rural homes, some were perceived as more backwoods than others, as Francis (1931/ 16 Cherokee) recalls:

They had little gangs, little clans I guess you'd call them. Like those bunch from Tahlequah and up in there, now they all stuck together pretty close. They was all hillbillies, and I mean hillbillies. [Laughter] Had to learn to wear shoes when they come down there. [Laughter] They stuck together, and they played a lot of fiddle and hoedown music. They were real good, they did jigs, Irish jigs, they get to playing music and a whole bunch of 'em would get to jigging.

There is still no clear pattern, however, among the narrators to indicate why some alumni discount tribalism as an important social factor at Chilocco and why others comment upon it. The next three narrators indicate there is a pattern of response embedded in this contradictory corpus of evidence, a pattern tied to the age boys arrived at Chilocco and to the kind of home from which they came, as well as to complexities of student interaction in a large institutional setting. Part of the reason people today have disparate memories of Chilocco is because they had disparate experiences at the school.

Little Boys, Big Boys

Edgar 1929/10 Creek:
I remember when I first came to Chilocco, we had rode on the Midland Valley train, all the way from Muskogee. Then to Arkansas City they sent a truck out to pick us up, my sister and I. As I walked up the steps of Home 2, which was the dormitory for the younger boys, old Sam Lincoln... Hippo, was up at the top. He looked at us, he grunted, and said, "Hm! White boy! You got no business here!" I'll never forget that, that was my first introduction: "White boy, you ain't got no business here." And I had two fights that night, before we went to bed. Of course, thereafter it was a matter of survival. Kids had to fight, but they were always fair fights. I could truthfully say that I never saw any student use a club or a knife or stomp or anything like that.

The men who speak next, Edgar, Curtis, and Mason, have some interesting things in common. They agree that tribalism was supremely important in gang membership at Chilocco. They are acutely cognizant of, and had intimate experience with, the violence among and between gangs. They emphasize how gangs physically protected their members, and the strong dichotomy between mixed bloods and full-bloods. This congruence of accounts reflects a fortuitous cluster of alumni who were closely related as students. Curtis, Edgar, and Mason are mixed bloods (Curtis and Edgar are mixed-blood Creek, Mason is mixed-blood Cherokee) who came from broken homes, with one or both parents gone. None were raised in a family with strong cultural ties to their respective tribes. They entered Chilocco as young boys (Curtis was nine, Edgar was ten, Mason was eleven) and joined small boys' gangs composed of noted troublemakers.

Curtis and Edgar ran with the same gang. Similar family backgrounds brought Curtis and Edgar to Chilocco, and similar experiences shaped their first few years as they hung out in the same gang. They rebelled strongly against the school's strict discipline and highly valued loyalty to their gang. They were in trouble a lot, and both remember that when rules were broken, they were called on the carpet as primary suspects. They were "overt resisters" par excellence. In their narratives we hear the strongest expressions of intertribal division, "intertribal warfare," and the strongest expressions of the divide between mixed blood and full-blood.

Curtis 1927/9 Creek:
There was a lot of intertribal warfare there, there was an awful lot of that went on. You belonged to one tribe, you hung out with that tribe. If you didn't have somebody to back you up, you could really get clobbered. These guys would lay for you and catch you out somewhere, so my brother and I stayed pretty close together to help each other. We got into an *awful* lot of scraps, we both seemed to enjoy it anyway! [Laughter] Because we'd get up every morning and fight over who's gonna make the beds. [Laughter]

Edgar 1929/10 Creek:
[I had few relatives at Chilocco]. I was pretty much alone. And I was called a *stahitkey*, which in Indian means "white man," and when they called me *stahitkey*, I called them *stalustey, stalustey's* "black man," and a fight started. The worse name that you could call me was white man, I mean to me there was nothing more despicable than to be called a white man. I was discriminated against, I guess. I had many, many fights over the fact that I was fair-skinned, and I know the reason that it was. Indians certainly would discriminate against a white person, they'd see white people discriminating against Indians, kind of a universal custom. There were certain tribes that were clannish, that ran around together strictly because they belonged to the same tribe. That wasn't so much true *generally*, I think all the students were pretty much thrown together, and you selected your friends not upon the basis of who roomed with you, or who was in your class, because you were pretty much thrown together with everybody. Now, your friends, naturally, were the ones in your own age group, and of course later on, the ones that you worked with. But I'd say that as you grew up there, your friends pretty much were just at random throughout the school.

Curtis emphasizes tribal differences in determining relations between students, and Edgar focuses on the distinction between full-blood and mixed blood, Indian and white, but then asserts a random pattern of friendship formation. A closer look at the differences between Curtis and Edgar sheds light on their different views of tribal affiliation.

Curtis entered Chilocco in 1927. By the early 1930s, he had begun a string of unsuccessful escapes, running away from school only to be returned. By 1935, at age sixteen or seventeen, he ran away from Chilocco never to return. His tenure at the school was dominated by his affiliation with his small boys gang. He never spent appreciable time in high school at Chilocco, and he never reached a rapprochement with school authorities. He remained rebellious throughout his stay. Edgar, on the other hand, underwent something of a transformation during his years at Chilocco. He came under the influence of a visiting Baptist missionary, who convinced him of his intelligence and promise, and under her guidance he became a star student. He graduated from high school at Chilocco at the head of his class. There is a crucial difference here between Edgar and Curtis and it has to do with age and the maturation process. Recall Edgar's statement that *"as you grew up there, your friends pretty much were just at random throughout the school."* The effect of the age difference is even more explicit in Mason's narrative.

Mason 1928/11 Cherokee:
The formative years, nine through ten, one learned he was either white – light complected; half breed – brown, light hair; or full-blood – dark. So gangs were formed, for individuals' protection, learning trust, to fight for each other, right or wrong. ...
TL: So the gangs, the full-bloods would hang together?
    Yes. You were categorized by that. That's the reason I mentioned it, you were categorized white or half breed, you were called that.
TL: Did people tend to stick together with their own tribe?
    Primarily. Because the Creeks would have their little forms, Cherokees would have theirs. It went by tribal, and locality, well, locality meant you were Cherokee. That's primarily the way they were categorized. After the tenth, eleventh grade, why you were pretty much old enough then to take care of yourself and you didn't have this business of the individuals ganging up, and they were kind of more sociable.

Mason's last comment reveals part of the pattern implicit in other answers to the ethnicity question. One of the reasons different people give such contradictory answers to the ethnicity question is because they experienced very different subcultures at Chilocco, depending on their age when they entered school. Gangs protected the smaller, younger boys and gang membership followed tribal and "blood" lines more than other criteria. This was true whether the boys came from strongly tribal homes or not. Neither Curtis nor Edgar came from homes where they had been surrounded by Creek culture. Curtis' home was in urban Wichita, and he and his brother had had almost no contact with Creeks (that is, Creeks as a tribal community, outside of immediate family) before they entered Chilocco. Yet Edgar, Curtis, and Curtis's brother

joined a mixed-blood Creek gang. For these small boys, gang membership was determined by tribal affiliation and degree of Indian blood.
Other narrators attest how important gangs were for mutual protection.

John 1931/16 Chickasaw:
Well it kind of wasn't too bad then [at the high school level], but for them
little guys, they would always kind of go around in groups, and you had to
join some group [for protection]. I didn't know, 'cause I went in there in
the tenth grade.
[...]

Tribal affiliation did not mean the same things to older and younger
students. Students who arrived at Chilocco in high school, often slightly
overage for their grade, had different experiences than the young boys.
Their relations with other students did in fact tend to be determined by
social factors other than tribal affiliation (except for small groups of
native language speakers for whom linguistic factors were important).
These other social factors included class attendance, mutual work
details, athletic team membership, and individual personality traits.
Age when entering school and family background emerge as important
correlates of a patterned response to the ethnicity question, and a partial
answer to the question, "Who resisted and who accommodated?"
     The link between age and family background was not accidental or
circumstantial. Young children who entered the elementary grades at
Chilocco in the 1920s and 1930s tended to come as orphans or from
broken homes. Federal policy at this time reserved off-reservation boarding-school enrollment for students aged twelve and older, with special
exceptions because of family circumstances. Children from stable
families attended public schools where available in rural Oklahoma
during the 1920s and 1930s and did not arrive at Chilocco until they
were at least twelve years old.
     Three factors emerge from this research as being important influences
on (but not determinants of) response to the boarding-school environment and disciplinary system: age when entered boarding school, family
background, and time when entered boarding school. Students who
entered very young, in the elementary grades, from broken homes, and
especially those whose attendance began in the 1920s, when military
regimentation was quite strict, tend to have had a negative response to
Chilocco. For boys at least, tribal affiliation dominated peer group
relations, even for boys who did not come to school well versed in
their own tribal culture.
     Students who entered Chilocco as high school students, often slightly
overage for their grade, from strong, stable family backgrounds, espe-

cially those who attended in the 1930s, when the military aspects of discipline were being phased out, were much more likely to have made a positive accommodation to the boarding-school environment. For these students, tribal affiliation was not the most important social factor in determining peer group associations, if it was important at all. Age differences in tribally determined association are more strongly evident for boys than for girls, for reasons that remain to be elucidated in future research. None of the factors cited, either singly or in concert, operated as complete determinants of individual response. They are indications of social and cultural factors that played a role in ordering student relations at Chilocco in the 1920s and 1930s.

The 1920s and the 1930s are not the 1980s, when the stories in these pages were told, nor less the 1990s, when many of them are being read for the first time. It has been said that history and memory are natural enemies rather than allies, but perhaps some truce can be found in the story, as well as the history, of Chilocco. Alumni narratives carry historical weight, literally and figuratively. They document the reality of an existence that barely crept onto the margins of the printed pages of federal records and correspondence. These narratives also carry, even configure, personal lives. They are fifty-one people's stories of childhood, adolescence and growing up. These stories fit into larger stories that make sense of fifty-one people's whole lives. For each of them, boarding school is only part of the story. For most of them, it is an important part.

A Valuable Education

Every surviving graduate or alum of Indian boarding schools has something to say about their education. Some people valued their education in the highest degree, others look back with regret and resentment, but everyone who attended Chilocco took something immutable and everlasting with them. It might be friendships, begun in school and strengthened over the years. It might be a trade that provided lifelong employment, or the self-reliance that provided the springboard to any career. It might be strength of character forged under difficult circumstances, or remembrances of a happy time without responsibility. It might be pain and anger and loss or confidence and joy and security or most likely it's all of the above all mixed up together. Fifty-one people have looked back on their lives and found meaning in fifty-one different ways.

Although Chilocco was closed in 1980, it persists as a social reality today in many communities across Oklahoma. Local chapters of the alumni association meet monthly or on a regular basis, and annually all the chapters come together for a big reunion. Less formally, families and friends share their memories and reinforce the bonds established years ago. For many students, Chilocco was a home they shared with their family; as alumni they still keep the family together.

> *Florence* 1933/7th Choctaw:
> The thing that I remember most about it, and I think it's probably the most valuable thing I learned, or the longest lasting, is the value of friendship. [We] were *very* close friends. And you never forget, you're always concerned about them, even though you don't see them often. You can still keep in touch.
> TL: Well, many people say that it was like family there.
> That's it! You develop a substitute, very close family relationship, and it's a different kind of sibling relationship.
> [. . .]

Students created a new kind of family life for themselves within the boarding school, which continues to have meaning today. Alumni also value other aspects of the school that were imposed on them by school authorities. In retrospect, they integrate Chilocco's discipline and work ethic with lessons learned throughout life to express an appreciation for the training they received.

> [. . .]
> *Edward* 1932/7th Cherokee, and *Rachel* 1929/4th Cherokee:
> Rachel: I feel we got a very well-rounded education, I never made below a *B* in P.E. or home ec, although I was never that great in academics. I'm what I wanted to be, a wife and a mother, a homemaker, a good neighbor and as good a Christian as I can be.
> Edward: And I got good training there: we never had to hire an electrician, or a carpenter, or a painter. There's something to being raised poor, too: you don't look to someone else to do things for you, you don't look to hire someone.

> *Charlie* 1934/9th Cherokee:
> TL: Do you think you got a good education there?
> I do. Maybe my academics wasn't as high as they would have been [elsewhere] but I think I got more than that, I picked up the academics later. I had to struggle a little bit in college. I made pretty good grades, but I recognized the fact, my first year in college, that I was behind some of those in the classroom. But I gained a lot of other things that they didn't have. One of the things that made America great was perseverance, and that you learned there [at Chilocco]. That's a lost art in society today. . . . They instilled that feeling of pride. Work was honorable, and you get out and hustle for what you get, and I think later years, they didn't have that. It

was a great experience. You have a feeling of brotherhood, that you just don't have going to public schools.

School trades did not usually pan out into lifetime careers, but Chilocco alumni believe they did provide critical bridges to other employment, or simply the confidence that one could do *any* job well once one had been trained at Chilocco. [. . .]

Retrospective evaluation of the boarding school features other prominent themes: the kinds of social training Chilocco provided and the simple opportunity to get an education, albeit not an academically advanced education, when no other options existed. Women alumni in particular comment on the social skills they learned at Chilocco, whereas both men and women are grateful for an education they could not have gotten anywhere else. They are glad they went to Chilocco: "Otherwise, I probably, I know I wouldn't have gone to high school. [I'd] probably be back in the hills somewhere, with the squirrels" (Frank 1923/14 Cherokee).

Alice 1925/7th Cherokee:
I think though, really and honestly, the *greatest* value that the Indian schools had over the public schools was the social development of the students. It wasn't the academic program, it wasn't the vocational program, very few of those kids from Chilocco that took a Vo-Tech course worked at it after they finished school. They went out and did something else. . . . They got the basics for life, but most of that basics was concerned with social development. We were taught how to introduce people. Now that was one thing we had to do, because that was one thing those old ladies pounded into us. You have to know how to meet people and you have to know what to say when you get there and you have to know how to act, how to look when you get there. Oh, my goodness yes, [Laughter] everything, everything that's happened to me has come from going to school at Chilocco, because I guess I'd still be living down in those hills [otherwise].

Nora 1943/10th Cherokee:
But I tell you, I wouldn't trade that education for all the public schools in the world. I really would not. It was really an experience, and I learned more there, maybe not academically, but overall, to take care of myself. To do on my own, and I matured. . . . Personality-wise and appearance-wise, now one rule, you *never* were seen in public with curlers in your hair, and to this day, I *cannot* go out with curlers in my hair. They really had a strong emphasis on personal appearance, and reputation.
[. . .]

Tillie 1939/13 Cherokee:
I think nothing can take the place of that mass discipline. Our parents were far away, or some didn't have parents. They sent their kids there because

they wanted them to get an education. It helped many, many people, thousands of them. There weren't school buses then, or money to board kids in town, without Chilocco, so many just wouldn't have gotten an education at all. It really was a marvelous school; I've always felt indebted for my education there.

I believe there is a moral to the story of Chilocco, and it falls somewhere between the depiction of boarding schools as irredeemably destructive institutions and Tillie's sentiment that Chilocco "really was a marvelous school." The moral is that no institution is total, no power is all-seeing, no federal Indian policy has ever been efficiently and rationally translated into practice, and much of the time practice produced unpredicted results anyway. I think that there has probably never been an off-reservation boarding school that was all bad or all good, all of the time (but I am still not willing to say it's impossible). We must *not*, however, confuse this generic moral of an internally complex and contradictory institution with individual reality. Certainly for the young man who drank poisoned liquor, and others, Chilocco was irredeemably destructive. It was fatal. For Tillie, and others, it was marvelous. The institution and the institutional experience were for each individual person what that person made of it. [. . .]

The fact that many alumni value their experience at Chilocco does not mean they fully endorse its educational policy and practice. The majority of alumni[,] after all, did not or would not send their own children to such an institution, especially at a young age. The three who did send children to boarding schools, sent them to a much-changed institution. The fact that many alumni value their Chilocco experience does not, I believe, constitute a justification or an endorsement of the school's "success." I believe it endorses the strengths and resources that students brought to, discovered at, and created within Chilocco, through their own ingenuity and through cooperation with and reliance on each other.

Recognition of student resourcefulness, however, should not be turned inside out into a reciprocal argument of student culpability. The obverse of the argument that Indian people were responsible for their own success during and after Indian school might be that they were also responsible for their own "failure." I abhor the twisted logic that would condemn young children who could not or would not adapt to Chilocco, or the young victim of poisoned liquor, as just not strong enough or creative enough to make it. The undeniable fact remains that children grew up away from their families in a very difficult, demanding, and occasionally physically violent environment. For better or for worse, they are different people now than they would have been had they never passed through Chilocco's doors.

Two last voices.

Robert 1933/10th Cherokee:
Like I said, I was getting a good education at a boarding school that some millionaire would send his son back East to a place like that, wouldn't be as good as Chilocco. That's the way I kind of looked at it. I felt like I was really in an elite place. Everything just went like clockwork and everybody got along, course there was fights, you know kids, once in awhile they'll have fights and so forth. It's just something, there'll never be another one like it. It was really a marvelous place, as far as I'm concerned. Like I said, I felt like, I never did say anything to anybody about it, but I felt like, I'm just as well off as some kid at some prep school back East. Everybody was interested in me, I had everything I needed. I didn't really need any money, but of course you can always use money [Laughter]. . . . You were kind of on your own and yet you were subject to controls. You do whatever you wanted to up to a certain point, it was democratic in that sense, and at the same time, it was kind of dictatorial. You had to march, you had to go in groups, to this and that, but it was for the good of all, I guess. They had to do it that way. When you've got a thousand kids on the campus like that, twenty-four hours a day, seven days a week, you got to have some controls . . . or you just have chaos. But most of the kids enjoyed it, there's always some that just couldn't quite make it. . . . There's always some who just felt they were being too restricted, and they broke over and then that's when they had to leave. You knew, at least I did, you knew what the limits were and I was always able to stay within 'em. Some of 'em could not, or didn't want to, or felt like they were in prison. But to me, that was teaching you to, that's the way life is. You can't just do whatever you want to do, whenever you want to do it. You got to have some control, I think that made it easier for me, later on. I learned there that if you stay with something long enough, pretty soon it's going to pay off for you.

Edgar 1929/10 Creek:
This school up there was certainly a great thing for all these homeless children and sometimes I think we got a little better bringing-up than some that had mothers and fathers at home. We may have lost out in some [things]. . . . I went to sleep at night crying, for various reasons, busted nose or lips . . . just so many things, you didn't have anybody to tuck you in bed, or whatever all that was. But you had so much, there was so much that was learned there on the good side. [The important thing] is this business of having to experience something, we're not going to learn other than by experience. There were things that you had to do and the discipline was such, that, it just didn't make any difference, there was no exceptions. And maybe that makes a better person out of you, at least you learn there's a lesson in all this, a *hard* lesson.

Chilocco taught hard lessons. Many students stuck with it and mined Chilocco for what it was worth. Many alumni set that worth highly today and value their experiences at the Light on the Prairie. We should value those alumni and treasure the lessons they teach us. I believe it is a tribute to the strength of Indian students that Chilocco alumni feel so strongly about their alma mater today. It is a tribute to the resilience of children, to the bonds of friendship, to creativity under duress, and to the loyalty of many lifetimes.

When Major Haworth reluctantly shouldered his responsibility to build and then fill the first school building on Chilocco Creek, he anticipated failure. Surely no federal boarding school located so close to Indian homes could survive. A product of his time and his place, he could not see a future when applications to enroll would outstrip space; when nieces and nephews and children and grandchildren would enroll; when Indian people would make Chilocco their home. Haworth's vision was not so much faulty as circumscribed, a human condition that hobbles so much prognostication. Similarly, the federal prediction of the dissolution of tribal and ethnic identity among Indians has not come completely to fruition. Close examination of student ties and cleavages has given us some clues as to how and why that is so. Family background, native language, degree of blood, hometown or home region – all interacted in a complex way as students structured school life into meaningful social units crosscut by age, tribe, gender, and individual attributes.

The story of Chilocco holds within it many stories – the shifts and vagaries of federal policy; the dedication of superintendents, teachers, and staff; the childhood of generations of Indian people; the survival of my father and our family. The story told in these pages began as many different and seemingly irreconcilable stories – accounts by female alumnae, male alumni, tribes from east or west, former employees; government documents detailing unreliable statistics and commissioners' cant. I have tried to make sense of them, and make them make sense, without suppressing or denying the kernel of truth of opinion held in each one. It is a cliché, but a true one, that I alone am responsible for the conclusions I have drawn based on these sources.

The richness, complexity, and variety of memories of boarding-school life convey to us an important message about the history of Native American education. Indian people at boarding schools were not passive consumers of an ideology or lifestyle imparted from above by federal administrators. They actively created an ongoing educational and social process. They marshaled personal and shared skills and resources to create a world within the confines of boarding-school life, and they occasionally stretched and penetrated school boundaries. In the process, an institution founded and controlled by the federal government was inhabited and possessed by those whose identities the institution was committed to erase.

Indian people made Chilocco their own.
Chilocco was an Indian school.

Documents

As the United States Commissioner of Indian Affairs during the height of the
boarding school movement, Thomas J. Morgan was instrumental in formulating the objectives and policies of government-sponsored Indian education. In
the introduction to his "Supplemental Report on Indian Education" (1889),
reprinted below, Morgan positioned schools as the crucial vehicle for rescuing
Indians from life on a "paltry reservation" and transforming them into ideal-
ized American citizens. In Morgan's view, what kind of people were Indians
supposed to become? Why should Indians change? And, what was wrong with
Indians as they were in 1889?

Supplemental Report on Indian Education

Thomas J. Morgan

DEPARTMENT OF THE INTERIOR,
OFFICE OF INDIAN AFFAIRS,
Washington, December 1, 1889.

SIR: I respectfully submit herewith a supplement to the foregoing
report, in which I have outlined a plan for Indian education. When the
regular annual report of this office was submitted, I had not at hand the
data necessary for formulating such a plan and hence could not present it
at that time. This plan, of course, is subject to modifications, as experience may show them to be desirable.

Very respectfully, your obedient servant,

T. J. MORGAN,
Commissioner.

The SECRETARY OF THE INTERIOR.

Morgan, Thomas J. "Supplemental Report on Indian Education." *House Executive
Document* No. 1, 51st Congress, 1st session, serial 2725, pp. 93-7.

A System of Education for Indians: General Principles

The American Indians, not including the so-called Indians of Alaska, are supposed to number about 250,000, and to have a school population (six to sixteen years) of perhaps 50,000. If we exclude the five civilized tribes which provide for the education of their own children and the New York Indians, who are provided for by that State, the number of Indians of school age to be educated by the Government does not exceed 36,000, of whom 15,000 were enrolled in schools last year, leaving but 21,000 to be provided with school privileges.

These people are separated into numerous tribes, and differ very widely in their language, religion, native characteristics, and modes of life. Some are very ignorant and degraded, living an indolent and brutish sort of life, while others have attained to a high degree of civilization, scarcely inferior to that of their white neighbors. Any generalizations regarding these people must, therefore, be considered as applicable to any particular tribe with such modifications as its peculiar place in the scale of civilization warrants. It is certainly true, however, that as a mass the Indians are far below the whites of this country in their general intelligence and mode of living. They enjoy very few of the comforts, and almost none of the luxuries, which are the pride and boast of their more fortunate neighbors.

When we speak of the education of the Indians, we mean that comprehensive system of training and instruction which will convert them into American citizens, put within their reach the blessings which the rest of us enjoy, and enable them to compete successfully with the white man on his own ground and with his own methods. Education is to be the medium through which the rising generation of Indians are to be brought into fraternal and harmonious relationship with their white fellow-citizens, and with them enjoy the sweets of refined homes, the delight of social intercourse, the emoluments of commerce and trade, the advantages of travel, together with the pleasures that come from literature, science, and philosophy, and the solace and stimulus afforded by a true religion.

That such a great revolution for these people is possible is becoming more and more evident to those who have watched with an intelligent interest the work which, notwithstanding all its hindrances and discouragements, has been accomplished for them during the last few years. It is no longer doubtful that, under a wise system of education, carefully administered, the condition of this whole people can be radically improved in a single generation.

Under the peculiar relations which the Indians sustain to the Government of the United States, the responsibility for their education rests primarily and almost wholly upon the nation. This grave responsibility, which has now been practically assumed by the Government, must be borne by it alone. It can not safely or honorably either shirk it or delegate it to any other party. The task is not by any means an herculean one. The entire Indian school population is less than that of Rhode Island. The Government of the United States, now one of the richest on the face of the earth, with an overflowing Treasury, has at its command unlimited means, and can undertake and complete this work without feeling it to be in any degree a burden. Although very imperfect in its details, and needing to be modified and improved in many particulars, the present system of schools is capable, under wise direction, of accomplishing all that can be desired.

In order that the Government shall be able to secure the best results in the education of the Indians, certain things are desirable, indeed, I might say necessary, viz:

First. Ample provision should be made at an early day for the accommodation of the entire mass of Indian school children and youth. To resist successfully and overcome the tremendous downward pressure of inherited prejudice and the stubborn conservatism of centuries, nothing less than universal education should be attempted.

Second. Whatever steps are necessary should be taken to place these children under proper educational influences. If, under any circumstances, compulsory education is justifiable, it certainly is in this case. Education, in the broad sense in which it is here used, is the Indians only salvation. With it they will become honorable, useful, happy citizens of a great republic, sharing on equal terms in all its blessings. Without it they are doomed either to destruction or to hopeless degradation.

Third. The work of Indian education should be completely systematized. The camp schools, agency boarding schools, and the great industrial schools should be related to each other so as to form a connected and complete whole. So far as possible there should be a uniform course of study, similar methods of instruction, the same textbooks, and a carefully organized and well-understood system of industrial training.

Fourth. The system should be conformed, so far as practicable, to the common-school system now universally adopted in all the States. It should be non-partisan, non-sectarian. The teachers and employes should be appointed only after the most rigid scrutiny into their qualifications for their work. They should have a stable tenure of office, being removed only for cause. They should receive for their service wages corresponding to those paid for similar service in the public schools. They should be carefully inspected and supervised by a sufficient number of properly qualified superintendents.

Fifth. While, for the present, special stress should be laid upon that kind of industrial training which will fit the Indians to earn an honest living in the various occupations which may be open to them, ample provision should also be made for that general literary culture which the experience of the white race has shown to be the very essence of education. Especial attention should be directed toward giving them a ready command of the English language. To this end, only English should be allowed to be spoken, and only English-speaking teachers should be employed in schools supported wholly or in part by the Government.

Sixth. The scheme should make ample provision for the higher education of the few who are endowed with special capacity or ambition, and are destined to leadership. There is an imperative necessity for this, if the Indians are to be assimilated into the national life.

Seventh. That which is fundamental in all this is the recognition of the complete manhood of the Indians, their individuality, their right to be recognized as citizens of the United States, with the same rights and privileges which we accord to any other class of people. They should be free to make for themselves homes wherever they will. The reservation system is an anachronism which has no place in our modern civilization. The Indian youth should be instructed in their rights, privileges, and duties as American citizens; should be taught to love the American flag; should be imbued with a genuine patriotism, and made to feel that the United States, and not some paltry reservation, is their home. Those charged with their education should constantly strive to awaken in them a sense of independence, self-reliance, and self-respect.

Eighth. Those educated in the large industrial boarding-schools should not be returned to the camps against their will, but should be not only allowed, but encouraged to choose their own vocations, and contend for the prizes of life wherever the opportunities are most favorable. Education should seek the disintegration of the tribes, and not their segregation. They should be educated, not as Indians, but as Americans. In short, the public school should do for them what it is so successfully doing for all the other races in this country, assimilate them.

Ninth. The work of education should begin with them while they are young and susceptible, and should continue until habits of industry and love of learning have taken the place of indolence and indifference. One of the chief defects which have heretofore characterized the efforts made for their education has been the failure to carry them far enough, so that they might compete successfully with the white youth, who have enjoyed the far greater advantages of our own system of education. Higher education is even more essential to them than it is for white children.

Tenth. Special pains should be taken to bring together in the large boarding-schools members of as many different tribes as possible, in order to destroy the tribal antagonism and to generate in them a feeling of common brotherhood and mutual respect. Wherever practicable, they should be admitted on terms of equality into the public schools, where, by daily contact with white children, they may learn to respect them and become respected in turn. Indeed, it is reasonable to expect that at no distant day, when the Indians shall have all taken up their lands in severalty and have become American citizens, there will cease to be any necessity for Indian schools maintained by the Government. The Indians, where it is impracticable for them to unite with their white neighbors, will maintain their own schools.

Eleventh. Co-education of the sexes is the surest and perhaps only way in which the Indian women can be lifted out of that position of servility and degradation which most of them now occupy, on to a plane where their husbands and the men generally will treat them with the same gallantry and respect which is accorded to their more favored white sisters.

Twelfth. The happy results already achieved at Carlisle, Hampton, and elsewhere, by the so-called "outing system," which consists in placing Indian pupils in white families where they are taught the ordinary routine of housekeeping, farming, etc., and are brought into intimate relationship with the highest type of American rural life, suggests the wisdom of a large extension of the system. By this means they acquire habits of industry, a practical acquaintance with civilized life, a sense of independence, enthusiasm for home, and the practical ability to earn their own living. This system has in it the "promise and the potency" of their complete emancipation.

Thirteenth. Of course, it is to be understood that, in addition to all of the work here outlined as belonging to the Government for the education and civilization of the Indians, there will be requisite the influence of the home, the Sabbath-school, the church, and religious institutions of learning. There will be urgent need of consecrated missionary work and liberal expenditure of money on the part of individuals and religious organizations in behalf of these people. Christian schools and colleges have already been established for them by missionary zeal, and others will doubtless follow. But just as the work of the public schools is supplemented in the States by Christian agencies, so will the work of Indian education by the Government be supplemented by the same agencies. There need be no conflict and no unseemly rivalry. The Indians, like any other class of citizens, will be free to patronize those schools which they believe to be best adapted to their purpose. [. . .]

* * *

Although many Indians saw their boarding school experiences as wrenching them away from their families, communities, and cultures, there were also many Indians who helped promote boarding schools. They saw that education offered Indians a means to survive in the twentieth century. Henry Roe Cloud (Winnebago), the most influential Indian educator in the early twentieth century, advocated schooling for Indian children but had doubts about the federal government's involvement in it. Roe Cloud started his own Indian high school, the American Indian Institute, in Wichita, Kansas, in 1915. Although the curriculum partly resembled that of government boarding schools in its emphasis on agriculture, religion, and self-sufficiency, Roe Cloud hoped to preserve Native cultures, not eliminate them. The following is a speech Roe Cloud gave in 1914 at the annual Lake Mohonk Conference, a gathering of self-proclaimed Indian reformers. (They wanted to reform Indians but, except for Roe Cloud and a few others, were not Indian themselves.) Why did Roe Cloud support Indian education? What were his criticisms of the government boarding school program?

Education of the American Indian

Henry Roe Cloud

Education is for life, – life in the workaday world with all its toil, successes, discouragements and heartaches. Education unrelated to life is of no use. "Educare" – education is the leading-out process of the young until they know themselves what they are best fitted for in life. Education is for complete living; that is, the educational process must involve the heart, head and hand. The unity of man is coming to the forefront in the thought of the day. We cannot pay exclusive attention to the education of one part and afford to let the other part or parts suffer. Education is for service; that is, the youth is led to see the responsibilities as well as the privileges of his education so that he lends a helping hand to those who are in need. Indian education is no exception to these general principles.

The educational needs of the Indian can be best seen in the light of his problem, – he has before him a twofold problem, the white man's

---

Roe Cloud, Henry. "Education of the American Indian." *Report of the Thirty-Second Annual Lake Mohonk Conference on the Indian and Other Dependent Peoples, October 14th, 15th and 16th, 1914.* Lake Mohonk, NY: Lake Mohonk Conference on the Indian and Other Dependent Peoples, 1914: 82–7.

problem and his own peculiar racial problem. The problem confronting the white child is the Indian's problem for, if the goal for the Indian is citizenship, it means sharing the responsibilities, as well as the opportunities, of this great Republic.

The task of educating the American young is a stupendous one. The future welfare of the American nation depends upon it. Children everywhere must be brought into an appreciation of the great fundamental principles of the Republic as well as the full realization of its dangers. It required a long, toilsome march of peoples beyond the sea to give us our present-day civilization. Trial by jury came by William the Conqueror. America's freedom was at the cost of centuries of struggle. America's democracy is the direct and indirect contribution of every civilized nation. The wide, open door of opportunity was paid for by untold sacrifice of life and labors. It involves the story of the sturdy and brave frontiersmen, the gradual extension of transportation facilities westward, the rise of cities on the plains. So great and rapid has been this progress that already the cry of the conservation of our natural resources is ringing in our ears.

To lead the white youth of the land into an appreciation of the history of American institutions, into their meaning for this generation and the generation to come, so that somewhere in the course of his education he feels possessed of some permanent interest which commands all his ambitions and devotion, is no small task.

Along with these great blessings there are the national dangers stalking through the land. I need but mention them.

The stupendous economic development has meant the amassing of great and unwieldy wealth into few hands. It has meant the creation of a wide gap between the rich and the poor. The industrial order has been revolutionized by the introduction of machinery. There has now grown up the problem of the relation of labor and capital. Our railroad strikes and mine wars are but symptoms of this gigantic problem. Immigration and the consequent congested districts in our cities has put the controlling political power in the hands of the "boss." There is the tenement problem – physical degeneracy and disease. It requires no prophet to foresee the increase of these problems and dangers owing to the war now raging across the sea. The desolation of those countries, the inevitable tax burdens, will mean an even greater influx of immigration into this country.

There is the problem of "fire water," that has burned out the souls of hundreds of thousands, to say nothing of the greater suffering of wives, mothers and children. There is the big national problem of race prejudice. Is America truly to be the "melting pot" of the nations?

These are the problems confronting the white youth, and, I repeat, they are the Indian's problems also.

Besides this, the Indian has his own peculiar race problem to meet. There is the problem of home education. Education in the home is almost universally lacking. The vast amount of education which the white child receives in the home – a great many of them cultured and Christian homes, where, between the age of ten and fourteen, the child reads book after book on travel, biography and current events – goes to make up for the deficiencies of the public schools. The Indian youth goes back into homes that have dominant interests altogether different from what he has been taught at school. I have seen many a young man and young woman bravely struggle to change home conditions in order to bring them into keeping with their training and they have at last gone down! The father and the mother have never been accustomed, in the modern sense, to a competitive form of existence. The father has no trade or vocation. The value of a dollar, of time, of labor is unknown in that home. The parents have not the insight into educational values to appreciate the boy's achievements and to inspire him further. What is to be done under such circumstances? In many cases he finds himself face to face with a shattered home. The marriage conditions, the very core of his social problem, stare him in the face. Many a young man and woman, realizing these home conditions, have gone away to establish a home of their own. As soon as the thrifty Indian accumulates a little property his relatives and tribesmen, in keeping with the old custom of communal ownership of property, come and live at his expense. There was virtual communal ownership of property in the old days under the unwritten laws of hospitality, but the omission, in these days, of that corresponding equal distribution of labor plays havoc with the young Indian homes.

The Indian has his own labor problem. He has here a race inertia to overcome. The sort of labor he is called upon to do these days is devoid of exploit. It is a change from the sporadic effort to that of routine labor calling for the qualities of self-control, patience, steady application and a long look ahead. Shall he seek labor outside the reservation? Shall he work his own allotment? What bearing has his annuity money and his lease money on his labor problem? Does it stifle effort on his part? Does it make him content to eke out a living from year to year without labor? If he works how is he to meet the ubiquitous grafter with his insistence upon chattel mortgages? How is he to avoid the maelstrom of credit into which so many have fallen?

The health problem of the Indian race may well engage the entire attention and life-work of many young Indian men and women. What about the seventy to eighty thousand Indians suffering now from trachoma? What about thirty thousand tubercular Indians? Is this due to housing conditions?

There is the legal problem to which special attention was just called. Is the Indian a ward of the Government, or a citizen? What are his rights and duties? His legal problem involves his land problem. Ought he to pay taxes? Will he ever secure his rights and be respected in the local courts unless he pays taxes? Is not this question most fundamental?

Shall the Indian youth ignore the problem of religion? Of the many religions on the reservation which one shall energize his life? Shall it be the sun dance, the medicine lodge, the mescal, or the Christian religion? Shall he take in all religions, as so many do? What do these different religions stand for?

There is finally the whole problem of self-support. If he is to pursue the lines of agriculture he must study the physical environment and topography of his particular reservation, for these in a large measure control the fortunes of his people. If the reservation is mountainous, covered with timber, he must relate his study to it. If it is a fertile plain, it means certain other studies. It involves the study of soils, of dry farming, irrigation, of stock-farming, of stock and sheep raising. The Indian must conquer nature if he is to achieve his race adaptation.

My friends, here are problems of unusual difficulty. In the face of these larger problems – city, state and national, as well as the Indian's own peculiar race problem, and the two are inextricably interwoven – what shall be the Indian's preparation to successfully meet them? What sort of an education must he have? Miss Kate Barnard told us something of the problem as it exists in Oklahoma. Into this maelstrom of political chicanery, of intrigue and corrupting influences of great vested interests shall we send Indian youth with only an eighth grade education? In vast sections of that Oklahoma country ninety per cent of the farms of white men were under mortgage last year. It means that even they with their education and inheritance were failing. Well might one rise up like Jeremiah of old and cry out, "My people perish for lack of knowledge," – knowledge of the truth as it exists in every department of life, – this can truly make us free.

The first effort, it seems to me, should be to give as many Indians as are able, all the education that the problems he faces clearly indicate he should have. This means all the education the grammar schools, secondary schools and colleges of the land can give him. This is not any too much for the final equipment for the leaders of the race. If we are to have leaders that will supply the disciplined mental power in our race development, they cannot be merely grammar school men. They must be trained to grapple with these economic, educational, political, religious and social problems. They must be men who will take up the righteous cause among their people, interpret civilization to their people, and restore race confidence, race virility. Only by such leaders can race segregation be overcome. Real segregation of the Indian consists in segregation of thought and inequality of education.

We would not be so foolish as to demand a college education for every Indian child in the land irrespective of mental powers and dominant vocational interests, but on the other hand we do not want to make the mistake of advocating a system of education adapted only to the average Indian child. If every person in the United States had only an eighth grade education with which to wrestle with the problems of life and the nation, this country would be in a bad way. We would accelerate the pace in the Government grammar schools of such Indian youth as show a capacity for more rapid progress. For the Indian of exceptional ability, who wishes to lay his hand upon the more serious problems of our race, the industrial work however valuable in itself, necessarily retards him in the grammar school until he is man-grown. He cannot afford to wait until he is twenty-four or twenty-five to enter the high school. This system is resulting in an absolute block upon the entrance of our ablest young people into the schools and colleges of the land which stand open to them. There are hundreds of the youth of the Oriental and other native races in our colleges. As an Indian it is impossible for me to believe that the fact that there are almost no Indians under such training today is due to a failure of my race in mental ability. The difficulty lies in the system rather than in the race. According to the census of the last decade, there were three hundred thousand college men and women to ninety millions of people in the United States, or one to every three hundred. In the same proportion there should be one thousand college Indian men and women in the United States, taking as a total population three hundred thousand Indians. Allowing for racial handicaps let us say there should be at least five hundred instead of one thousand Indian college men and women. Actually there is not one in thirty thousand and most of these in early life escaped the retarding process in the Government schools.

This is not in any way disparaging the so-called industrial education in the Government Indian grammar schools, such as Carlisle, Haskell, Chilocco. Education – as education that seeks to lead the Indians into outdoor vocational pursuits, is most necessary. Our Government Indian Bureau feels the need for vocational training among the Indians, and I am very glad that it does. Productive skill we must have if we are to live on in this competitive age. However, in this policy of industrial training for the Indian youth, the Government should not use the labor of the students to reduce the running expenses of the different schools, but only where the aim is educational, to develop the Indian's efficiency, and mastery of the trade. Recent Congressional charges of shifting students from one trade to another so that they master no trade have been made and the charges sustained. I worked two years in turning a washing machine in a Government school to reduce the running expenses of the institution. It did not take me long to learn how to run the machine and the rest of the two years I nursed a growing hatred for it. Such work is not educative. It begets a hatred for work, especially where there is no pay for such labor. The Indian will work under such conditions because he is under authority, but the moment he becomes free he is going to get as far as he can from it. I, personally, would hail the day with joy when the Government Indian schools can redeem the moral discipline of even drudgery work connected with the schools by some system of compensation of value received for work expended. Others before me, such as Dr. Walter C. Roe, have dreamed of founding a Christian, educational institution for developing a strong native, Christian leadership for the Indians of the United States. I, too, have dreamed. For, after all, it is Christian education that is going to solve these great problems confronting the Indian. Such an institution is to recognize the principle that man shall not live by bread alone and yet at the same time to show the dignity and divineness of toil by the sweat of one's brow. The school is to teach self-support. The Indian himself must rise up and do for himself by the help of Almighty God. It is to be Christian education because every problem that confronts us is in the last analysis, a moral problem. In the words of Summer, "Capital is another word for self denial." The gift of millions for Indian education is the peoples' self denial. In whatever activity we may enter for life work, we must pay the price of self-control if we are to achieve any degree of success. The moral qualities therefore are so necessary for our successful advance. Where shall we look for our final authority in these moral questions? We must look to nothing this side of the "Great Spirit" for our final authority. Having then brought into the forefront of the Indian race men of sound morality, intellectual grasp and productive skill, we shall have leaders who are like the great oak tree on the hill. Storm after storm may break upon them, but they will stand because they are deeply rooted, and the texture of their soul is strong.

Further Reading

Adams, David Wallace. Education for Extinction: *American Indians and the Boarding School Experience, 1875–1928.* Lawrence: University Press of Kansas, 1995.

Child, Brenda J. *Boarding School Seasons: American Indian Families, 1900–1940.* Lincoln: University of Nebraska Press, 1998.

Crum, Steven J. "Henry Roe Cloud, A Winnebago Indian Reformer: His Quest for American Indian Higher Education." *Kansas History* 11 (Autumn, 1988): 171–84.

Pratt, Richard Henry. *Battlefield and Classroom: Four Decades with the American Indian, 1867–1904*. Ed. Robert M. Utley. New Haven: Yale University Press, 1964.

Szasz, Margaret Connell. *Education and the American Indian: The Road to Self-Determination Since 1928*. Revised edn. Albuquerque: University of New Mexico Press, 1999.

Red Power

Introduction

In 1969 a group of American Indian activists, most of whom were students in the San Francisco Bay Area, occupied Alcatraz Island, site of the infamous but by that time abandoned federal penitentiary. To the rising number of young Indian activists around the country, Alcatraz introduced the idea of the radical takeover as a political strategy for bringing grievances and demands to a wider public. Other militant takeovers followed Alcatraz, culminating in the American Indian Movement's occupation of the town of Wounded Knee, South Dakota, in 1973. This was, of course, a time period of protest everywhere in America, not just among Indians. Although Alcatraz fits within this larger social upheaval, Indian activists spoke from the vantage-point of a distinct history, their grievances and demands were rooted in indigenous claims to American land, and as members of tribes, they had a unique relationship to the federal government compared to other racial and ethnic minorities.

The Alcatraz protesters, who called themselves Indians of All Tribes, failed in their immediate objectives. Their demands were not met, and after about a year and a half, the few occupiers who had not yet left were quietly removed by federal authorities. Alcatraz's long-term impact has been tremendous, however. Troy Johnson and Joane Nagel explain why Alcatraz ranks as a momentous historic event in "Remembering Alcatraz: Twenty-five Years After," their introduction to a commemorative issue of the *American Indian Culture and Research Journal* devoted to the Alcatraz takeover. Whether these dramatic, controversial takeovers and occupations helped Indian causes is debatable. Since takeovers attracted the media, they provided a forum for asserting Indians' civil rights and treaty rights, but media attention could both help and hurt Indian causes. And in terms of bringing about concrete changes, should Alcatraz be judged by its short-term objectives or its long-term impact? Alcatraz failed in bringing about any tangible, institutionalized changes for the San Francisco Indian community, but it did have an enduring impact as a catalyst in mobilizing the spirit of an entire generation.

Remembering Alcatraz: Twenty-five Years After

Troy Johnson and Joane Nagel

In the early morning hours of 20 November 1969, eighty-nine American Indians landed on Alcatraz Island in San Francisco Bay. Identifying themselves as "Indians of All Tribes," the group claimed the island by "right of discovery" and by the terms of the 1868 Treaty of Fort Laramie which gave Indians the right to unused federal property that had been Indian land previously. Except for a small caretaking staff, Alcatraz Island had been abandoned by the federal government since the early 1960s, when the federal penitentiary was closed. In a press statement, Indians of All Tribes set the tone of the occupation and the agenda for negotiations during the nineteen-month occupation:

> We, the native Americans, re-claim the land known as Alcatraz Island in the name of all American Indians. ... [W]e plan to develop on this island several Indian institutions: 1. A CENTER FOR NATIVE AMERICAN STUDIES...2. AN AMERICAN INDIAN SPIRITUAL CEN-TER...3. AN INDIAN CENTER OF ECOLOGY...4. A GREAT INDIAN TRAINING SCHOOL...[and] an AMERICAN INDIAN MUSEUM. ... In the name of all Indians, therefore, we reclaim this island for our Indian nations. ...We feel this claim is just and proper, and that this land should rightfully be granted to us for as long as the rivers shall run and the sun shall shine. Signed, INDIANS OF ALL TRIBES.

Johnson, Troy and Joane Nagel. "Remembering Alcatraz: Twenty-five Years After." *American Indian Culture and Research Journal*, 18: 4 (1994): 9–23. Reprinted by permission of the American Indian Studies Center, UCLA. Copyright © Regents of the University of California.

In the months that followed, thousands of protesters and visitors spent time on Alcatraz Island. They came from a large number of Indian tribes, including the Sioux, Navajo, Cherokee, Mohawk, Puyallup, Yakima, Hoopa, Omaha. The months of occupation were marked by proclamations, news conferences, powwows, celebrations, "assaults" with arrows on passing vessels, and negotiations with federal officials. In the beginning months of the occupation, workers from the San Francisco Indian Center gathered food and supplies on the mainland and transported them to Alcatraz. However, as time went by, the occupying force, which generally numbered around one hundred, confronted increasing hardships as federal officials interfered with delivery boats and cut off the supply of water and electricity to the island, and as tensions on the island grew.

The negotiations between Indians of All Tribes and the federal government eventually collapsed, and Alcatraz Island was never developed in accordance with the goals of the Indian protesters. In June 1971, the dozen or so remaining protesters were removed by federal marshals, more than a year-and-a-half after Indians of All Tribes first took over the island. Despite their failure to achieve their demands, Alcatraz represented a watershed moment in Native American protest and resulted in an escalation of Indian activism around the country.

The occupation, which caught the attention of the entire country, provided a forum for airing long-standing Indian grievances and for the expression of Indian pride. Vine Deloria noted its importance, referring to the occupation as a "master stroke of Indian activism" and recognizing its impact on Indian ethnic self-awareness and identity

> "Indianness" was judged on whether or not one was present at Alcatraz, Fort Lawson, Mt. Rushmore, Detroit, Sheep Mountain, Plymouth Rock, or Pitt River. . . . The activists controlled the language, the issues, and the attention.[1]

The Alcatraz occupation and the activist events that followed it offered firm evidence to counter commonly held views of Indians as powerless in the face of history, as weakened remnants of disappearing cultures and communities. In contrast, the events on Alcatraz and the activism that spread in its wake fueled American Indian ethnic pride and strengthened native individuals' sense of personal empowerment and community membership.

For example, Wilma Mankiller, now principal chief of the Cherokee Nation of Oklahoma, visited the island many times during the months of occupation. She describes the personal impact of the event as "an awakening that ultimately changed the course of my life." The life-changing impact of the Alcatraz occupation emerged as a recurrent theme in our interviews with Native Americans who participated in or observed the protests of that period:

George Horse Capture. In World War II, the marines were island-hopping; they'd do the groundwork, and then the army and the civilians would come in and build things. Without the first wave, nothing would happen. Alcatraz and the militants were like that. They put themselves at risk, could be arrested or killed. You have to give them their due. We were in the second wave. In the regular Indian world, we're very complacent; it takes leadership to get things moving. But scratch a real Indian since then, and you're going to find a militant. Alcatraz tapped into something. It was the lance that burst the boil.

John Echohawk. Alcatraz just seemed to be kind of another event – what a lot of people had been thinking, wanting to do. We were studying Indian law for the first time. We had a lot of frustration and anger. People were fed up with the status quo. That's just what we were thinking. Starting in 1967 at the University of New Mexico Law School, we read treaties, Indian legal history. It was just astounding how unfair it was, how wrong it was. It [Alcatraz] was the kind of thing we needed.

Leonard Peltier. I was in Seattle when Alcatraz happened. It was the first event that received such publicity. In Seattle, we were in solidarity with the demands of Alcatraz. We were inspired and encouraged by Alcatraz. I realized their goals were mine. The Indian organizations I was working with shared the same needs: an Indian college to keep students from dropping out, a cultural center to keep Indian traditions. We were all really encouraged – not only those who were active, but those who were not active as well.

Frances Wise. The Alcatraz takeover had an enormous impact. I was living in Waco, Texas, at the time. I would see little blurbs on TV. I thought, These Indians are really doing something at Alcatraz. . . . And when they called for the land back, I realized that, finally, what Indian people have gone through is finally being recognized. . . . It affected how I think of myself. If someone asks me who I am, I say, well, I have a name, but Waco/Caddo – that's who I *am*. I have a good feeling about who I am now. And you need this in the presence of all this negative stuff, for example, celebrating the Oklahoma Land Run.

Rosalie McKay-Want. In the final analysis, however, the occupation of this small territory could be considered a victory for the cause of Indian activism and one of the most noteworthy expressions of patriotism and self-determination by Indian people in the twentieth century.

Grace Thorpe. Alcatraz was the catalyst and the most important event in the Indian movement to date. It made me put my furniture into storage and spend my life savings.

These voices speak to the central importance of the Alcatraz occupation as the symbol of long-standing Indian grievances and increasing impatience with a political system slow to respond to native rights. They also express the feelings of empowerment that witnessing and participating in protest can foster. Loretta Flores did not become an activist herself until several years after the events on Alcatraz, but she eloquently describes the sense of self and community that activism can produce:

> The night before the protest, I was talking to a younger person who had never been in a march before. I told her, "Tomorrow when we get through with this march, you're going to have a feeling like you've never had before. It's going to change your life." Those kids from Haskell (Indian Nations University) will never forget this. The spirits of our ancestors were looking down on us smiling.

The impact of the Alcatraz occupation went beyond the individual lives and consciousnesses it helped to reshape. The events on Alcatraz marked the beginning of a national Indian activist movement, sometimes referred to as "Red Power," that kept national attention on Indian rights and grievances. The founding of D-Q University in California, the Trail of Broken Treaties, the takeovers of the BIA, the siege at Wounded Knee, the Longest Walk: All of these followed in the wake of Alcatraz.

Despite its influence, the occupation of Alcatraz Island has largely been overlooked by those who write or speak today of American Indian activism. Much has been written about the battles fought by Indian people for their rights regarding access to hunting and fishing areas reserved by treaties in the states of Washington and Oregon, the continuing struggles for those same rights in Wisconsin and Minnesota, and the efforts of the Six Nations to secure guaranteed treaty rights in the northeastern United States. The 1972 takeover of the Bureau of Indian Affairs (BIA) headquarters in Washington, D.C., and the 1973 occupation of Wounded Knee are well known as well, as is the killing of an Indian man, Joseph Stuntz, and two FBI agents on the Pine Ridge Reservation in 1975. Yet it is to the occupation of Alcatraz Island twenty-five years ago that one must look to find the genesis of modern-day American Indian activism. The movement began in 1969 and continues to this day.

A large number of occupations began shortly after the 20 November 1969 landing on Alcatraz Island. Most scholars and the general public who follow Indian issues frequently and incorrectly credit this new Indian activism to the American Indian Movement (AIM). AIM was founded on 28 July 1968 in Minneapolis, Minnesota, by Dennis Banks,

George Mitchell, and Vernon and Clyde Bellecourt. Although AIM became a central actor in and organizer of much Native American protest during the 1970s and after, in 1969, at the time of the Alcatraz occupation, AIM was largely an urban movement concerned with overcoming discrimination and pervasive abuse by police, and its membership was not directly involved in the Alcatraz occupation. Only after visiting the Indians on Alcatraz Island and realizing the possibilities available through demonstration and seizure of federal facilities did AIM actually enter into a national activist role.

AIM leaders recognized the opportunities when they met with the Indian occupiers on Alcatraz Island during the summer of 1970 and were caught up in the momentum of the occupation. On a broader scale, they realized the possibilities of a national activist movement. Additionally, AIM leaders had seen firsthand, during their visit to Alcatraz, that the bureaucracy inherent in the federal government had resulted in immobility: No punitive action had been taken against the Indian people on the island. This provided an additional impetus for AIM's kind of national Indian activism and was congruent with the rising tide of national unrest, particularly among young college students. AIM's first attempt at a national protest action came on Thanksgiving Day 1970, when AIM members seized the *Mayflower II* in Plymouth, Massachusetts, to challenge a celebration of colonial expansion into what then was mistakenly considered to be a "new world." During this action, AIM leaders acknowledged the occupation of Alcatraz Island as the symbol of a newly awakened desire among Indians for unity and authority in a white world.

Background of the Alcatraz Occupation

The 1960s and early 1970s was a time of urban unrest across the nation. The United States was deeply involved in an unpopular war in Vietnam. The civil rights movement, Black Power, the rise of LaRaza, the Latino movement, the stirring of the new feminism, the rise of the New Left, and the Third World strikes were sweeping the nation, particularly college campuses. While US armed forces were involved in the clandestine invasion and bombing of Cambodia, the announcement of the massacre of innocent civilians in a hamlet in My Lai, Vietnam, burned across the front pages of American newspapers. Ubiquitous campus demonstrations raised the level of consciousness of college students. People of all ages were becoming sensitized to the unrest among emerging minority and gender groups, who were staging demonstrations and proclaiming their points of view, many of which were incorporated by student activists. White students faced with the draft and an "unjust" war ultimately empathized with minority populations, thus adding numbers and support to their causes. Sit-ins, sleep-ins, teach-ins, lock-outs, and boycotts became everyday occurrences on college campuses. And from these college campuses – specifically the University of California, Santa Cruz; San Francisco State; the University of California, Berkeley; and the University of California, Los Angeles – emerged the Native Americans who would comprise the first occupation force on Alcatraz Island.

Latino, Black, white, and native protests each had different sources and goals. The roots of American Indian activism were buried in centuries of mistreatment of Indian people. The latest was the federal government's relocation program of the 1950s and 1960s, which promised to move reservation residents to major urban areas for vocational training and to assist them in finding jobs, adequate housing, and financial assistance while training was underway. More than one hundred thousand Indian people were relocated as a result of this process. The training, which generally was supposed to last three months, often lasted only three weeks; the job assistance was usually one referral, at best; the housing was 1950s and 1960s skid row; and the financial support ran out long before the training was started or any hope of a job was realized. The history of the San Francisco Bay Area relocation effort is replete with examples of Indian people – men, women, boys, and young girls – who sat for days and weeks at bus stations, waiting for the government representative who was to meet them and start them on the road to a new, successful urban life.

Another group of Indian people who relocated to the Bay Area were those who had served in the military during World War II and then chose to settle in urban areas after the war. These veterans often brought their families with them. The majority of the thirty thousand Indians who served in the armed forces during the war had left the reservation for the first time in their lives to join up. During the war, they got used to regular employment and regular paychecks; in addition, they became accustomed to living with electricity, modern appliances, and hot and cold running water. These conveniences, taken for granted in non-Indian homes, were rare or nonexistent on Indian reservations. It was only natural that, once exposed to such basic services, Indian veterans would want to establish a more modern lifestyle for themselves and their families. Their relatives, too, sought the "good life" offered in the urban areas. Many Indian people wanted to see what was available in the cities that older brothers or uncles talked about as a part of their military experience. With relatives now living in urban areas such as New York, San Diego, Los Angeles, and San Francisco, many relocated and some found employment, but most returned home to the reservation.

Still other Indian people migrated to the Bay Area in the war years to work in defense industries, and they remained there. Because of the industrial need fed by the war and in keeping with the policy of termination of tribal groups and assimilation of Indians into non-Indian society, the government also relocated thousands of Indian workers to San Francisco.

In the Bay Area – one of the largest of more than a dozen relocation sites – the newly urban Indians formed their own organizations to provide the support that the government had promised but failed to provide. Generally, these groups were known by tribal names such as the Sioux Club and the Navajo Club, but there were also sports clubs, dance clubs, and the very early urban powwow clubs. Eventually, some thirty social clubs were formed to meet the needs of the urban Indians and their children – children who would, in the 1960s, want the opportunity to go to college and better themselves.

By the early 1960s, a growing and increasingly organized urban Indian population, dissatisfied with the federal relocation program and with conditions both on the reservations and in the city, began to search for a means to communicate their concerns and grievances. Alcatraz Island appeared to be a promising site for launching an information and protest campaign.

The Occupations

In actuality, there were three separate occupations of Alcatraz Island. The first was a brief, four-hour occupation on 9 March 1964, during which five Sioux Indians, representing the urban Indians of the Bay Area, occupied the island. The event was planned by Belva Cottier, the wife of one of the occupiers. The federal penitentiary on the island had been closed in 1963, and the government was in the process of transferring the island to the city of San Francisco for development. Meanwhile, Belva Cottier and her Sioux cousin developed plans of their own. They recalled having heard of a provision in the 1868 Sioux treaty with the federal government that stated that all abandoned federal lands reverted to ownership by the Sioux people. Using this interpretation of the treaty, they encouraged five Sioux men to occupy Alcatraz Island and claim it for the Sioux people. They issued press releases claiming the island in accordance with the 1868 Sioux treaty and demanded better treatment for urban Indians. Richard McKenzie, the most outspoken of the group, pressed the claim for title to the island through the court system, only to have the courts rule against him. More importantly, however, the Indians of the Bay Area were becoming vocal and united in their efforts to improve their lives.

The 1964 occupation of Alcatraz Island was a forewarning of the unrest that was fermenting, quietly but surely, in the urban Indian population. Prior to the 1964 occupation, the Bay Area newspapers contained a large number of articles about the federal government's abandonment of the urban Indian and the state and local government's refusal to meet their needs. The social clubs that had been formed for support became meeting places for Indian people to discuss the discrimination they were facing in schools, housing, employment, and health care. They also talked about the police, who, like law officers in other areas of the country, would wait outside of Indian bars at closing time to harass, beat, and arrest Indian patrons. Indian centers began to appear in all the urban relocation areas and became nesting grounds for new pan-Indian, and eventually activist, organization.

The second Alcatraz occupation came out of the Bay Area colleges and universities and other California college campuses where young, educated Indian students joined with other minority groups during the 1969 Third World Liberation Front strike and began demanding that colleges offer courses that were relevant to Indian students. Indian history written and taught by non-Indian instructors was no longer acceptable to these young students, who were awakened to the possibility of social protest to bring attention to the shameful treatment of Indian people.

Among the Indian students at San Francisco State was a young Mohawk named Richard Oakes. Oakes came from the St. Regis Reservation, had worked on high steel in New York, and had traveled across the United States, visiting various Indian reservations. He eventually had wound up in California, where he married a Kashia Pomo woman, Anne, who had five children from a previous marriage. Oakes worked in an Indian bar in Oakland for a period of time and eventually was admitted to San Francisco State. In September 1969, he and several other Indian students began discussing the possibility of occupying Alcatraz Island as a symbolic protest, a call for Indian self-determination. Preliminary plans were made for a symbolic occupation to take place in the summer of 1970, but other events caused an earlier execution of the plan.

The catalyst for the occupation was the destruction of the San Francisco Indian Center by fire in late October 1969. The center had become the meeting place for the Bay Area Indian organizations and the newly formed United Bay Area Indian Council, which had brought the thirty private clubs together into one large council headed by Adam Nordwall (later to be known as Adam Fortunate Eagle). The destruction of the Indian center united the council and the American Indian student organizations as never before. The council needed a new meeting place, and the students needed a forum for their new activist voice.

After the fire, the second occupation of Alcatraz Island was planned for 9 November 1969. Richard Oakes and the other Indian college students, along with a group of people from the San Francisco Indian Center, chartered a boat and headed for Alcatraz Island. Since many different tribes were represented, the name *Indians of All Tribes* was adopted for the group.

The initial plan was to circle the island and symbolically claim it for Indian people. During the circling maneuver, however, Richard and four others jumped from the boat and swam to the island. They claimed Alcatraz in the name of Indians of All Tribes and left the island after meeting with the caretaker, who asked them to leave. Later that same evening, Oakes and fourteen others returned to the island with sleeping bags and food sufficient for two or three days; they left the island the following morning without incident.

In meetings following the 9 November occupation, Oakes and his fellow students realized that a prolonged occupation was possible. It was clear that the federal government had only a token force on the island and that no physical harm had come to anyone involved. A new plan began to emerge.

Following the brief 9 November occupation, Oakes traveled to UCLA, where he met with Ray Spang and Edward Castillo and asked for their assistance in recruiting Indian students for what would become the longest Indian occupation of a federal facility to this very day. Spang, Castillo, and Oakes met in UCLA's Campbell Hall, now the home of the American Indian Studies Center and the editorial offices of the *American Indian Culture and Research Journal,* in private homes, and in Indian bars in Los Angeles. On 20 November 1969, the eighty Indian people who occupied Alcatraz Island included seventy Indian students from UCLA.

The occupation of Alcatraz would last nineteen months and would bring together Indian people from across the United States, Alaska, Canada, Mexico, and South America. Most importantly, Alcatraz would force the federal government to take a new look at the situation faced by urban Indian people, the long-forgotten victims of a failed relocation program.

Life on the Rock

Once on the island, the people began to organize themselves immediately. An elected council was put into place. Everyone was assigned a job: security, sanitation, day-care, housing, cooking, laundry. All decisions were made by unanimous consent of the people. Sometimes meetings were held five, six, seven times per day to discuss the rapidly developing occupation.

The federal government, for its part, insisted that the Indian people leave and placed an ineffective coast guard barricade around the island. Eventually, the government agreed to the Indian council's demands for formal negotiations. But, from the Indians' side, the demands were nonnegotiable. They wanted the deed to the island; they wanted to establish an Indian university, a cultural center, and a museum; and they wanted federal funding to establish all of these. The government negotiators turned down their demands and insisted that they leave the island.

It is important to remember that, while the urban Indian population supported the concept of an occupation and provided the logistical support, the occupation force itself was made up initially of young, urban Indian college students. The most inspiring person, if not the recognized leader, was Richard Oakes, who is described as handsome, charismatic, a talented orator, and a natural leader. Oakes was strongly influenced by an Iroquois organization known as the White Roots of Peace, which had been revitalized by a Mohawk, Ray Fadden, and an Iroquois holy man, Mad Bear Anderson. The White Roots of Peace was an old Iroquois organization that taught Iroquois traditions and attempted to influence Mohawk youths to take up leadership roles in the Mohawk Longhouse. This was an effort to revive and preserve Iroquois traditional life.

In the autumn of 1969, Jerry Gambill, a counselor for White Roots of Peace, visited the campus of San Francisco State and inspired many of the students, none more than Oakes, with whom he stayed. Gambill found a willing student and later a student leader in Richard Oakes. But Oakes's position as leader on the island, a title he himself never claimed, quickly created a problem. Not all of the students knew Oakes, and, in keeping with the true concepts underlying the occupation, many wanted an egalitarian society on the island, with no one as their leader. Although this may have been a workable form of organization on the island, it was not comprehensible to the non-Indian media. Newspapers, magazines, and television and radio stations across the nation sent reporters to the island to interview those in charge. They wanted to know who the leaders were. Oakes was the most knowledgeable about the landing and the most often sought out and identified as the leader, the "chief," the "mayor of Alcatraz."

By the end of 1969, the Indian organization on the island began to fall into disarray. Two groups rose in opposition to Richard Oakes, and, as the Indian students began returning to school in January 1970, they were replaced by Indian people from urban areas and reservations who had not been involved in the initial occupation. Where Oakes and the other students claimed title to the island by right of discovery, the new arrivals harked back to the rhetoric of the 1964 occupation and the Sioux treaty, a claim that had been pressed through the court system by Richard McKenzie and had been found invalid. Additionally, some non-Indians now began taking up residency on the island, many from the San Francisco hippie and drug culture. Drugs and liquor had been banned from the island by the original occupiers, but they now became commonplace.

The final blow to the early student occupation occurred on 5 January 1970, when Richard Oakes's twelve-year-old stepdaughter fell three floors down a stairwell to her death. Yvonne Oakes and some other children apparently had been playing unsupervised near an open stairwell when she slipped and fell. Following Yvonne's death, the Oakes family left the island, and the two remaining groups maneuvered back and forth for leadership. Despite changes of leadership, however, the demands of the occupiers remained consistent: title to Alcatraz Island, the development of an Indian university, and the construction of a museum and cultural center that would display and teach the valuable contributions of Indian people to the non-Indian society.

By this time, the attention of the federal government had shifted from negotiations with the island occupants to restoration of navigational aids to the Bay Area – aids that had been discontinued as the result of a fire on Alcatraz Island and the discontinuance of electrical service. The government's inability to restore the navigational aids brought criticism from the coast guard, the Bay Area Pilot's Association, and local newspapers. The federal government now became impatient. On 11 June 1971, the message went out to end the occupation of Alcatraz Island, which had begun on 20 November 1969.

The success or failure of the Indian occupation of Alcatraz Island should not be judged by whether the demands for title to the island and the establishment of educational and cultural institutions were realized. If one were to make such a judgment, the only possible answer would be that the occupation was a failure. Such is not the case, however. The underlying goals of the Indians on Alcatraz were to awaken the American public to the reality of the plight of the first Americans and to assert the need for Indian self-determination. In this they were indeed successful. Additionally, the occupation of Alcatraz Island was a springboard for Indian activism, inspiring the large number of takeovers and demonstrations that began shortly after the 20 November 1969 landing and continued into the late 1970s. These included the Trail of Broken Treaties, the BIA headquarters takeover in 1972, and Wounded Knee II in 1973. Many of the approximately seventy-four occupations that followed Alcatraz were either planned by or included people who had been involved in the Alcatraz occupation or who certainly had gained their strength from the new "Indianness" that grew out of that movement.

Remembering Alcatraz

[...] Alcatraz was a defining moment in the lives of the American Indian people who participated either directly or in support of those on the island. Many of the individuals who were involved in the occupation have gone on to become prominent leaders in Indian education, law, and tribal government. [...]

Alcatraz Island remains a strong symbol of Indian activism and self-determination, and a rallying point for unified Indian political activities. On 11 February 1978, Indian participants began the "Longest Walk" to Washington, D.C. to protest the government's ill treatment of Indian people. That walk began on Alcatraz Island. On 11 February 1994, AIM leaders Dennis Banks, Clyde Bellecourt, and Mary Wilson met with Indian people to begin the nationwide "Walk for Justice." The walk was organized to protest the continuing imprisonment of Leonard Peltier as a result of the 26 June 1975 shootout between AIM members and FBI agents on the Pine Ridge Reservation in South Dakota. That walk also began on Alcatraz Island. On Thanksgiving Day of each year since 1969, Indian people have gathered on Alcatraz Island to honor those who participated in the occupation and those who continue the struggle for Indian self-determination. In the final analysis, the occupation of Alcatraz Island was a major victory for the cause of Indian activism and remains one of the most noteworthy expressions of renewed ethnic pride and self-determination by Indian people in this century.

Note

1   Vine Deloria, Jr., "The Rise of Indian Activism," in *The Social Reality of Ethnic America*, ed. R. Gomez, C. Collingham, R. Endo, and K. Jackson (Lexington, MA: D.C. Heath, 1974), 184–5.

Documents

No reader in American Indian history would be complete without something by political activist, lawyer, and writer Vine Deloria, Jr. Here, Deloria reflects back on Alcatraz, which he was closely involved with but as an outsider. At the time, Deloria's own political connections were to the National Congress of American Indians (NCAI), a pan-tribal Indian organization founded in Denver at the end of the Second World War. Like the National Association for the Advancement of Colored People (NAACP) for African Americans, NCAI was an established political organization whose methods were challenged by the younger, more radical generation of political activists of the 1960s. NCAI sought to improve the political status of Indians by working through institutionalized channels for change, such as the legislature and courts. Despite the urban setting of its first meeting, NCAI's focus was on the rights of tribes and dealt substantially with concrete issues relating to reservation lands, tribes' land-based resources, and claims cases. This may partly explain Deloria's frustrations with the ill-defined aims of the Alcatraz takeover and why "Indians of All Tribes" had difficulty formulating an agenda that would succeed in redressing their grievances.

Alcatraz, Activism, and Accommodation

Vine Deloria, Jr

Alcatraz and Wounded Knee 1973 have come to symbolize the revival of Indian fortunes in the late twentieth century, so we hesitate to discuss the realities of the time or to look critically at their actual place in modern Indian history. We conclude that it is better to wrap these events in romantic notions and broker that feeling in exchange for further concessions from the federal; government; consequently, we fail to learn from them the hard lessons that will serve us well in leaner times.

Activism in the 1950s was sporadic but intense. In 1957, Lumbee people surrounded a Ku Klux Klan gathering in North Carolina and escorted the hooded representatives of white supremacy back to their homes sans weapons and costumes. In 1961, a strange mixture of Six Nations people and non-Indian supporters attempted a citizens' arrest of the secretary of the interior, and, sometime during this period, a band of "True Utes" briefly took over the agency offices at Fort Duchesne. The only context for these events was the long suffering of small groups of

Deloria, Vine, Jr. "Alcatraz, Activism, and Accommodation." *American Indian Culture and Research Journal*, 18: 4 (1994): 25–32. Reprinted by permission of the American Indian Studies Center, UCLA. Copyright © Regents of the University of California.

people bursting forth in an incident that illustrated oppression but suggested no answer to pressing problems. In 1964, the "fish-ins" in the Pacific Northwest produced the first activism with an avowed goal; continual agitation in that region eventually resulted in *U.S. v. Washington*, which affirmed once and for all the property rights of Northwest tribes for both subsistence and commercial fishing.

Indians benefited substantially from the civil rights movement of the 1960s and the ensuing doctrines concerning the poor, which surfaced in the Economic Opportunity Act and more particularly in its administration. The civil rights movement had roots in a hundred small gatherings of concerned attorneys brought together by Jack Greenberg and Thurgood Marshall to determine the legal and philosophical basis for overturning *Plessy v. Ferguson*. Concentrating on the concept of *equality*, a series of test cases involving access to professional education in the border states cut away the unexamined assumption that separate facilities for higher education automatically meant equality of treatment and equality of the substance of education.

In 1954, *Brown v. Topeka Board of Education* stripped away the cloak of indifference and hypocrisy and required the dismantling of segregated schools. By extension, if schools were to be integrated, why not lunch counters and buses, and why not equality under the law in all public places and programs? The *Brown* strategy was created on behalf of the oppressed multitudes of African-Americans but did not involve the rank and file people until the movement went into the streets and lunch counters of the South. With the announcement of "Black Power" by Stokely Carmichael and SNCC in 1966 – made possible in some measure by the insistence of federal War on Poverty administrators that the "poor" knew better than anyone else what poverty was and how to combat it – the civil rights movement became a people's movement.

A people's movement has many benefits – the mass of minority groups are involved, and political strength increases dramatically – but it also has immense vulnerability in that goals that can be seen, articulated, and achieved are surrendered in favor of symbolic acts that illustrate and demonstrate the suffering and frustrations of the people. Symbolic acts demand attention from an otherwise unaware general public, but they also fail to articulate the necessity of specific actions that can and must be taken by the government at the local, state, and federal levels to alleviate the crisis. Consequently, the choice of remedy is given to the institutional structure that oppresses people and to the good and bad politicians and career bureaucrats who operate the institution.

The Poor People's March of 1968 best exemplifies the problem of a people's movement unable to articulate specific solutions and see them through to completion. Organized partially in memory of the slain

Martin Luther King and partially as an effort to secure increases in the
funding of social programs, the march floundered when participants
spent their time harassing members of the cabinet about problems that
had no immediate solution and demanding sympathy and understanding
from federal officials who could not translate these concerns into pro-
grammatic responses. Smaller protests had maintained a decent level of
funding for poverty programs in past years, but, this time, the march
faced the bitter reality of the Vietnam War and the impossibility of
continuing to expand the federal budget into unrealistic deficits.

It is important to note that, while the Indian fishing rights struggle
maintained itself with measurable goals, Alcatraz represented an Indian
version of the Poor People's March. The proclamation presented by the
first invaders of the island demanded a bewildering set of responses from
the federal government, focusing on transfer of the island's title to an
Indian organization and the funding of an educational center on the
island for the thousands of Indians who had made the Bay Area their
home. The popular interpretation of the occupation was that Indians
were entitled to own the island because it was federal surplus property
and therefore qualified under a provision of the 1868 treaty of Fort
Laramie.

Unfortunately, the treaty provision was a myth. Red Cloud had simply
remained in the Powder River country until the government withdrew its
troops from the Bozeman Trail and then, satisfied that the trail was
closed, arrived at Fort Laramie in November 1868 to sign the treaty.
During the Alcatraz occupation, when White House staff and Department of Interior lawyers looked at the treaty, they could find no phrase
that justified returning the island to the Indian occupants; consequently,
they were blocked from using any executive powers to resolve the crisis.

The initial group of Indian occupants was composed of students from
Bay Area colleges and universities, but, as the occupation continued,
these people were replaced with enthusiastic recruits from across the
nation and with unemployed people who had nowhere else to go. The
mood of the occupants was that they should use the press as often as
possible; thus the goal of the movement quickly became confused, with
various spokespeople articulating different philosophies on different
occasions.

The difference between Alcatraz and the fishing rights fight, and
between the Brown litigation and the Black Power movement, should
be made clear: Behind the sit-ins and the fish-ins was the almost certain
probability that, should activists be convicted at the trial court level, they
would have their convictions overturned by a higher court and/or the
object of their protest would be upheld at a higher level of litigation.
Brown and the Medicine Creek fishing rights treaty were already federal

law before people went out to protest; the protests were made on behalf of impartial enforcement of existing law. This foundation of legality did not exist for either the Poor People's March or the occupation of Alcatraz. Therefore, in legal terms, these activities meant nothing.

My role in Alcatraz was sporadic and, in a few instances, not welcomed by some of the activists on the rock. While I was director of the National Congress of American Indians (NCAI), I had worked for several years with people in the Bay Area as part of the NCAI's concern for relocated Indians. I entered law school in the fall of 1967 and, by the time of the occupation, had already written *Custer Died for Your Sins*, which was released in early October 1969. Some years before, Richard McKenzie and others had briefly landed on Alcatraz, and, in the years since that first invasion, Bay Area activists such as Adam Nordwall had disrupted Columbus Day celebrations and, with some modest successes, generally tried to focus the attention of Bay Area politics on urban Indian problems. Ironically, some of the people who were now shouting "Red Power" into every microphone they could find had called me a communist the year before for doing a Frank McGee NBC news interview that advocated Red Power.

Adam Nordwall saw that the occupation would flounder unless it was tied to some larger philosophical issue that could be seen by the American public as important to their own concerns for justice. During the fall of 1969, I was asked several times to come out to Alcatraz to discuss how the people on the island could transform the occupation into a federal issue that could be resolved by congressional action. I favored announcing that not only did Indians want the island, we wanted a federal policy of land restoration that would provide a decent land base for small reservations, return submarginal lands to tribes that had them, and, in some cases, restore original reservation boundaries.

On Christmas Eve 1969, I flew out to California to discuss the land issue with people on the island, but the meeting never got off the ground. Instead of listening to our presentation on land restoration, the activists began quarreling about who was in charge of the operation. Richard Oakes had many supporters, but he also had many rivals. Adam and I were considered intruders because we had not been in the original invasion. About all we got out of the meeting was the sneer that the activists had the whole world watching them, and they were in control of Indian policy. We pointed out that a sensible program had to be articulated so that the administration could act, but we got no positive response.

In January 1970, hoping to highlight a land and treaty issue, I invited Merv Griffin to come out to Alcatraz and do part of a show from there. Unfortunately, many of the people on the Rock had not moved forward in their thinking; Merv got the old response of how the island belonged to Indians under the 1868 treaty and how they wanted to establish an educational and vocational training facility on the island.

In the spring of 1970, a group of us held a national urban Indian conference on Alcatraz in another effort to provide a context for securing the island. In November 1969, this same urban group had held its conference the weekend before the San Francisco Indian center burned, but now, under different leadership, we were trying to focus everything on the Bay Area in the hope of defining an issue that the public would embrace. The meeting was not long under way when a man and woman began to scream at each other across the room, viciously and seemingly without any provocation. Every time anyone would propose a course of action, one or the other would jump up and let loose a string of curses designed to infuriate everyone. Most people sat there politely listening to the nonsense, but eventually the meeting just dissolved. Later, we discovered they were a husband and wife who went through this performance at every meeting they attended.

While our meeting was being held, we learned that Richard Oakes and his supporters had been thrown off the island the day before and that they were likely to confront us when we returned to the mainland. We met only one sullen young man who warned us that he was going to remember our names and faces. Later that evening, as we sat around trying to figure out what to do, we hit on a plan. We had someone call Oakes's headquarters and, in his best reservation English, relate that he was supervising two buses of Navajo boys who were traveling to the Hoopa Bear Dance and wanted to be housed for the night. The Oakes contingent immediately tried to enlist these Navajo as a force to help Oakes recapture the island. They gave us directions for finding their headquarters, and we promised to come help them. A few minutes after hanging up the phone, we decided it would be even better to include buses of Navajo girls, so we had a rather prominent Indian woman call the headquarters and pretend that she was matron over two busloads of girls from Navajo Community College who were looking to make contact with the Navajo boys. This phone call created a dilemma for us and for Oakes's people. They wanted to get the two busloads of girls and lose the boys; we wondered how long we could continue to drive four phantom buses around the Bay Area.

Our pretend Navajo man then called Oakes's people back and said he had gotten lost and was in Oakland, and we got new directions for reaching their headquarters. Our woman then got back on the phone and told Oakes's group that the girls' buses were only a few blocks away. Their response was that they would go out and buy food and get ready to welcome the girls, apparently forgetting that the boys' buses would be along shortly also. We hung up and pondered the situation we had created. The consensus was that we should call back and confess the whole thing before everyone was inconvenienced. We were just about to confess when one of our group said, "Wait a minute! Real Indians would just go their own way and not say a word; we are thinking like responsible, educated Indians." So we just went back to our hotel to bed.

The next morning, as we embarked for Alcatraz to finish the meeting, we were greeted by two surly Oakes supporters. They told us to go ahead and visit the island, but they assured us that we would not stay long because they had reinforcements of four hundred Navajo arriving momentarily and we would be thrown off the Rock along with the anti-Oakes people. Needless to say, our meeting went well, and the Navajo never did arrive. I will not mention the names in our little group, but I can confess that they are still prominent, responsible, national Indian leaders.

The occupation of Alcatraz lingered on. A rougher group of people occupied the island, and it became useless to try to make sense of the occupation. Increasingly, it became a hazard to go out there. Eventually, many of the buildings were burned, and feeble, nonsensical ultimatums were issued by the declining population on the Rock. Finally, the government swooped down and took the remaining people away. I visited the island about a decade later and heard a surprisingly mild and pro-Indian explanation of the occupation from a Park Service guide. I walked around the grounds and remembered some of the difficult meetings we had held there and how, several times, we almost had a coalition that could have affected land policy. Unfortunately, most of the people involved in the occupation had no experience in formulating policy and saw their activities as primarily aimed at awakening the American public to the plight of Indians. Thus a great opportunity to change federal programs for Indians was lost.

The Trail of Broken Treaties came along in the fall of 1972. By that time, the activists had devised the Twenty Points, which, in my opinion, is the best summary document of reforms put forth in this century. Written primarily by Hank Adams, who supervised the fishing rights struggle until the Supreme Court ruled in favor of Indians, it is comprehensive and philosophical and has broad policy lines that can still be adopted to create some sense of fairness and symmetry in federal Indian policy.

Then came the Wounded Knee occupation, with its aftermath of trials and further violence. Indians were well represented in the media from the Alcatraz occupation through the Wounded Knee trials, but, unfortunately, each event dealt primarily with the symbols of oppression and did not project possible courses of action that might be taken to solve problems.

The policy posture of Indians at Alcatraz was part of a historical process begun during the War on Poverty when people demanded action from the government but failed to articulate the changes they wanted. With the incoming Nixon administration in 1969, we clamored for an Indian to be appointed as commissioner. Because we failed to support Robert Bennett, who was already occupying the office, the inept Louie Bruce was installed. Bruce's chaotic administration produced an era in which résumés were enhanced and job descriptions were watered down so that the respective administrations could appoint Indian puppets to symbolize the presence of Indians in the policymaking process. Today the government, under Ada Deer, is at work trying to create a new set of categories – "historic" and "nonhistoric" tribes – so that benefits and services can be radically reduced. When Indians do not clearly articulate what they want, the government feels free to improvise, even if it means creating new policies that have no roots in anything except the fantasies of the creator.

Alcatraz was more than a protest against the oppressive conditions under which Indians lived. In large part, it was a message that we wanted to determine our own destiny and make our own decisions. That burden is still upon us and weighs heavily when contemporary tribal chairpeople are consulted about policy directions. Almost always, immediate concerns or irritating technicalities are regarded as important in the consultative process, and, consequently, it is increasingly difficult to determine exactly where people think we are going. Like the activists at Alcatraz, we often mill around, keenly aware that we have the ears of the public but uncertain what to do next. Until we can sketch out realistic scenarios of human and resource goals, we continue to resemble those occupants of the Rock a quarter of a century ago: We want change, but we do not know what change.

★   ★   ★

A child of the city, Wilma Mankiller would later in life return to the Cherokee Nation of Oklahoma and, eventually, be elected to the position of Principal Chief. In her autobiography, Mankiller tells of her family's move to San Francisco from Oklahoma under the auspices of the federal relocation program of the 1950s, when Mankiller was a child. At the time of the Alcatraz occupation, Mankiller was in her twenties, still living in the Bay Area, a wife, mother, and college student at San Francisco State. In this except from her autobiography, she describes Alcatraz as a turning point in her life and the beginning of a lifelong commitment to Indian community activism. Like the children at Chilocco, Mankiller reaffirmed her identity as Cherokee through her associations with Indians from other nations.

Mankiller: A Chief and Her People

Wilma Mankiller and Michael Wallis

[...] Although Alcatraz ultimately would not remain a sovereign Indian nation, the incredible publicity generated by the occupation served all of us well by dramatizing the injustices that the modern Native Americans have endured at the hands of white America. The Alcatraz experience nurtured a sense among us that anything was possible – even, perhaps, justice for native people. [...]

Before it was over, four of my brothers and sisters and their children had joined the original band on the island. I, too, would become totally engulfed by the Native American movement, largely because of the impact that the Alcatraz occupation made on me. Ironically, the occupation of Alcatraz – a former prison – was extremely liberating for me. As a result, I consciously took a path I still find myself on today as I continue to work for the revitalization of tribal communities.

From those unforgettable events that flashed like bright comets years ago, I have tried to retain valuable chunks of experience along with some of youth's raw courage. It is my hope that those idealistic moments have blended with the perspective that luckily comes with maturity. It makes for a vintage mixture that has helped to sustain me against all odds, against real and imaginary foes, and even against death itself.

Still, no matter where my path leads me, I must always remember where the journey started. It was in San Francisco – at Alcatraz, and at the American Indian Center, and in my own home where, starting about the time of the Alcatraz takeover, native people often came to sip coffee, make plans, and build indestructible dreams. The occupation of Alcatraz excited me like nothing ever had before. It helped to center me and caused me to focus on my own rich and valuable Cherokee heritage.

My brother Richard, six years my junior, was the first of the Mankiller siblings who joined the other native people at Alcatraz. He later

Mankiller, Wilma and Michael Wallis. *Mankiller: A Chief and Her People*. New York: St Martin's Press, 1993: 192–205.

served on the Alcatraz Council, the panel of men and women who tried to maintain a semblance of order on the island. After Richard, the next ones to go were my younger sister Vanessa and our little brother James.

Finally, my sister Linda wanted to go out and be with the others. Only twenty years old, Linda already had three small children, and she was separated from her husband. She and her kids were temporarily staying with Hugo [WM's husband] and me. When she made up her mind to go, I accompanied Linda and her children to the island. At the docks, we saw a lot of people we knew. We rode out together in a boat supplied by Credence Clearwater Revival that was called the *Clearwater*. Of the four Mankillers who went to Alcatraz, Linda ended up staying there the longest. She remained until June of 1971, when federal marshals finally removed the last few native occupants.

I will always be very proud of my brothers and sisters for going to Alcatraz. I did not stay there, but always returned to the mainland, where I felt I could be of more service by remaining active in the various support efforts. I found myself spending more time at the new home of the American Indian Center. It was a key command post where much of the fund-raising activities for Alcatraz took place, and almost all of the communications were funneled to and from the island.

The entire Alcatraz occupation was such an important period for me. Every day that passed seemed to give me more self-respect and sense of pride. Much of the credit for that awakening has to go to the young men and women who first went to Alcatraz and helped so many of us return to the correct way of thinking. One of the most influential was Richard Oakes.

Oakes was a student at San Francisco State. Formerly an ironworker in New York, he moved to California, where he drove a truck. He then worked at Warren's, an Indian bar in the Mission District, while he went back to college. He was instrumental in starting the Native American studies program at San Francisco State, and he soon became one of the strongest voices of activism and social protest at the American Indian Center.

I became well acquainted with Richard Oakes during the occupation, and I found him to be one of our most articulate leaders. Although only in his late twenties when I met him, Richard spoke persuasively about treaty rights and the need for America to honor its legal commitments to native people. He spoke of the various tribal histories and diverse cultures, and of the many contributions Native Americans have made to contemporary society. His words, considered so radical in the 1970s, are strikingly similar to the language of many of the relatively moderate tribal leaders of today. [. . .]

Richard and his wife, Anne, a Pomo woman, had five young children and took care of several others. In January of 1970, after they had resided on the island for almost three months, one of their daughters, Yvonne, was playing in a deserted prison building when she fell down a three-story stairwell. She was rushed to the mainland, but she died two days later. Annie had had a premonition that something bad was going to happen to her family.

The girl's death cast a veil of sorrow over the island. Although Richard explained that even in death his daughter was still within the circle of life, the grief was too much. He and Annie packed up their few possessions and left with their other children. Later that year, Richard helped the Pit River Indians in their struggle over land rights with a powerful utility company. He endured tear gas, billy clubs, and getting tossed in jail, only to end up in a bar brawl back in San Francisco where two men beat him to a pulp with pool cues. Richard survived, but he was never able to return to his earlier level of activism. He moved farther north to settle in the Pomo country near Santa Rosa. In September of 1972, a caretaker of a YMCA camp claimed that Richard had threatened him with a knife. The white man pulled a gun and shot Richard Oakes dead. He was in his thirtieth year.

Annie floundered after Richard's death. I made it a point to visit her several times at her home. Gradually, she began to withdraw more and more from community work, and finally we lost touch. But whenever I hear the name Annie or see a Cherokee woman whose demeanor reminds me of my friend, I think of that resilient Pomo woman and of her children and of the daughter who fell to her death on Alcatraz, and I always feel profoundly sad. I pray that Annie is doing well. I also think of Richard Oakes, the visionary young man whose turbulence helped us all find harmony. [. . .]

Another of the eloquent native leaders to emerge from the Alcatraz Island experience was John Trudell, a wiry young Lakota man – one of the best thinkers I have ever met. Immensely creative and irreverent, Trudell is still absolutely committed to whatever he is doing. That has not changed.

John and his wife Lou and their two daughters, Maurie and Tara, came up from Los Angeles to join the Indians of All Tribes, as the group at Alcatraz was called. I thought they were the most incompatible couple I had ever met. John was hyperactive and serious, while Lou was level and steady but with a great sense of humor. She became the consummate earth mother on the island and later for the entire East Bay Indian community. John and Lou did have one common interest – a great love of politics. Their third child, a son they named Wovoka after the Paiute medicine man who had originated the Ghost Dance, was born on Alcatraz.

During the occupation, John served as the announcer on Radio Free Alcatraz, which was beamed for thirty minutes each evening over Berkeley's radio station KPFA. He often spoke of creating a complex on Alcatraz that would include an educational center for Native American studies, a historical archives and museum, and a spiritual center. Grace Thorpe, a Sac and Fox and the daughter of all-time Olympic hero Jim Thorpe of Oklahoma, was a guest on his program, as were many other activists.

Lou became a close friend of mine, and I always have maintained a great deal of affection and respect for John. Even when the federal government rejected all Native American claims to Alcatraz and suggested that the island be used as a park, John and the others would not budge. [...]

Throughout the Alcatraz experience and afterward, I met so many people from other tribes who had a major and enduring effect on me. They changed how I perceived myself as a woman and as a Cherokee.

Gustine Moppin – the Klamath woman whom I had known since I was a young girl, the person who had convinced me to continue my education – was a true inspiration. Gustine was the personification of the Cherokee concept of "having a good mind." Unfailingly cheerful even in the worst of circumstances, she devoted every waking moment to helping others.

Gustine thought I had the potential to do something with my life. She encouraged and supported me through those years as my marriage eroded and I struggled for independence. I appreciated that. I was always happy that we reconnected during the Alcatraz experience. Years later when she developed diabetes, we had many talks about the toll this dreaded disease takes on native people. She lost an arm to diabetes and then had to undergo dialysis when her kidneys failed. Ultimately, she was confined to a wheelchair. When I last saw her in the winter of 1990, Gustine was quite frail, but she had not stopped helping people. She was busy counseling other amputees on independent living. She still served on the boards of several Indian agencies. Soon after that visit, Gustine passed into the other world. I lost a sister. The Bay area Native American community lost its matriarch.

Another California relocatee from those bittersweet years whom I stayed in contact with was Bill Wahpepah, who was Kickapoo and Sac and Fox. I worked very closely with Bill on several projects, including an alternative school, youth services, and an Indian adult education center. He brought some of the primary AIM leaders – Dennis Banks, Carter Camp, and Vernon and Clyde Bellecourt – to his home. Clyde Bellecourt, one of AIM's founders, was especially likable. He came to the Bay area with an entourage of native children. It was obvious how much he cared about them and how hard he worked to help them.

Leonard Crow Dog, a vital cog in the Native American movement, also came to Wahpepah's place. I liked him quite well. He maintained a certain presence that reminded me of the Cherokee elders I knew when I was a little girl back in Oklahoma. On one occasion, Leonard led an impressive Lakota ceremony in the adult education building in Oakland. He and his wife, Mary, their young son, and other people traveled in a large truck. They carried a sacred buffalo skull with them wherever they went.

Bill Wahpepah was always there for us. He opened his home to everyone, especially the Indian children. Most of them were second-generation relocatees who would have been out on the streets without Bill's guidance. I saw Bill weep in utter frustration over a young man who continued to sniff paint. I knew those tears were real. They came from a man who had survived alcoholism and heroin addiction to emerge in the 1970s as one of our finest spokespersons for native rights. He traveled all over the world, telling anyone who would listen about the problems of Native Americans, while he searched for answers and solutions.

Bill, whose life had been hard, died much too young. He was in his late forties and at the height of his activism when he walked into spirit country after a sudden illness. Like so many others who had been relocated, Bill had always spoken of someday returning to live among his people in Oklahoma. That was not to be. He was taken home to Shawnee, Oklahoma, for a tribal burial.

The same was true for my own father. Only in death did he return to the place where he was born.

My father's death tore through my spirit like a blade of lightning. It came during the Alcatraz occupation. By that time, my parents had long since left San Francisco and Hunter's Point. The spice company my father worked for had relocated, so my folks had moved farther south, down the coast to a small town not too far from Salinas and Monterey, places that John Steinbeck had immortalized in his books. Life had finally leveled out for my father and mother. It was the best period of their life together. At last, they had a decent place to live. Most of their kids were grown and making their ways in the world, and several of us were deeply involved in the Native American rights movement.

Just when it appeared that all was well, more misfortune came calling. My father began to experience high blood pressure and severe kidney problems. The diagnosis was not good – end-stage polycystic kidney disease. At that time, the options for treatment were quite limited. Kidney transplants, which are widely performed today, were experimental and not available at all to persons older than fifty-five. That meant my father was just barely eliminated from consideration. Dialysis, although readily available, was not nearly as efficient as it is now.

We were only starting to adjust to the shock of my father's illness when I experienced more health problems of my own. Once again, I began to have urinary-tract infections and the discomfort associated with kidney problems, just as I had when I was pregnant with my first daughter. After extensive testing to find out why I continued to be plagued with the infections, I also was diagnosed with polycystic kidney disease. I had inherited it from my father. All of us were stunned.

The physicians told me that this genetic condition is characterized by the appearance of many cysts on the kidneys which may continue to grow and overcome the healthy tissue until the kidneys fail. They said that in mild cases of the disease, total kidney loss is certainly not inevitable. In fact, some people live out their lives without even knowing they have the disease because it has produced no symptoms.

But further tests revealed that just like my father, I had a severe form of the disease. In both of our cases, the disease was progressive and incurable. Mine was not nearly as advanced as it was with my father, but all predictions were that I could expect to experience kidney failure by the time I reached my early to mid-thirties, sometime in the 1980s. I reacted to the diagnosis almost with relief. At least I finally had an explanation for the repeated infections, which sometimes required days of hospitalization.

My doctor asked me to limit my protein intake, have my kidney functions monitored regularly, and rest as much as possible. Afterwards the woman in the hospital bed next to mine, who had overheard the discussion, asked if there was anything she could do for me. I told her yes she could, and I asked her for a cigarette. I had not smoked for about a year, but from that moment forward, it became a habit again until I stopped once and for all in 1980.

Because of the hereditary question, I immediately had my two girls, Gina and Felicia, tested for any possible signs of kidney disease. Thankfully, the results were negative, and both of them were clear of any symptoms. Then I arranged for a tubal ligation. I considered it unfair to risk having another child who might end up with a deadly illness.

Dad's health steadily declined, but we tried to make him as comfortable as possible. His approval and support were always very important to me, even after I was a grown woman with children of my own. We had always shared an interest in political debate, in the community around us, and in books. Now we shared this family disease.

It was so difficult to watch my father slowly leave us. He hated being sick, he hated having to give up his job, and he hated taking medicine. My mother practically had to force him to see the doctor for regular visits. We all went to see him as often as we could. He understood our involvement in Alcatraz – that we were fighting for native rights. A conservative Cherokee full-blood, Dad was pleased that his children were taking a stand. I have a strong memory of a Thanksgiving visit with my dad. He was bedfast, and while the rest of the family was busy out in the kitchen getting all the little ones fed, I brought him a plate of food. We ate together, just the two of us, a rare treat in a family as large as ours. He smiled at me and told me he was proud to have a daughter who had become a revolutionary. As it turned out, that was to be his final Thanksgiving dinner.

The end was very sad. Because my parents had no health insurance, we children brought Dad to San Francisco General Hospital, where he could be placed on dialysis. His reaction to the procedure was not at all good. He had to undergo cardiac surgery to remove fluid that was gathering in his chest. Afterward, I went to his room and walked over to his bed. A huge scar and dressing were across his heart. My father looked up and said, "Look what they have done to me now."

After undergoing that surgery, he failed very quickly. We sent the boat out to Alcatraz to retrieve my brothers and sisters. The good doctors worked ever so hard to save him. They ran up and down the halls and did all they could. It was not enough. With his children and his wife gathered around his bed, my father died. He was fifty-six years old. It was February of 1971.

We never even considered leaving him in California. We brought Charley Mankiller back home to his everlasting hills of Oklahoma. My brother Don and my mother made the arrangements. Some of us flew back to Oklahoma, others drove across country to get there. Even though the lives of my brothers and sisters had taken different paths, my father's death brought us together. We took him to Echota Cemetery, just a few miles from where I now live. Waiting for him were the graves and spirits of his parents, grandparents, cousins, aunts, and old friends, all of them long departed to the other world. It was a cold February day. We formed a line of cars and pickups and followed the hearse from the funeral home in Stilwell out to the graveyard.

Even in my grief, the countryside looked so familiar to me. I was back home again. Rocky Mountain is sparsely populated, but as our procession of vehicles wound slowly down the road to the cemetery, people came outside and stood in their yards to watch us pass. You could almost hear them saying, "There goes Charley Mankiller. They are bringing Charley Mankiller home." [...]

Most people who spoke or sang at my father's funeral service did so in our Cherokee language. Some people literally walked out of the woods to attend the service. Others came from as far away as Kansas and North Carolina. He was buried beside his parents and a child my mother had miscarried between my birth and Linda's. There was something very natural about laying him to rest in that ground near people he loved. It was so peaceful, and I knew the trees would protect him.

Still, as we left and made our way back to California, we were all numb. The anchor that had always kept our family together was gone. In many ways, none of us would ever be the same again.

For my mother, it was a most terrible time. Part of her spirit went with my father. They had jointly fought for his life. Now that he was gone, she looked as if she had waged her last great battle. From then on, life for her would never be the same. They were so connected. She had done her best to prepare for his loss, but the transition was difficult. She had been married to him since she was a fifteen-year-old girl, and over the course of more than thirty years, they had gone through so much together. They had raised a family, buried children, and gone through the trials of relocation. Besides loving him, my mother truly respected and liked my father. Watching someone you care so much about suffer through such indignity and dehumanization is not easy. But she made the necessary adjustments and, like the rest of us, she persevered.

I returned to Native American issues for my comfort. The Alcatraz occupation came to a halt a few months after my father's death. Then I became even more involved with community work. I knew for sure that I could no longer remain content as a housewife.

Hugo was not at all in favor of my involvement in Alcatraz or any of the other projects I became associated with in the Bay area. During that period of my awakening, he was most unhappy whenever I held meetings at our home. He also opposed the idea of my traveling anywhere without him, even if only for a short time. Of course, he neglected to remember that a few years earlier, when he had got itchy feet and was gone for weeks at a stretch traveling around the world with his cousins in the merchant marine, I had learned to adjust.

Times for the two of us had changed so radically. I had become a much stronger person and was more than ready to assert my independence. So when Hugo informed me that I could not have a car, I did not acquiesce. Instead, I went straight to the bank, withdrew some money, and bought an inexpensive Mazda. It took a little bit of doing, but I figured out how to operate the stick shift on those terrific San Francisco hills.

Buying that little red car without my husband's consent or knowledge was my first act of rebellion against a lifestyle that I had come to believe was too narrow and confining for me. I wanted to break free to experience all the changes going on around me – the politics, literature, art, music, and the role of women. But until I bought that little red Mazda, I was unwilling to take any risks to achieve more independence. Once

I had the car, I traveled to many tribal events throughout California and even in Oregon and Washington. [. . .]

All around me, there was so much going on. There was a great deal to accomplish. One task I took on was acting as director of the Native American Youth Center in East Oakland. I literally discovered the building that housed the organization, on the corner of Fruitvale and East Fourteenth streets. I drafted some volunteers to slap fresh paint on the place, pulled together some school curricula and a cultural program, and opened the doors. My experience at the San Francisco Indian Center was put to good use. Some of the young people who made their way to this new youth center were dropouts. Others came there at the end of the school day.

I suppose there is much to be said for ignorance. I had no idea what I was doing when I became involved at the youth center, but I learned quickly – on the job. My enthusiasm seemed to make up for any lack of skills. There were field trips to plan and coordinate, and visits to various tribal functions all over northern California. At the center, while the kids did their homework after school, they listened to the music of Paul Ortega, Jim Pepper, or some of the other talented native singers and musicians who came there. All the while, we tried to instill pride in our Native American heritage and history, and to encourage our young people to use that pride as a source of strength to survive the tough streets of East Oakland.

We also worked on basic educational needs. I worked very hard with a young Klamath girl to get her to return to school. I scraped up a little bit of money to pay her, and she helped me with the center's office work. She was just fine with running errands, but when it came to jotting down telephone messages or filing, she became terrified. Finally, she broke down and admitted that she had absolutely no reading skills at all. I immediately got her into a literacy program.

At the youth center, I also learned valuable lessons about self-help. When I had no clue where I was going to come up with the money needed for a renovation project, I went to a bar about a block from the center called Chicken's Place. The sister of my friend Gustine was the owner, and many of the native people of East Oakland went there. I stepped inside and asked for volunteers. Suddenly, to my great surprise and delight, I had several people on their feet, all ready to get to work. I was even more amazed by their ability and commitment. From then on, whenever we needed funds for a field trip or warm bodies to do some work, I went straight to Chicken's Place. The folks there never let me down.

A little of that absolute faith in our ability to get things done by helping one another sustained me later when I returned to Oklahoma.

But it was in Oakland where I formed a belief that poor people, particularly poor American Indian people, have a lot more potential and many more answers to problems than they are ever given a chance to realize.

Beyond the youth center, I also became a volunteer worker for the Pit River people in their fierce legal battle with the powerful Pacific Gas and Electric Company over the rights to millions of acres of the tribe's northern California land. This was the tribe that my old friend Richard Oakes had tried to help. I saw a story on the six o'clock television news about the tribe's efforts to reclaim ancestral lands. They were rural people – a very gutsy tribe just trying to get back what was rightfully theirs. Something about them reminded me of the Cherokees. I heard their lawyer speaking on the news, and afterward I called him up and said that I would like to volunteer my services. He said that would be just fine, and I began an almost five-year association with that tribe. It lasted until the mid-1970s, when I finally left Hugo and California behind.

During the time I volunteered for the Pit River people, I absorbed a great deal of the history and culture of the native tribes in California. Most of the time, I stayed quite busy at the tribe's legal offices in San Francisco, where I helped to organize a legal defense fund. But frequently, my daughters and I would visit the traditional leaders out on their land. Whenever we went to Pit River country, we stayed in a small cabin not far from the home of Raymond and Marie Lego.

Raymond was a traditional tribal leader, and the Lego home became the center of activity for those of us taking part in the land fight. Often in the evening, we sat on the front porch, and Raymond and Marie told us about their long struggle to get back the land. Sometimes Raymond would bring out an old cardboard box filled with tribal letters and documents, which he treated as though they were sacred objects. We were privileged to be able to see those things and to spend that time with such people. I felt at home there. The Legos grew a garden. They hunted, and lived a simple life. The demeanor and lifestyle of the Pit River people put me in mind of my own people back in eastern Oklahoma.

From my time with the Pit River tribe, I came away with so much information I would later use. I learned about treaty rights and international law. Everywhere my girls and I went during the 1970s in California, we received an education. Those were fine trips. We drove to Mendocino on the northern shore of a half-moon-shaped bay. We followed the Pacific coast. We visited with Pomo people I had met at Alcatraz, and we gathered seaweed with them along the shore. Collecting seaweed was one of their seasonal rituals, and we placed what we found in special baskets that were family heirlooms. The seaweed was quickly fried in very hot grease and wrapped in thick bread. It was delicious.

We went to Kashia, a Pomo *rancheria* in the mountains near Santa Rosa. Only about five acres in size, Kashia is where some of the activists sought refuge after the 1973 AIM takeover at the hamlet of Wounded Knee on the Pine Ridge Reservation in South Dakota. Wounded Knee was the site of the 1890 massacre where, it is said, the Lakota Nation's sacred hoop was broken and where many dreams died with the slaughtered native people. Some of the soldiers who participated in the killings even received medals from the United States government. Russell Means, John Trudell, and other strong activists went to Wounded Knee in 1973 to demand reforms. Their seventy-two-day standoff with the FBI ended in a shoot-out and deaths on both sides, but it focused more attention on the injustices in Indian life.

My brother Richard was at Wounded Knee. After Alcatraz, he had worked at a television station in San Francisco, but he left to go to Wounded Knee because he felt it was important. My mother was so worried that he would end up getting shot, but he was not hurt. Like many other young native men of that time, Richard heard the call to help the people at Pine Ridge, and he went. Whether the occupation of Wounded Knee helped or hurt Pine Ridge continues to be the subject of debate among the people most affected – those who live on Pine Ridge Reservation.

There was still much talk of the bloodshed at Wounded Knee when my girls and I camped at Kashia. We stayed with the parents of my friend Maxine Steele. Her brother Charles had gone to Wounded Knee. We cooked our meals outside, and we talked. We felt it was a magical place. It still is today. There are several Indian doctors there, mostly women. We attended dances in the traditional Pomo round house. Under the stars, we listened to stories of history, medicine, and ceremonies.

All of it was a remarkable experience. All of those trips and visits. All of the music and dancing. All of the hard, hard work. All of the time spent in the fight for Alcatraz, at the youth center, with the Pit River people gave me precious knowledge. All of the people I encountered – the militants, the wise elders, the keepers of the medicine, the storytellers – were my teachers, my best teachers. I knew my education would never be complete. In a way, it was only beginning. I felt like a newborn whose eyes have just opened to the first light.

More and more, I found my eyes turning away from the sea and the setting sun. I looked to the east, where the sun begins its daily journey. That was where I had to go, not to heal for a few weeks after a marital squabble, not to lay a loved one to rest and then leave again – I had to go back to stay. Back to the land of my birth, back to the soil and trees my grandfather had touched, back to the animals and birds whose calls I had memorized as a girl when we packed our things and left on a westbound train so very long ago. The circle had to be completed. It was so simple, so easy.

I was going home.

Further Reading

Cornell, Stephen. *The Return of the Native: American Indian Political Resurgence*. New York: Oxford University Press, 1988.

Crow Dog, Mary, with Richard Erdoes. *Lakota Woman*. New York: HarperCollins, 1990.

Nagel, Joane. *American Indian Ethnic Renewal: Red Power and the Resurgence of Identity and Culture*. New York: Oxford University Press, 1995.

Smith, Paul Chaat and Robert Allen Warrior. *Like a Hurricane: The Indian Movement from Alcatraz to Wounded Knee*. New York: New Press, 1996.

Index

Note: page numbers in italic denote illustrations.